SFML Game Development

Learn how to use SFML 2.0 to develop your own
feature-packed game

Jan Haller

Henrik Vogelius Hansson

Artur Moreira

PUBLISHING

BIRMINGHAM - MUMBAI

SFML Game Development

Copyright © 2013 Packt Publishing

First published: June 2013

Production Reference: 1170613

Published by Packt Publishing Ltd.
Livery Place
35 Livery Street
Birmingham B3 2PB, UK.

ISBN 978-1-84969-684-5

www.packtpub.com

Cover Image by Vivek Sinha (vivek.ratan.sinha@gmail.com)

Credits

Foreword

I'm really honored to write the first words of this book, the very first one about SFML. When I started to write this library, in 2006, I couldn't imagine that it would become so much popular. Around 100,000 visitors per month, 100 new forum posts everyday... this is huge! And this is just the beginning; with the release of SFML 2.0, the library makes an important step forward. While SFML 1 is a constantly evolving (understand "unstable") API, SFML 2.0 is meant to be a robust, stable, and mature foundation for the future. And hopefully a solid base for more and more great games.

Increasing popularity also means more effort from the authors to provide complete and quality documentation. Sadly, this is often overlooked by developers.

Although I do my best to provide detailed tutorials for SFML, they are nothing more than an improved API documentation. Users often ask me where they can find a more complete guide to start programming games with SFML. And until today, I had nowhere to direct them to. But Artur, Henrik, and Jan did a great job to fill this hole. They have gathered their wisdom and experience into a unique book that covers the basics of game programming, as well as everything that SFML has to offer—from audio to network, through advanced graphics. What I really appreciate about this book is that it is written with the same philosophy that is behind SFML: good design, simplicity, and modern code.

I hope you will enjoy reading this book as much as I did and find what you're looking for; whether you're a beginner who wants to learn game programming with SFML, or a more experienced programmer who wants to improve his design and technical skills. And don't hesitate to come to the SFML forum if you have questions or comments. I, the authors of this book, and all the community will be glad to answer you.

Laurent Gomila

Author of SFML

Software Engineer, Tegesoft, France

About the Authors

Artur Moreira is a game development enthusiast who ultimately aims to start a new game development company in his home country. He has been programming games and game-related software for over 4 years. Most of the effort in that time was put in creating an open source game-making library with lots of flexibility and portability. The library is called *Nephilim* and is known for supporting all major desktop and mobile operating systems, making game development fully cross-platform and fast. Alongside this big project, he keeps making his own prototypes and games for educational and commercial purposes.

Aside from the programming, he also puts some focus in creative areas such as 3D modeling, digital painting, and music composing.

I would like to thank, first of all, my girlfriend for her patience and unconditional support every single time the writing was taking all of my time and energy. Also, I can't be thankful enough for the support of my parents and sisters, along with all the closest relatives, whose support is ever-present and always helpful. On the technical side, I would like to directly thank Jan Haller and Henrik Vogelius Hansson, the co-authors of the book, for their remarkable collaboration, skill, and teamwork. It's been always a pleasure to work with them.

Henrik Vogelius Hansson has always been in love with both games and programming. He started his education fairly early and continued on into the indie scene with Defrost Games and their game *Project Temporality*. The next company that hired him was Paradox Development Studio where he got to work on titles such as *Crusader Kings 2*.

Beside the game companies, Henrik has also been very active in the SFML community and has even provided a binding for Ruby called *rbSFML*.

I would like to thank my co-authors, Jan and Artur, for the amazing cooperation and great times. I am also very happy and would like to thank my family that encouraged me to pursue this line of work. Also special thanks to my grandmother.

Jan Haller is a Master's degree student of Electrical Engineering and Information Technology. In his free time, he occasionally develops games in C++. He is also interested in the creation of graphics and 3D models.

In 2008, Jan stumbled upon SFML. Since then, he has used the library for many of his works. One of his bigger projects was a 2D Jump'n'Run game, where the character has to find its way through different levels, defeating enemies and collecting various items. During the years, Jan has actively participated in the SFML community, getting a lot of insights into the development of SFML 2. He has also written a C++ library called *Thor*, which extends SFML by ready-to-use features such as particle systems or animations.

I would like to thank Laurent Gomila for the passion and huge efforts he invested into the Simple and Fast Multimedia Library. It has always been interesting to discuss with him about the library and its development process. I would also like to thank my co-authors, Artur Moreira and Henrik Vogelius Hansson, who have been a very nice team to work with.

About the Reviewers

Brandon DeRosier is a free software supporter, software engineer, and a hobbyist game developer living in the Greater Boston area. Driven by an early interest in programming, he took to the reverse engineering of his favorite games of his childhood; he would later write several small augmentation tools to run alongside these games. Over time, he developed his skills as a programmer — as well as an interest in music composition, animation, and interactive media. Currently, he is directing these skills and interests towards game design.

As a member of the Free Software Foundation, he understands that the concealing of source code is unethical and regressive; dedicated to the digital rights of users everywhere, he has actively participated in the development and distribution of free software.

Brandon is currently pursuing a Bachelor of Science degree in Computer Science at Wentworth Institute of Technology in Boston and takes pride in helping others learn. Occasionally, he gives lectures in classes and clubs, with hopes of encouraging interest in interactive media development with frameworks such as SFML and LWJGL.

I'd like to thank my partner, Yamilah Atallah, for brainstorming game ideas with me, coming up with meaningful concepts and wonderful designs, and changing my life in so many positive ways; with this support, my interest in game development has grown.

Karol Gasiński is a programmer, entrepreneur, and traveler living in Poland, Europe. He works as a Graphic Software Engineer at an Intel Research & Development facility, and has worked on 6 generations of Intel graphic cards. As a member of KHRONOS group, Karol contributes to the development of OpenGL and OpenGL ES Specifications — the industry standard for high-performance graphics.

Outside of his work, Karol's biggest passion is game development and low-level programming. He has been associated with the games industry for over 6 years. In the past, he has worked on mobile versions of games such as *Medieval Total War*, *Pro Evolution Soccer*, and *Silent Hill*. Currently he is the founder and chairman of the Polish Conference on Computer Games Development — the biggest and fastest growing industry event in the country.

Karol gives lectures on most Polish conferences and events for game developers including WGK, GameDay, SWPC, the DigitalFrontier course, IGK, and others. You can also meet him on GDC Europe and GDC San Francisco, where each year he gathers inspiration for his new games.

Eyal Kalderon is a self-taught computer programmer and high school student. Having been introduced to the programming scene at a fairly young age, Eyal developed his early skills in Visual Basic and made a switch to C# early on. Eyal has made himself at home for several years now programming with C and C++ and using shell scripts to automate every task he finds boring. After trying SDL, Eyal switched to SFML in 2010, enjoyed it, and has been following its progress closely ever since.

Understanding the power of print, having gained much from the Internet and professional publications, Eyal chose to erect 'nullpwd' (`nullpwd.wordpress.com`) in March of 2010, a casual software-centered blog that acts as an unintimidating front for various software topics, such as programming, penetration systems, and the current happenings of the open source community.

www.PacktPub.com

Support files, eBooks, discount offers and more

You might want to visit www.PacktPub.com for support files and downloads related to your book.

Did you know that Packt offers eBook versions of every book published, with PDF and ePub files available? You can upgrade to the eBook version at www.PacktPub.com and as a print book customer, you are entitled to a discount on the eBook copy. Get in touch with us at service@packtpub.com for more details.

At www.PacktPub.com, you can also read a collection of free technical articles, sign up for a range of free newsletters and receive exclusive discounts and offers on Packt books and eBooks.

http://PacktLib.PacktPub.com

Do you need instant solutions to your IT questions? PacktLib is Packt's online digital book library. Here, you can access, read and search across Packt's entire library of books.

Why Subscribe?

- Fully searchable across every book published by Packt
- Copy and paste, print and bookmark content
- On demand and accessible via web browser

Free Access for Packt account holders

If you have an account with Packt at www.PacktPub.com, you can use this to access PacktLib today and view nine entirely free books. Simply use your login credentials for immediate access.

Table of Contents

Preface

Welcome to the pages of *SFML Game Development*!

Whether you are just grabbing our book in a store, previewing it in your e-book reader, or you have already bought it—you have taken your first step in becoming a game developer by picking up this book.

Game development is a very interesting topic, as it combines many different fields such as software development, graphical design, music composition, and storytelling. Nowadays, there is an enormous variety of games available, yet developers never cease to be creative and to come up with innovations. This book conveys the process of game development in a way that covers state-of-the-art techniques, leaving you ready to implement your own ideas.

It does not matter if you are already an experienced developer or an ambitious newcomer to the field of making games. Although the book requires no previous knowledge on game development, we also teach valuable concepts and techniques that will help you grow as a game developer.

Throughout the book, we develop a 2D game with SFML. We focus on a top-scrolling aircraft shooter, where the player acts as a pilot and is confronted with various challenges. We begin with the bare bones of each element and continuously add functionality as we progress in the book. In every chapter, new features are introduced, and the code is updated accordingly. Therefore, you will not only see the concepts in theory, but also will have a direct implementation at hand, which you can investigate and extend the way you like.

That said, we would like to wish you a great journey through the chapters of this book. May it be a good experience in all its extent! Please enjoy!

What this book covers

Chapter 1, Making a Game Tick, introduces the SFML library and shows you basic concepts such as the game loop and rendering.

Chapter 2, Keeping Track of Your Textures – Resource Management, covers the loading and management of external resources such as images, fonts, and sounds.

Chapter 3, Forge of the Gods – Shaping Our World, builds up the framework of the game world and addresses the concept of scene graphs and game entities.

Chapter 4, Command and Control – Input Handling, shows how to react to user input from the keyboard, mouse, and joystick.

Chapter 5, Diverting the Game Flow – State Stack, covers switching between application states such as different menus, or between menus and the game itself.

Chapter 6, Waiting and Maintenance Area – Menus, introduces a simple graphical user interface in the menus.

Chapter 7, Warfare Unleashed – Implementing Gameplay, approaches actual gameplay mechanisms. Enemies, bullets, missiles, power-ups and collision detection are implemented.

Chapter 8, Every Pixel Counts – Adding Visual Effects, enhances the graphical appearance of the game by adding animations, particle systems, and shaders.

Chapter 9, Cranking Up the Bass – Music and Sound Effects, explains a way to integrate audio into the game.

Chapter 10, Company Atop The Clouds – Co-op Multiplayer, covers networking basics and a multiplayer implementation over the network.

What you need for this book

Since this book is built around the SFML library, you need to download and install it. You can get SFML at `www.sfml-dev.org`; the first chapter gives a brief installation guide.

In case you decide to recompile SFML yourself, you will also require the cross-platform build tool CMake, which can be downloaded from `www.cmake.org`.

Who this book is for

SFML Game Development is aimed at audiences of all ages who already know how to program in C++, at least to an intermediate level. It is optimal if the reader already has some experience in programming and knows the language well.

The ideal reader for such a book would be a person who is experienced in C++ and would now like to enter the world of game development in a simple yet serious way. However, if the reader already knows a good deal of it and still wants to read through the pages to see different approaches, or if he simply wants to learn more about SFML in a bigger practical example, we strongly encourage to read on!

Conventions

In this book, you will find a number of styles of text that distinguish between different kinds of information. Here are some examples of these styles, and an explanation of their meaning.

Code words in text are shown as follows: "To manage all these screens and transitions, we create the StateStack class."

A block of code is set as follows:

```
namespace GUI
{
    class Component : public sf::Drawable,
                      public sf::Transformable
    {
        public:
            typedef std::shared_ptr<Component> Ptr;

                        Component();
```

When we wish to draw your attention to a particular part of a code block, the relevant lines or items are set in bold:

```
: mChildren()
, mSelectedChild(-1)
{
}

void Container::pack(std::shared_ptr<GUI::Component> component)
{
```

New terms and **important words** are shown in bold. Words that you see on the screen, in menus or dialog boxes for example, appear in the text like this: "It shows a background with a little information about the game, besides its title and then blinks a big old **Press any key to continue** message".

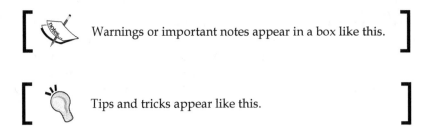

Warnings or important notes appear in a box like this.

Tips and tricks appear like this.

Reader feedback

Feedback from our readers is always welcome. Let us know what you think about this book—what you liked or may have disliked. Reader feedback is important for us to develop titles that you really get the most out of.

To send us general feedback, simply send an e-mail to feedback@packtpub.com, and mention the book title via the subject of your message.

If there is a topic that you have expertise in and you are interested in either writing or contributing to a book, see our author guide on www.packtpub.com/authors.

Customer support

Now that you are the proud owner of a Packt book, we have a number of things to help you to get the most from your purchase.

Downloading the example code

You can download the example code files for all Packt books you have purchased from your account at http://www.packtpub.com. If you purchased this book elsewhere, you can visit http://www.packtpub.com/support and register to have the files e-mailed directly to you.

Errata

Although we have taken every care to ensure the accuracy of our content, mistakes do happen. If you find a mistake in one of our books—maybe a mistake in the text or the code—we would be grateful if you would report this to us. By doing so, you can save other readers from frustration and help us improve subsequent versions of this book. If you find any errata, please report them by visiting http://www.packtpub.com/submit-errata, selecting your book, clicking on the **errata submission form** link, and entering the details of your errata. Once your errata are verified, your submission will be accepted and the errata will be uploaded on our website, or added to any list of existing errata, under the Errata section of that title. Any existing errata can be viewed by selecting your title from http://www.packtpub.com/support.

Piracy

Piracy of copyright material on the Internet is an ongoing problem across all media. At Packt, we take the protection of our copyright and licenses very seriously. If you come across any illegal copies of our works, in any form, on the Internet, please provide us with the location address or website name immediately so that we can pursue a remedy.

Please contact us at copyright@packtpub.com with a link to the suspected pirated material.

We appreciate your help in protecting our authors, and our ability to bring you valuable content.

Questions

You can contact us at questions@packtpub.com if you are having a problem with any aspect of the book, and we will do our best to address it.

1
Making a Game Tick

Through the words in this book, we will attempt to convey the best knowledge we possibly can. We aim to teach techniques that we learned along the years, techniques that we would like to have been told about in our early days of game development. We now write this book to save your time, by showing you directly the solution to common problems, and why things work the way they do.

Alongside our attempt to teach the basics and a little beyond game development, we will especially focus on the **Simple and Fast Multimedia Library (SFML)**. Every part of this book will be about developing a game and leveraging the advantages that SFML is able to provide us. To spice things up a little, and since we use the C++ programming language, we will try our best to use the language in a modern way, applying more recent language features, techniques, and programming styles, in a fully object-oriented approach. C++ is a great tool and it always has been, however, it is a good thing if we grow with it and adapt to the possibilities it has to offer in the present day.

This chapter introduces the SFML library and shows you its capabilities by creating a small application. We are going to address the basic concepts relevant to game development, namely; rendering, game loops, and code organization. Furthermore, the first part of our game code developed, will serve as a basis for the coming chapters.

Introducing SFML

Before we start developing a game, we would like to tell you a little bit about the library we will use throughout the book. SFML is an object-oriented C++ framework. As can be guessed by the name, its philosophy consists of having a simple, user-friendly **application programming interface (API)**, and allowing for both high performances and fast development.

SFML is a multimedia library, meaning that it provides a layer between you and the hardware. It is split into five modules:

- **System**: This is a core module upon which all other modules are built. It provides two-dimensional and three-dimensional vector classes, clocks, threads, and Unicode strings, among other things.

- **Window**: The Window module makes it possible to create application windows, and to collect user input, such as mouse movement or key presses.

- **Graphics**: This module provides all functionalities that are related to two-dimensional rendering, such as images, texts, shapes, and colors.

- **Audio**: SFML also offers a module to work with sound. When you want to load a music theme and play it on the computer's loudspeakers, this is the module you have to look for.

- **Network**: Another medium SFML covers is the network, a more and more important part of our interconnected world. This module allows you to send data over LAN or the Internet; it also lets you work with protocols, such as HTTP or FTP.

If you don't need all the modules, it is possible to use only a part of SFML. We will cover every module in SFML, but of course we are not able to use every single class. We recommend having a look at the SFML documentation, which is available at www.sfml-dev.org/documentation.php. The documentation explains every class and function in a detailed manner, and is an invaluable tool when developing a game using SFML.

SFML is open source, which means that you have access to its complete source code. Usually, the implementations aren't relevant to the user, but if you are interested in how something was solved, don't hesitate to skim through SFML's code.

The library uses the zlib/libpng license, which is extremely permissive. You can use SFML in both open and closed source projects, both free and commercial.

Downloading and installation

There are two possibilities when using SFML: download the pre-built libraries, or recompile them yourself. The first option is simpler, but you have to wait for major versions (2.0, 2.1, and so on) to be released. If you want to use the latest development sources, you can download the current Git revision. The configuration software CMake is used to prepare the sources for compilation with a compiler of your choice. For example, CMake creates Visual Studio solutions or g++ Makefiles. The recompilation process is explained in detail in the SFML tutorials, which can be found at www.sfml-dev.org/tutorials.php.

As mentioned, SFML is split into five modules. There are five headers to include a complete module (and its dependencies). To include the whole Audio module, you can write:

```
#include <SFML/Audio.hpp>
```

On the other hand, if you need a specific header file, you can find it in the directory of the corresponding module:

```
#include <SFML/Audio/Sound.hpp>
```

Each module is compiled to a separate library, which makes it possible to use only the modules you need. SFML can be built for release or debug mode, and it can be linked statically or dynamically. The resulting libraries are named according to the scheme `sfml-module[-s][-d]`. The `-s` postfix is required if you link statically; the `-d` postfix specifies debug mode. For example, to link the Graphics module statically in release mode, you have to specify the library `sfml-graphics-s` in your linker options. Depending on your compiler, a file extension (such as `.lib`) might be necessary. Keep in mind that some modules depend on others; therefore, you have to link the dependencies too. For example, Graphics depends on Window, which depends on System; therefore, you should link the three (in this order).

An important point to note is that if you link SFML statically, you have to define the macro `SFML_STATIC` in your projects, so that the linker knows what functions to resolve.

In case you do not know how linking a library works for a specific compiler, please refer to the online tutorials. They explain how to install everything correctly, and are always up-to-date.

A minimal example

Before you go deeper into the book and SFML itself, let's take a look at a minimal application example to show how an application that uses this library looks like, its general flow of execution, and some basic functionality.

```
#include <SFML/Graphics.hpp>

int main()
{
    sf::RenderWindow window(sf::VideoMode(640, 480), "SFML
Application");
    sf::CircleShape shape;
    shape.setRadius(40.f);
    shape.setPosition(100.f, 100.f);
```

```
shape.setFillColor(sf::Color::Cyan);
while (window.isOpen())
{
sf::Event event;
while (window.pollEvent(event))
{
    if (event.type == sf::Event::Closed)
        window.close();
}
window.clear();
window.draw(shape);
window.display();
}
}
```

All this application does is to open a window onto which we can render, with a width of 640 pixels and a height of 480 pixels. Its title says "SFML Application". Then, a cyan geometric circle is created, and while the window is open, it is drawn to the screen. Finally, for each time the circle is drawn, the program checks for user input that may have arrived from the underlying window. In our case, we only handle the sf::Event::Closed event, which arrives every time the application is requested to terminate, such as when we click on the close button, or press an application-terminating shortcut, such as *Alt + F4*.

If you failed to understand a part of or the whole snippet of code, don't fear. This book contains all you need to know about this and much more.

A few notes on C++

C++ is a very powerful, but also very complex programming language; even after years one never stops learning. We expect you to understand the basic language features (variables, data types, functions, classes, polymorphism, pointers, and templates), as well as the most important parts of the standard library (strings, streams, and the STL). If you feel unsure, we recommend reading a good C++ book, before or in parallel to this book, since SFML and our code sometimes uses advanced techniques. Game development is a difficult topic on its own; it is very frustrating if you additionally have to fight C++. Even if it takes some time to reasonably learn the programming language, it is a good investment, since it will save you days of tedious debugging.

You may have heard that in 2011, a new C++ standard was released, which introduced a lot of extremely useful features. We are going to use a few C++11 features in the book, and show how they can improve code. Each time we use a new C++11 technique, we will briefly explain it.

An issue that is widely underestimated, especially by beginners, is the importance of clean code. Before making a game, it is always a good idea to have a rough imagination of the game features and their implementation. It may help to draw sketches on a paper, in order to visualize contexts better. Also during development, it is crucial to keep an eye on the code design, and to refactor messy code where necessary.

Some key aspects of good code are as follows:

- **Modularity**: In this the functionalities are separated, and dependencies between them are reduced to a minimum. This allows you to maintain and debug application parts locally, as well as, to change the implementation of a module without affecting the other modules. Concretely, we achieve this by widely avoiding global variables, distributing functionality to different classes, and keeping interfaces between them small. We also split the code base to different headers and implementation files, and try to include only what is really necessary.

- **Abstraction**: In this, the functionality is encapsulated into classes and functions. Code duplication is avoided. The usage of low-level operations, such as manual memory management (`new`/`delete`) is minimized, because it is inherently error-prone, and replaced with idioms such as RAII. In short, keep most of your code on a high abstraction level, such that it is expressive and achieves a lot of actions within a few lines. When you need boilerplate code, wrap it into functions, so that the code using it still looks clean.

- **Code style**: One thing, be consistent. It does not matter what naming convention you use, or if you have a space between `if` and the opening parenthesis, so long as you stick to one style. It is important that you keep the code readable and expressive, so that you still recognize what you have done after several weeks. Use comments where appropriate.

After this initial sermon, we hope that you have recognized how a well-structured code can keep up your motivation to develop, while on the other hand, a total mess is contra-productive and frustrating, when it comes to maintenance, debugging, or integration of new features. Don't be afraid if this advice sounds very abstract; you will automatically gain experience while developing projects.

By the way, the code we are going to develop during the chapters is available for download on the Packt Publishing website.

Developing the first game

Now that we got the boring parts finished, we can finally start making a game. So where do we start? What do we do first? First, you should have an idea of what kind of game you want to develop, and what elements it will incorporate. For the purpose of this book, we have chosen to create a shoot-em-up game. The player controls an aircraft viewed from the top, and has to find its way through a level full of enemies.

In order to tease you a little, we show you a screenshot we will have at the end of this chapter.

It might not be the most amazing game you have seen so far, but it exemplifies a good point. To make a game, we need a medium for communicating what is going on to the user. For us, that amounts to showing images on the screen to the player, and having a way for the player to manipulate the game.

The Game class

In this chapter, we implement the basis for your game that will get you going. The root for us is a class called Game; instead of doing our logic in the main() function as we did in the minimal example, we move everything into the Game class instead. This is a good starting point—it gives us a better overview of our code, as we can extract separate functionality into their own functions, and use them within the Game class. If we look at the minimal example, we had three distinct areas in the code: initialization, event processing, and rendering. Now if we continued to develop there, these three parts would grow quite a lot, and we would end up with a gigantic wall of code, which would be nearly impossible to navigate. The Game class helps us out here.

Here is the general design of the class and its intended usage:

```
class Game
{
    public:
                            Game();
        void                run();

    private:
        void                processEvents();
        void                update();
        void                render();

    private:
        sf::RenderWindow    mWindow;
        sf::CircleShape     mPlayer;
};

int main()
{
    Game game;
    game.run();
}
```

As you can clearly see, we replaced all the code in the main() function from the minimal example with just a Game object and a call to its run() function. The idea here is that we have hidden the loop we had previously in the run() function. It doesn't happen very often that we have to fiddle with it anyway. Now, we can move the actual code that updates the game to the update() function, and the code that renders it to the render() function. The method processEvents() is responsible for player input. So if we want to get something actually done, we implement it in one of the three private functions.

Let's have a look at the code now:

```
Game::Game()
: mWindow(sf::VideoMode(640, 480), "SFML Application")
, mPlayer()
{
    mPlayer.setRadius(40.f);
    mPlayer.setPosition(100.f, 100.f);
    mPlayer.setFillColor(sf::Color::Cyan);
}
void Game::run()
{
    while (mWindow.isOpen())
    {
        processEvents();
        update();
        render();
    }
}
```

The function processEvents() handles user input. It polls the application window for any input events, and will close the window if a Closed event occurs (the user clicks on the window's **X** button).

```
void Game::processEvents()
{
    sf::Event event;
    while (mWindow.pollEvent(event))
    {
        if (event.type == sf::Event::Closed)
            mWindow.close();
    }
}
```

The method update() updates the game logic, that is, everything that happens in the game. For the moment, we leave the implementation empty. We are going to fill it as we add functionality to the game.

```
void Game::update()
{
}
```

The render() method renders our game to the screen. It consists of three parts. First, we clear the window with a color, usually black. Therefore, the output of the last rendering is completely overridden. Then, we draw all the objects of the current frame by calling the sf::RenderWindow::draw() method. After we have drawn everything, we need to actually display it on the screen. The render() method looks as follows:

```
void Game::render()
{
    mWindow.clear();
    mWindow.draw(mPlayer);
    mWindow.display();
}
```

Later in the chapter, when we display something more interesting than a cyan circle, we are going to have a deeper look at the rendering step.

Even though this actually is more code than what we started with, it still looks like it is less, because at any given time, our eyes only have to rest on a smaller part.

And with this you should still get the same result as you would in the SFML minimal example: a cyan-colored circle in a window with a black background. Nothing fancy yet, but we are well on our way.

Game loops and frames

Now talking a little more in-depth about the loop we have placed in the run() function. This loop is most often called the **main loop** or the **game loop** because it controls the lifetime of an application. As long as this one continues to iterate, the application will stay alive. In our case, we would like our application to terminate its execution as soon as the window ceases to exist.

Now what do we do during an iteration of this loop? First we process the events from the window, then we update the game, and finally we render the results on the screen. An iteration of the game loop is most often called a **frame** or a **tick**. You might have heard of the term **frames per second (FPS)**. This is a measurement of how many loop iterations the game can do during a second. Sometimes, the concept of FPS only accounts for rendering times, but it is not unusual for it to encompass the input processing and logic updates as well.

We can explain this visually with a flow chart to further help you see clearly the logic of our loop.

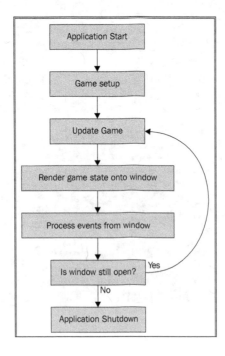

It accurately describes what our application does at the moment. The only thing left out is the event processing. That functionality could have its own flow chart. But it does one task only in our basic example. It tells the window to close itself if the user requests it.

Now, the way we work with the computer in C++ is very linear. Everything is done in the set order that we give it, and the computer does nothing for us unless we explicitly tell it to. So, if we don't tell it to draw the circle, it won't draw it. If the state of the game somehow changes, and we don't tell the computer how to render a new frame, then nothing will change on the screen because the computer won't know that the graphics have changed.

Now that we got this sorted out, let's see if we can get something to happen over several frames. We make the circle move by pressing keys on our keyboard.

Input over several frames

First we have to be able to detect that the user is pressing down a key on his keyboard. SFML provides this functionality in several ways, but for now we will settle with input detection by responding to *events*.

What are events? The word itself implies something that is happening with our window, emitting a notice of the happening. As soon as the user somehow interacts with our window, the operating system sends an event that we can process. For our convenience, SFML translates events from the underlying operating systems to a uniform structure that we can use with ease: `sf::Event`. Once the window internally detects that some kind of input has happened, it will store an `sf::Event` object containing information about that input. We will then poll all those events as fast as we can, in order to respond to them.

SFML supports a wide variety of events, but there are two event types that interest us here: `sf::Event::KeyPressed` and `sf::Event::KeyReleased`. They represent a key being pressed and released respectively.

So let's change our code so that it can handle this. We again poll the window for events, and have a case differentiation on the event type.

```
void Game::processEvents()
{
    sf::Event event;
    while (mWindow.pollEvent(event))
    {
        switch (event.type)
        {
```

For each time the `while` loop iterates, it means a new event that was registered by the window is being handled. While there can be many different events, we will only check for some types of events, which are of our interest right now.

```
case sf::Event::KeyPressed:
    handlePlayerInput(event.key.code, true);
    break;
case sf::Event::KeyReleased:
    handlePlayerInput(event.key.code, false);
    break;
case sf::Event::Closed:
    mWindow.close();
    break;
        }
    }
}
```

In the `handlePlayerInput()` function, we check which key on the keyboard has been pressed or released. To store this information, we use four Boolean member variables: `mIsMovingUp`, `mIsMovingDown`, `mIsMovingLeft`, and `mIsMovingRight`. We set the corresponding variable depending on the key being pressed or released.

```
void Game::handlePlayerInput(sf::Keyboard::Key key,
bool isPressed)
{
    if (key == sf::Keyboard::W)
        mIsMovingUp = isPressed;
    else if (key == sf::Keyboard::S)
        mIsMovingDown = isPressed;
    else if (key == sf::Keyboard::A)
        mIsMovingLeft = isPressed;
    else if (key == sf::Keyboard::D)
        mIsMovingRight = isPressed;
}
```

In `Game::handlePlayerInput()` we receive the enumerator describing the key that was pressed or released. The flag describing whether a press or release occurred is passed as the second argument. So we check what key the user is manipulating, and change our state depending on that.

Now, we have a way to perceive that the user is pressing a key. We know when we want to move up, down, left, and right. We know at each iteration of the main loop exactly, what the user wants; we just have to update the circle with a new position depending on this input. This method gives us a great advantage. So finally we can write something in our `update()` function, namely, the movement of our player. We check which of the four Boolean member variables is true, and determine the movement accordingly. By using `+=` (instead of `=`) and `if` (instead of `else if`), we implicitly handle the case where two opposite keys, such as right and left are pressed at the same time — the `movement` stays zero. The `update()` function is shown in the following code snippet:

```
void Game::update()
{
    sf::Vector2f movement(0.f, 0.f);
    if (mIsMovingUp)
        movement.y -= 1.f;
    if (mIsMovingDown)
        movement.y += 1.f;
    if (mIsMovingLeft)
        movement.x -= 1.f;
    if (mIsMovingRight)
        movement.x += 1.f;

    mPlayer.move(movement);
}
```

We introduce two new things here: a vector and the `move()` function on the circle shape. The `move()` function does what its name says, it moves the shape by the amount we provide it.

Vector algebra

Vectors are an important part of algebraic mathematics. They imply lots of rules and definitions, which go beyond the scope of our book. However, SFML's `sf::Vector2` class template is way more practical, both in concept and functionality. To be as simple as we could possibly be, we know that a coordinate in a two-dimensional Cartesian system would need two components: x and y. Because in graphics all coordinates are expressed with the decimal `float` data type, `sf::Vector2` is instantiated as `sf::Vector2<float>`, which conveniently has a typedef named `sf::Vector2f`. Such an object is made to contain two member variables, x and y. This makes our life simpler, because now we don't need to pass two variables to functions, as we can fit both in a single `sf::Vector2f` object. `sf::Vector2f` also defines common vector operations, such as additions and subtractions with other vectors, or multiplications and divisions with scalars (single values), effectively shortening our code.

To be a little more precise in the explanation, vectors are not only used to define positions, but they also are a perfect fit to define orientations. So, a vector is great to store a two-component coordinate, be it an absolute or relative position, or even to express a direction to follow, or to shoot a bullet towards. There is a little more to know about two-dimensional vectors, especially if they are directions, such as the concept of normalization or unit vector. This operation applies only to directions, as it makes no sense in positions. We consider a vector normalized if it has length one (hence the term unit vector) and the vector still expresses the same direction as before normalization. The following figure visualizes the vector (2, 3). This vector represents a translation of 2 units to the right and 3 units down.

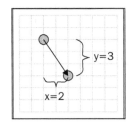

Please do not confuse `sf::Vector2f` with `std::vector`. While their names are similar, the first refers to the mathematical concept; the latter is simply a dynamically allocated array from the standard C++ library.

In our case, our vector called `movement` expresses a movement from the origin of the current coordinate system. For us, this origin is the shape's position. It might be a bit tricky getting into the whole way of thinking in different spaces if you don't like math.

Vector algebra is very interesting, and definitely something very useful if you know it. So we recommend you study it. Mathematics is your friend as soon as you stop fighting it; it really makes a lot of things easier for you in programming. It is almost safe to claim that this subsection of math is the single most important topic when we need to implement gameplay mechanics. A wide range of problems that you will face in almost any kind of game are already solved and well-studied before, so you're better off learning this subject than reinventing the wheel every time. To avoid leaving you hanging, here's an example: Let's say you have point A and point B, which represent two characters in an action game. When the enemy at point A wants to shoot our player at point B, it needs to know the direction in which to shoot the projectile. Why waste your brains thinking on how to solve this problem if this field of math defines this operation as one of its most basic rules? All you need is to find the direction vector C, which is obtained by calculating B minus A. The difference between two positions gives us the direction between the two. Yes, that easy!

Frame-independent movement

If you run everything we have done so far, you will be able to move the circle, but it won't move uniformly. It will probably be very fast, because currently we have done the movement in a very naive way. Right now your computer will be running the update() function as fast as it can, which means it will probably call it a couple of hundreds of times each second, if not more. If we move the shape by one pixel for every frame, this can count up to several 100 pixels every second, making our little player fly all over the screen. You cannot just change the movement value to something lower, as it will only fix the problem for your computer. If you move to a slower or faster computer, the speed will change again.

So how do we solve this? Well, let's look at the problem we are facing. We are having a problem because our movement is frame-dependent. We want to provide the speed in a way that changes depending on the time a frame takes. There is a simple formula you should remember from your old school days. It's the formula that goes: *distance = speed * time*. Now why is this relevant for us? Because with this formula we can calculate a relevant speed for every frame, so that the circle always travels exactly the distance we want it to travel over one second, no matter what computer we are sitting on. So let's modify the function to what we actually need to make this work.

```cpp
void Game::update(sf::Time deltaTime)
{
    sf::Vector2f movement(0.f, 0.f);
    if (mIsMovingUp)
        movement.y -= PlayerSpeed;
    if (mIsMovingDown)
        movement.y += PlayerSpeed;
    if (mIsMovingLeft)
        movement.x -= PlayerSpeed;
    if (mIsMovingRight)
        movement.x += PlayerSpeed;

    mPlayer.move(movement * deltaTime.asSeconds());
}
```

The major difference we have made here is that we now receive a time value every time we call the update. We calculate the distance we want to travel every frame, depending on how much time has elapsed. We call the time that has elapsed since the last frame **delta time** (or **time step**), and often abbreviate it as dt in the code. But how do we get this time? We are lucky because SFML provides the utilities for it.

In SFML, there is a class that measures the time from when it was started. What we have to do is to measure the time each frame takes. We are talking about the class `sf::Clock`. It has a function called `restart()`, which lets the clock return the elapsed time since its start, and restarts the clock from zero, making it ideal for our current situation. SFML uses the class `sf::Time` for all time formats; it is a convenient data type that can be converted from and to seconds, milliseconds, and microseconds. Here's the modified `Game::run()` member function:

```cpp
void Game::run()
{
    sf::Clock clock;
    while (mWindow.isOpen())
    {
        sf::Time deltaTime = clock.restart();
        processEvents();
        update(deltaTime);
        render();
    }
}
```

There is no big difference; we create a `clock`, and in every frame we query it for its current elapsed time, restart the `clock`, and then pass this time to the update function.

Fixed time steps

The solution we have come up with so far is sufficient for many cases. But it is not a perfect solution, because you can have problems in certain scenarios where delta times vary strongly. The code can be quite hard to debug, because it is impossible to get 100 percent reproducible results, since every frame is unique, and you can't guarantee that the delta time remains the same.

Consider that a frame may sometimes take three times the average delta time. This can lead to severe mistakes in the game logic, for example, when a player moves three times the distance and passes through a wall he would normally collide with. This is why physics engines expect the delta time to be fixed.

The following is a figure describing the problem we are referring to:

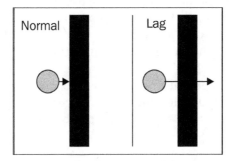

What we will do now is use a technique called fixed time steps. We write code that guarantees that in any circumstances, we always give the same delta time to the update function, no matter what happens. If you find that sounding difficult, there is no big difference from what we already have. We just have to do some book-keeping in our code for how much time has passed since we last called the update() function.

```
void Game::run()
{
    sf::Clock clock;
    sf::Time timeSinceLastUpdate = sf::Time::Zero;
    while (mWindow.isOpen())
    {
        processEvents();
        timeSinceLastUpdate += clock.restart();
        while (timeSinceLastUpdate > TimePerFrame)
        {
            timeSinceLastUpdate -= TimePerFrame;
            processEvents();
            update(TimePerFrame);
        }
        render();
    }
}
```

The actual effect of this change is that we accumulate how much time has elapsed in a variable timeSinceLastUpdate. When we are over the required amount for one frame, we subtract the desired length of this frame (namely TimePerFrame), and update the game. We do this until we are below the required amount again. This solves the problem with variable delta times, as we are guaranteed that the same amount of frames is always run. In the application you can download, the logic frame rate will be set to 60 frames per second by having the TimePerFrame constant equal to sf::seconds(1.f / 60.f).

Eventually, we have two while loops. The outer one is the game loop as we know it, and calls the render() method. The inner one collects user input, and computes the game logic; this loop is executed at a constant rate. If rendering is slow, it may happen that processEvents() and update() are called multiple times before one render() call. As a result, the game occasionally stutters, since, not every update is rendered, but the game doesn't slow down. On the other hand, fast rendering can lead to render() being called multiple times without a logic update in between. Rendering the same state multiple times does not change anything on the screen, but it allows for techniques such as interpolations between two states to smoothen the game flow.

If you are interested in the topic, there is a famous article with detailed explanations at http://gafferongames.com/game-physics/fix-your-timestep.

Other techniques related to frame rates

SFML provides a few utilities that are worth knowing with respect to time handling and frame updates. One of them is sf::sleep(), a function that interrupts the execution for a given time, which gives the processor an opportunity to work on other tasks. Sleeping is not very accurate, so you should not use it for exact timing purposes. The method sf::RenderWindow::setFramerateLimit() tries to achieve the specified frame rate by calling sf::sleep() internally. It is a nice function for testing purposes, but it also lacks precision.

Another important technique is **vertical synchronization**, also known as **V-Sync**. Enabled V-Sync adapts the rate of graphical updates (calls of sf::RenderWindow::display()) to the refresh rate of the monitor, usually around 60Hz. This can avoid graphical artifacts such as screen tearing, where a part of your window shows the old frame, and another the new one. You can enable or disable V-Sync using the method sf::RenderWindow::setVerticalSyncEnabled().

Displaying sprites on the screen

Now let's get something interesting on the screen. Instead of just rendering a boring single color circle to the screen, let's actually render an image. To do this, SFML provides a couple of tools to make your life easy. First we have the sf::Texture class that holds the actual image data loaded from the hard drive. Next is the sf::Sprite class that represents an instance with position and orientation in the scene. The texture describes the image, while the sprite describes where and how to put one on the screen.

A simple example of their relationship is as follows:

```
sf::Texture texture;
if (!texture.loadFromFile("path/to/file.png"))
{
  // Handle loading error
}
sf::Sprite sprite(texture);
sprite.setPosition(100.f, 100.f);
window.clear();
window.draw(sprite);
window.display();
```

Here, we load a `texture` from the hard drive, and check if loading has succeeded. We construct a new sprite to use the texture and set its position to (100, 100), relative to the upper-left window corner.

File paths and working directories

About file paths, it would be useful to make some things clear. First, the slashes that separate directories in a path in order to locate a file will be most often forward slashes (/), especially in Unix-like operating systems. In Windows, you will occasionally see back slashes (\) used instead, but probably not everywhere. Do not let this confuse you, the only true cross-platform way to specify a file path is using forward slashes, so make sure they are always your choice, even in Windows.

Also, it is of extreme importance to note that every program being run in the operating systems that SFML supports has a working directory while being executed. Usually, when you run the program from a graphical window manager, the working directory is exactly where the executable is located; however, this is not always the case. It is possible to run a program with any working directory, and it is even possible to change the working directory programmatically from inside the program. In the context of a game, the point of understanding working directories is for loading files, which are loaded in paths relative to the executable in most cases. All paths passed on to SFML are relative to the working directory, unless you make them absolute by starting them with a slash in Unix-like operating systems, or with a drive letter in Windows.

Real-time rendering

In a game simulation, it is highly likely that there will be changes to what's drawn in every frame. Even when there is no player input, you will observe in most cases some kind of animation, which will effectively change the end result on the screen for that given frame.

Many programs use a render-on-demand approach. They will only redraw a new frame on the screen when a change actually happens, minimizing the performance costs in applications where the screen doesn't change very often. But, by the nature of gaming software, this approach would be made redundant, as we would be requesting new frames all the time. Because of this, game programmers adopted entirely the concept of **real-time rendering**, which ignores frame requests as they were previously known, and blindly draws to the screen as fast as possible. If while playing your favorite game you eventually noticed a usual FPS count of 30 or 60, this is due to the fact that our eyes can't perceive, in regular circumstances, more frames than that amount in a second. Because it makes virtually no difference to the end user, the programmers limit the FPS count to such a number, and save the processor power for other tasks, such as logic processing. In short, nowadays, the whole scene is rendered again and again, independently of what changed since the last frame.

To explain the notion of real-time rendering a bit further, we would like to mention the concept of **double buffering** that comes inherently attached to it. Double buffering is a technique that was created to negate graphical glitches derived from asynchronies in the rendering tasks. Before this technique became widely used, programmers needed to have additional concerns when drawing to the screen, to ensure that only what belongs to a frame is drawn in it, and that there are no remains of pixels from previous frames.

Double buffering defines two virtual screens to draw graphics to. The front buffer and the back buffer are the names chosen to address these render targets. The front buffer is what is currently displayed on the screen, while the back buffer is the one we are drawing to at the moment, preparing a new frame. Once our frame is fully drawn in the back buffer, we use the SFML's `sf::RenderWindow::display()` function to put the contents of the back buffer on the screen. The back buffer becomes the front buffer, while the front buffer that was set will now be the back buffer to draw on. This way we ensure that we always have a buffer with the previous frame unharmed, as well as a working buffer that we can safely change at any time, without affecting what is on the screen. By clearing, drawing, and then displaying these buffers in an interleaved manner, we achieve double buffering.

Adapting the code

In our code, we replace `sf::CircleShape` with `sf::Sprite`, which only requires minor modifications. We load an image file called `Eagle.png`. The relative path to it is `Media/Textures`. Don't worry if you don't have the file; you can download it together with the whole source code.

```cpp
// Game.hpp
class Game
{
    public:
                        Game();
        ...
    private:
        sf::Texture mTexture;
        sf::Sprite  mPlayer;
        ...
};

// Game.cpp
Game::Game()
: ...
, mTexture()
, mPlayer()
{
    if (!mTexture.loadFromFile("Media/Textures/Eagle.png"))
    {
        // Handle loading error
    }
    mPlayer.setTexture(mTexture);
    mPlayer.setPosition(100.f, 100.f);
}
```

No code changes have to be done to get our `render()` function to work with sprites instead of shapes. SFML is nice in that way. Everything that can be drawn to a window has to inherit from the abstract class `sf::Drawable`. As long as it is possible, the SFML API keeps a consistency to it. This makes it a lot easier to use, because if you have used a function on one class, you can be pretty sure there will be identical or similar functions in other classes.

Now you have achieved the results you observed in the screenshot we had in the beginning of the chapter. You are also very well on the way to making your game. With these few tools alone you would be able to make a simple game, such as Snake or Pac-Man with ease.

Summary

We had to cover a lot of ground in this chapter. We have explained the most basic concepts that are required to create a game; concepts that you should always have present in order to save yourself from losing time in such issues, and instead, focus on making a great game.

In this chapter we:

- Learned what SFML is, and what functionality it provides
- Listened to input, and moved the player over several frames
- Rendered an image to the screen
- Learned about game loops and delta times, and saw the strengths and weaknesses of different approaches to handle time steps.

And if you are interested in how you would measure your FPS and render that to the screen, then have a look at the code base. We have implemented that functionality there, and it is based on the subjects we have already covered. We would recommend you try yourself; the only things you need are `sf::Text` and `sf::Font` in order to render text on the screen. You can learn more about these classes in SFML's API documentation at `www.sfml-dev.org`.

This concludes our introduction chapter. From now on we are going to investigate different aspects of SFML and game development in a more detailed manner. In the next chapter, we start with resource handling, which explains the backgrounds behind textures, fonts, and other resources.

2
Keeping Track of Your Textures – Resource Management

In the previous chapter, you have learned how to load a texture, and display a sprite that uses the texture. During the process of game development, you encounter such situations again and again: you need to load data from the hard disk, be it images, fonts, or sounds. This chapter intends to give you a broader understanding of the following points:

- What is the motivation behind external resources
- Which classes for resource handling and manipulation does the Simple and Fast Multimedia Library (SFML) provide
- What might a typical use case in a game look like
- How do we cope with the constantly recurring need to manage resources in a simple way

Defining resources

In game development, the term **resource** denotes an external component, which the application loads during runtime. Another often-used term for a resource is **asset**.

Mostly, resources are heavyweight multimedia items, such as images, music themes, or fonts. "Heavyweight" refers to the fact that those objects occupy a lot of memory, and that operations on them, especially copying, perform slowly. This affects the way we use them in our application, as we try to restrict slow operations on them to a minimum.

Non-multimedia items such as scripts that describe the in-game world, menu content, or artificial intelligence are also considered resources. Configuration files containing user settings such as the screen resolution and the music volume are good examples of resources as well. However, when we mention resources in the book, we mostly refer to multimedia resources.

Resources are usually loaded from a file on the hard disk. Although being the most common approach, it is not the only one—other possible examples are the RAM or the network.

Resources in SFML

SFML offers classes to deal with a wide variety of resources. Often, the resource classes are not directly used to output multimedia on the periphery. Instead, there is an intermediate front-end class, which refers to the resource. In contrast to the resource class which holds all the data, the front-end class is lightweight and can be copied without severe performance impacts.

All resource classes contain member functions to load from different places. Depending on the exact resource type, there may be slight deviations. A typical method to load a resource from a file has the following signature:

```
bool loadFromFile(const std::string& filename);
```

The function parameter contains the path to the file, where the resource is stored, and the return value is a `bool`, which is `true` if loading was successful, and `false` if it failed. It is important to check return values in order to react to possible errors, such as invalid file paths.

SFML resources also provide methods to load resources from media other than the hard disk. The function `loadFromMemory()` loads a resource from RAM, which may be useful to load resources that are directly embedded into the executable. The member function `loadFromStream()` loads the resource using a custom `sf::InputStream` instance. This allows the user to exactly specify the loading process. Important use cases of user-defined streams are encrypted and/or compressed file archives.

SFML's resource classes are explained in more detail in the following sections. For this game, we will focus on loading from files.

Textures

The class `sf::Texture` represents a graphical image. The image is stored as an array of pixels in the graphics card's video memory, that is, it does not reside in the RAM. Each pixel is a 32 bit RGBA value, specifying a color with the components red, green, blue, and alpha (transparency), at a certain position in the image. Many common image formats are supported by SFML, for example, JPEG, BMP, PNG, or GIF.

Textures can be drawn on the screen with the `sf::Sprite` class. A sprite is a lightweight object that refers to a texture or a rectangular part of it. It stores attributes such as the position, rotation, scale, or color to affect the way the texture is represented on the screen. Multiple sprites can refer to the same texture and have different attributes, while the texture itself is not affected. The separation between sprites and textures has a big advantage that we have a simple possibility to deal with graphics using `sf::Sprite`, while the heavyweight `sf::Texture` need not be modified.

Images

The `sf::Image` class is a container for pixel values. It behaves similarly to `sf::Texture`; however it stores its pixels on the RAM instead of the video memory, which makes it possible to manipulate single pixels. `sf::Image` is able to load the same image formats as `sf::Texture`. It is also capable of saving the stored image back to a file. It is interesting to know that `sf::Texture` loads the data using an intermediate `sf::Image`, more exactly, the `sf::Texture::loadFromX()` functions are just a shortcut for combined `sf::Image::loadFromX()` and `sf::Texture::loadFromImage()` calls.

When we want to display a `sf::Image` on the screen, we first have to convert it into a `sf::Texture`, and create a `sf::Sprite` referring to it. It is also possible to construct a texture only from a rectangular part of an image, in situations where not all the pixels are going to be displayed. As a result, no memory on the graphics card is wasted. In cases where we do not need to access the single pixels of an image after loading, we are better off when we directly use `sf::Texture`.

An important use case for `sf::Image` is the situation where big textures are required. `sf::Texture` can only store textures on the graphics card that do not exceed a hardware-dependent size. This limit can be retrieved with `sf::Texture::getMaximumSize()`. If you try to load bigger textures into `sf::Texture`, loading will fail. However, you sometimes still need to draw big sprites, for example, a static background for the whole window. What you can do is to load the pixels into `sf::Image`, which does not use the graphics card's memory to store them. Afterwards, you can create multiple `sf::Texture` objects, of which each one is only loaded from a rectangular part of the image. Eventually, the whole image can be drawn by using multiple `sf::Sprite` objects, where each sprite references one texture.

Fonts

The `sf::Font` class is SFML's resource type that stores a character font and provides an interface to manipulate it. A font consists of glyphs, where a glyph is the visual representation of a character. Glyphs are loaded on demand, that is, when the user needs to render a certain character with a certain font size, the corresponding glyph is sought in the font file. Therefore, `sf::Font` does not load the complete font data into memory. As a consequence, the font source (file, memory location, or stream) must remain accessible throughout the font's lifetime. SFML supports many font formats, most notably, **true type fonts (TTF)** and **open type fonts (OTF)**.

To display text on the screen, we use the class `sf::Text`. Analogous to sprites, texts are lightweight objects that refer to fonts. In a game, there are usually only a few fonts, but many different places where text is rendered. Therefore, we have many `sf::Text` instances that refer to a small amount of `sf::Font` objects.

Shaders

A shader is a program that operates directly on the graphics card. Shaders are used to apply a variety of graphical effects to rendered objects. Examples include a bloom shader that amplifies bright parts of the scene, a toon shader that makes objects look like in a cartoon, or a blur effect which simulates flickering hot air. Since SFML builds upon OpenGL, its shader instances use the **OpenGL Shading Language (GLSL)**, a programming language similar to C. SFML supports vertex shaders (which affect the geometry of objects in the scene) and fragment shaders (which manipulate pixels of the scene).

`sf::Shader` can be created from a `std::string` containing the GLSL code of a vertex or a fragment shader. It can also hold both shaders at once; in this case it can be loaded from two strings. It is also possible to initialize a `sf::Shader` instance by passing the filename of a GLSL source file to its constructor.

Sound buffers

The `sf::SoundBuffer` class is used to store a sound effect. It holds an array of 16 bit audio samples, where each sample specifies the amplitude of the audio waveform at a given time. A sound buffer allows access and modification of the samples, but it cannot play audio. Supported file formats are WAV, OGG, AIFF, and many more. The MP3 format is not supported because of its restrictive license.

`sf::Sound` is the class that plays audio from a sound buffer. Like a sprite refers to a texture containing the pixels, a sound refers to a sound buffer containing the audio samples. Analogous to textures, sound buffers must remain alive while they are used by sounds. `sf::Sound` objects can be played, paused, and stopped and have configurable attributes such as volume or pitch. Note that a `sf::Sound` object must stay valid as long as it is played, destroying it ceases to play the sound effect immediately.

Music

`sf::Music` is the class to play music. While `sf::SoundBuffer` is appropriate for short sound effects (explosions, button clicks, and so on.), `sf::Music` is designed to handle music themes. Themes are usually much longer and thus require more memory than sound effects. As a result, `sf::Music` does not load all data at once. Instead, it streams the music, meaning that it continuously loads small chunks of samples. The streaming semantics imply that the source of the music (for example, a file or memory location) must remain valid while the music is in use. That is also why `sf::Music` methods are called `openFromX()` instead of `loadFromX()`, where "X" denotes a source media such as "File". The supported audio formats are the same as for `sf::SoundBuffer`.

For music themes, there is no separation between heavyweight resource and lightweight front-end. `sf::Music` manages all at once: in addition to the loading functionality, it offers many of the `sf::Sound` methods to play, pause, or stop a theme or to configure other parameters. Its objects must also remain alive while the music plays.

The difference between sound buffers and music is shown in the following diagram. On the left, you see a sound buffer object, which loads the whole audio data from the hard disk at once. It can be played using a separate sound object. On the right, a music object streams from the hard disk, that is, it continuously loads small chunks. It can be played on its own.

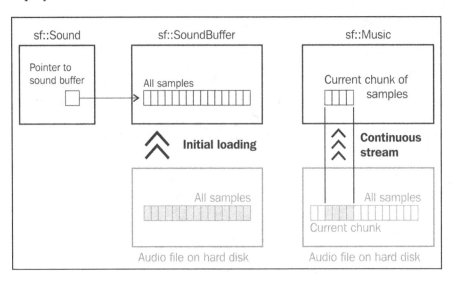

A typical use case

Now we have seen what kinds of different resources there are, but we do not know yet how to apply this knowledge to our game. While the approach you have seen in *Chapter 1, Making a Game Tick*, may work for simple examples, it does not scale well to a bigger project. As our game grows, we have to reflect about how the resources are going to be used. This is explained in the next sections.

Graphics

In our game, a crucial part will be the visual representation of the world and different objects in it. We need to think about how we get from an image on the hard disk to its visualization on the screen.

- Game entities such as the player's airplane, enemies, or the landscape are represented with sprites and possibly texts. They do not own the heavy textures and fonts; instead they use the front-end classes to refer to them.

- As a consequence, the resources (textures and fonts) need to be accessible by the entities. We must make sure that the resource objects stay alive as long as any front-end object refers to them, so we have to find an appropriate scope to declare the resources.

- A sprite in the airplane must somehow get a reference to the texture stored outside. Therefore, we have to transport this information via constructor parameter to the airplane class.

Audio

Another important resource is audio, which can be divided into sound effects and background music. We have to consider how to make both of them audible in the final application, when all we start with is a bunch of audio files in a directory:

- Sound effects are not tied to a specific game entity such as an airplane; they persist independently of the object that causes them. Imagine an airplane that explodes and creates an explosion sound. When we destroy the plane object, we still want the explosion to be audible for some time. As a result, we do not store `sf::Sound` instances in the game entities, but in an object which remains alive throughout a mission. The same applies to the underlying `sf::SoundBuffer` objects which are used by `sf::Sound`.

- For music themes, the semantics are similar. It may even occur that the same theme is played across multiple missions. Ideally, the `sf::Music` objects exist in a scope that outlives a single mission.

- Although the game entities do not own sound effects, they are supposed to play them. As a consequence, we shall provide an interface that allows playing new sound effects.

Acquiring, releasing, and accessing resources

Once we have decided which resources are required by the application, the next step is to investigate how long and by whom they are used. This allows us to decide how the resources are stored in the application, as well as who is responsible of loading and releasing them.

- We want to load the resource in advance, for example, at the time the game starts or the player begins a new mission. In contrast to loading on demand (as soon as a resource is needed), this approach has the advantage that possible loading times occur in the beginning and not during a game. Therefore, the game itself remains fluent and is not interrupted because of resources.

- When resources are likely to not be needed anymore, we can release them and free the memory. This is usually the case at the end of a mission or when the application is quit. We do not want to release resources too early if we risk reloading them shortly after. For example, we do not release the explosion sound buffer as soon as the sound effect is over, because the next explosion may follow a few seconds later.

- There must be a possibility to get a reference to a certain resource after it has been loaded – using a resource identifier. This identifier (ID) could be the file path as a `std::string`. This has some disadvantages: all classes that use a resource must hardcode the path, so if it changes, a lot of code needs to be refactored. Strings are also quite error-prone regarding typographic or case errors. An alternative to strings are enums, where each enumerator denotes an ID. Since an enum has a predefined set of possible states, we get some compile-time safety, and we can handle the paths in a central place.

In conclusion, we have the heavy resource classes which shall be loaded when appropriate, but before the game. Throughout their lifetime, front-end classes such as sprites or sounds may reference them, so we must keep the resources alive. When they are not needed anymore, we can release them.

An automated approach

Our goal is to encapsulate the just mentioned functionality into a class that relieves us from managing resources again and again. For resource management, the C++ idiom **Resource Acquisition Is Initialization (RAII)** comes in handy.

RAII describes the principle that resources are acquired in a class' constructor and released in its destructor. Since both constructor and destructor are invoked automatically when the object is created or goes out of scope, there is no need to track resources manually. RAII is mostly used for automatic memory management (as in smart pointers), but it can be applied to any kind of resources. A great advantage of RAII over manual allocation and deallocation (such as `new`/`delete` pairs) is that deallocation is guaranteed to take place, even when there are multiple return statements or exceptions in a function. To achieve the same safety with manual memory management, every possible path would have to be protected with a `delete` operator. As a result, the code becomes quickly unreadable and error-prone.

In our application, we want to take advantage of RAII to determine the construction (loading) and destruction (release) of SFML resource objects.

Let's begin with a class that holds sf::Texture objects and loads them from files. We call it TextureHolder. Once we have implemented the semantics for textures, we can generalize the implementation to work with other resource types.

Finding an appropriate container

First, we must find the right data structure to store the textures. We ought to choose an STL container that does not perform unnecessary copies. std::vector is the wrong choice, since inserting new textures can trigger a reallocation of the dynamic array and the copying of all textures. Not only is this slow, but also all references and pointers to the textures are invalidated. As mentioned before, we like to access the textures by an enum, so the associative container std::map looks like the perfect choice. The key type is our enumeration, the value type is the sf::Texture.

> The C++11 standard introduces **strongly typed enumerations**, also known as enum class. Unlike traditional enums, they do not offer implicit conversion to integers, and their enumerators reside in the scope of the enum type itself. Since C++11 is still being implemented by compiler vendors, not all features are widely supported yet. In this book, we focus on C++11 features that have already been implemented for a few years. Unfortunately, strongly typed enums do not fall into this category, that's why we do not use them in the book. If they are supported by your compiler, we still recommend using them.

We call our enum as ID, and let it contain three texture identifiers Landscape, Airplane, and Missile. We nest it into a namespace Textures. The namespace gives us a scope for the enumerators. Instead of writing just Airplane, we have Textures::Airplane which clearly describes the intention and avoids possible name collisions in the global scope:

```
namespace Textures
{
    enum ID { Landscape, Airplane, Missile };
}
```

We do not store the sf::Texture directly, but we wrap it into a std::unique_ptr.

> **Unique pointers** are class templates that act like pointers. They automatically call the delete operator in their destructor, thus they provide means of RAII for pointers. They support C++11 move semantics, which allow to transfer ownership between objects without copying. A std::unique_ptr<T> instance is the sole owner of the T object it points to, hence the name "unique".

Unique pointers give us a lot of flexibility; we can basically pass around heavyweight objects without creating copies. In particular, we can store classes that are non-copyable, such as, `sf::Shader`. Our class then looks as shown in the following code:

```
class TextureHolder
{
    private:
        std::map<Textures::ID,
                 std::unique_ptr<sf::Texture>> mTextureMap;
};
```

The compiler-generated default constructor is fine, our map is initially empty. Same for the destructor, `std::map` and `std::unique_ptr` take care of the proper deallocation, so we do not need to define our own destructor.

Loading from files

What we have to write now is a member function to load a resource. It has to take a parameter for the filename and one for the identifier. The identifier is used as a key to store the resource in the map:

```
void load(Textures::ID id, const std::string& filename);
```

In the function definition, we first create a `sf::Texture` object and store it in the unique pointer. Then, we load the texture from the given filename. After loading, we can insert the texture to the map `mTextureMap`. Here, we use `std::move()` to take ownership from the variable `texture` and transfer it as an argument to `std::make_pair()`, which constructs a key-value pair for the map:

```
void TextureHolder::load(Textures::ID id, const std::string& filename)
{
    std::unique_ptr<sf::Texture> texture(new sf::Texture());
    texture->loadFromFile(filename);

    mTextureMap.insert(std::make_pair(id, std::move(texture)));
}
```

Accessing the textures

So far, we have seen how to load resources. Now we finally want to use them. We write a method `get()` that returns a reference to a texture. The method has one parameter, namely the identifier for the resource. The method signature looks as follows:

```
sf::Texture& get(Textures::ID id);
```

Concerning the implementation, there is not much to do. We perform a lookup in the map to find the corresponding texture entry for the passed key. The method `std::map::find()` returns an iterator to the found element, or `end()` if nothing is found. Since the iterator points to a `std::pair<const Textures::ID, std::unique_ptr<sf::Texture>>`, we have to access its second member to get the unique pointer, and dereference it to get the texture:

```
sf::Texture& TextureHolder::get(Textures::ID id)
{
    auto found = mTextureMap.find(id);
    return *found->second;
}
```

Type inference is a language feature that has been introduced with C++11, which allows the compiler to find out the type of expressions. The `decltype` keyword returns the type of an expression, while the `auto` keyword deduces the correct type at initialization. Type inference is very useful for complex types such as iterators, where the syntactic details of the declaration are irrelevant. In the following code, all three lines are semantically equivalent:

```
int         a = 7;
decltype(7) a = 7;    // decltype(7) is int
auto        a = 7;    // auto is deduced as int
```

In order to be able to invoke `get()` also, if we only have a pointer or reference to a `const TextureHolder` at hand, we need to provide a const-qualified overload. This new member function returns a reference to a `const sf::Texture`, therefore the caller cannot change the texture. The signature is slightly different:

```
const sf::Texture& get(Textures::ID id) const;
```

The implementation stays the same, so it is not listed again. Our class now looks as follows:

```
class TextureHolder
{
    public:
        void                    load(Textures::ID id,
                                    const std::string& filename);
        sf::Texture&            get(Textures::ID id);
        const sf::Texture&      get(Textures::ID id) const;
    private:
        std::map<Textures::ID,
                std::unique_ptr<sf::Texture>> mTextureMap;
};
```

Now the `get()` method is easy to use and can directly be invoked when a texture is requested:

```
TextureHolder textures;
textures.load(Textures::Airplane, "Media/Textures/Airplane.png");

sf::Sprite playerPlane;
playerPlane.setTexture(textures.get(Textures::Airplane));
```

Error handling

The basic steps are done, the main functionality is implemented. However, there may be errors which we have to recognize and handle meaningfully. The first error can occur during the loading of the texture. For example, the specified file might not exist, or the file might have an invalid image format, or be too big for the video memory of the graphics card. To handle such errors, the method `sf::Texture::loadFromFile()` returns a Boolean value that is true in case of success, and false in case of failure.

There are several strategies to react to resource loading errors. In our case, we have to consider that the texture is later needed by sprites that are rendered on the screen—if such a sprite requests the texture, we must give something back. One possibility would be to provide a default texture (for example, plain white), so the sprites are just drawn as a white rectangle. However, we do not want the player of our game to fiddle around with rectangles; he should either have a proper airplane or nothing. But how can we implement "nothing"? We have to notify the caller of our `load()` method that something did not work. A possibility to implement these notifications is shown in the next sections.

Boolean return values

We could follow SFML's philosophy and return a Boolean value denoting success or failure. This approach has some disadvantages. We cannot use the return type for something else. Additionally, the caller has to check the returned value every time he calls `load()`. This is easily overlooked, and if it is not, it leads to messy usage code that is full of error checks. That is not what we want, as initially stated our objective consists of performing as much work as possible in the `TextureHolder`, to relieve the user from writing boilerplate code.

Throwing exceptions

Another approach to react to a loading failure is to throw an exception. We choose the standard exception type `std::runtime_error`. To its constructor, we pass an error message describing the problem as clearly as possible, including the filename:

```
if (!texture->loadFromFile(filename))
    throw std::runtime_error("TextureHolder::load - Failed to load "
    + filename);
```

Exceptions have the big advantage that user code can be kept clean of error handling. Clients can now have the following code:

```
TextureHolder textures;
textures.load(Textures::Landscape, "Media/Textures/Desert.png");
textures.load(Textures::Airplane, "Media/Textures/Airplane.png");
textures.load(Textures::Missile, "Media/Textures/Missile.png");
```

We do not need to check every single call. If an error occurs, an exception will be thrown until a `try-catch` block catches it and reacts meaningfully. It is possible that the exception passes several functions before it is eventually handled.

Once the resource is loaded, we insert it into the map. Here, we have to be aware of possible error sources too. When the given ID is already stored, the map will refuse to insert our ID-resource pair, as it cannot contain duplicate keys. The member function `std::map::insert()` returns a pair with an iterator to the inserted element and a Boolean value which is true if inserting was successful. We store this returned pair and check its second member (the Boolean value). Instead of writing `std::pair<std::map<Textures::ID, std::unique_ptr<sf::Texture>>::iterator, bool>`, we can use C++11 type inference:

```
auto inserted = mTextureMap.insert(std::make_pair(id,
std::move(resource)));
```

Now, `inserted` is our pair containing an iterator and a Boolean value, `inserted`. `second` is the Boolean value denoting the success of the insertion. If it is false, we know that the ID is already stored in the map. How do we react to this situation?

We could throw a `std::runtime_error` exception again. However, in contrast to a loading failure, double insertion is not a runtime error. The attempt to insert the same ID twice in the map is a logic error, meaning, there is a mistake in the application logic—in other words, a bug. A well-formed program would not attempt to load the same resource twice. In comparison, runtime errors occur in correctly written programs too, for example, if the user renames or moves the resource files. For logic errors, the standard library provides the exception class `std::logic_error`.

This raises already the next question: how do you handle such exceptions? It is not that once you have thrown an exception, you can forget about it and the world is in harmony. Somebody has to catch those exceptions, and it had better be you and not the operating system (unless you like crashing applications). In the case of a loading failure, we can tell the player that the files were not found, and prevent him from starting the game. But what in our double insertion case? Are we supposed to tell the player that the programmer accidentally called `load()` twice? Certainly not. This bug must not occur in the final application. There is no way to recover from it—continuing the application is dangerous, because its logic is broken, and we risk upsetting even more if we ignore the error. What if the two `load()` calls are passed the same ID, but different filenames? We do not know with which resource the ID is associated. If we later want to access a resource by its ID, we might get the wrong resource, and thus display a wrong image on the screen. In this manner, errors can propagate further and further, sometimes remaining for a long time before being noticed. In case of a logic error, we would like the program to interrupt immediately.

Assertions

Clearly, a mechanism apart from exceptions is appropriate, which shows us directly and inevitably when something goes wrong. This is where assertions come into play. The macro `assert` evaluates its expression; if it is false in debug mode, a breakpoint is triggered, halting the program execution and directly pointing to the source of the error. In release mode, assertions are optimized away, so we do not waste any performance to check for errors that cannot occur. The `assert` expression is completely removed in release mode, so make sure you only use it for error checks, and not to implement actual functionality with possible side effects.

We have to insert a single line, we expect that the Boolean member of the pair returned by `std::map::insert()` is true:

```
assert(inserted.second);
```

That is already it. The whole method looks now as follows:

```
void TextureHolder::load(Textures::ID id, const std::string& filename)
{
    std::unique_ptr<sf::Texture> texture(new sf::Texture());
    if (!texture->loadFromFile(filename))
        throw std::runtime_error("TextureHolder::load -
        Failed to load "     + filename);

    auto inserted = mTextureMap.insert(std::make_pair(id,
    std::move(texture)));
    assert(inserted.second);
}
```

In our method `get()`, there are things that may go wrong too. The requested texture might not exist in the map. This is also a logic error; we are supposed to load the textures before we access them. Consequently, we verify whether the texture has been found, again using `assert`:

```
sf::Texture& TextureHolder::get(Textures::ID id)
{
    auto found = mTextureMap.find(id);
    assert(found != mTextureMap.end());

    return *found->second;
}
```

Generalizing the approach

We have implemented everything we need for textures, but we would like to handle other resources such as fonts and sound buffers too. As the implementation looks extremely similar for them, it would be a bad idea to write new classes `FontHolder` and `SoundBufferHolder` with exactly the same functionality. Instead, we write a class template, which we instantiate for different resource classes.

We call our template `ResourceHolder` and equip it with two template parameters:

- **Resource**: The type of resource, for example, `sf::Texture`. We design the class template to work the SFML classes, but if you have your own resource class which conforms to the required interface (providing `loadFromFile()` methods), nothing keeps you from using it together with `ResourceHolder`.

- **Identifier**: The ID type for resource access, for example, `Textures::ID`. This will usually be an enum, but the type is not restricted to enumerations. Any type that supports an `operator<` can be used as identifier, for example, `std::string`.

The transition from `TextureHolder` to `ResourceHolder<Resource,` `Identifier>` is straightforward. We replace the used types with the generic template parameters: `sf::Texture` becomes `Resource`, and `Textures::ID` becomes `Identifier`. Furthermore, we rename some variables to reflect the fact that we are talking about resources in general, not only textures. We also adapt the member functions accordingly.

One thing we have to note when using templates is that the complete implementation needs to be in the header. We cannot use `.cpp` files for the method definitions anymore, but we would still like to separate interface and implementation. That is why we use a file `ResourceHolder.hpp` for the class definition, and a file `ResourceHolder.inl` for the method definitions. At the end of the `.hpp` file, we include the `.inl` file containing the implementation. `.inl` is a common file extension for inline template implementations.

The generalized class definition has the following interface:

```cpp
template <typename Resource, typename Identifier>
class ResourceHolder
{
    public:
        void            load(Identifier id,
                            const std::string& filename);

        Resource&       get(Identifier id);
        const Resource& get(Identifier id) const;

    private:
        std::map<Identifier,
                std::unique_ptr<Resource>> mResourceMap;
};
```

The `load()` method can be written in the following way. Like before, we attempt to load the resource from a file, and then we insert the unique pointer into the map and make sure the insertion was successful:

```cpp
template <typename Resource, typename Identifier>
void ResourceHolder<Resource, Identifier>::load(Identifier id,
const std::string& filename)
{
    std::unique_ptr<Resource> resource(new Resource());
    if (!resource->loadFromFile(filename))
        throw std::runtime_error("ResourceHolder::load - Failed to
        load " + filename);
```

```
auto inserted = mResourceMap.insert(
std::make_pair(id, std::move(resource)));
    assert(inserted.second);
}
```

The two overloaded `get()` member functions are generalized using the same principle, that is why they are not listed here. You can refer to the online code base for a complete implementation.

Compatibility with sf::Music

As initially mentioned, the class `sf::Music` has semantics that are very different from other resource types. This begins already with its `openFromFile()` method that is not compatible to the `loadFromFile()` call in our implementation. Because of its streaming nature, a music object cannot be shared between multiple clients—each object represents one point in time of a certain music theme. No object contains the whole music data at once.

Instead of forcing `sf::Music` into a concept it does not fit, we decide to not store it inside `ResourceHolder` instances. This does not imply that there will be no encapsulation for music; we are rather going to cover music handling in-depth during *Chapter 9, Cranking Up the Bass – Music and Sound Effects*.

A special case – sf::Shader

There is one resource type we have yet to cover: shaders. Since a SFML shader object can consist of a fragment and/or a vertex shader, the interface of `sf::Shader` deviates slightly from the other resource classes in SFML. `sf::Shader` provides two methods to load from a file:

```
bool loadFromFile(const std::string& filename, sf::Shader::Type type);
bool loadFromFile(const std::string& vertexShaderFilename,
const std::string& fragmentShaderFilename);
```

The first function loads either a fragment or a vertex shader (which one is specified by the second parameter). The second function loads both a vertex and a fragment shader.

This interface is an issue for our generic implementation, because `ResourceHolder::load()` contains the following expression:

```
resource->loadFromFile(filename)
```

Which assumes that `loadFromFile()` is invoked with one argument. For `sf::Shader`, we have to specify two instead.

The solution is simple: we write an overloaded `ResourceHolder::load()` function that takes an additional parameter and forwards it directly as the second argument to `sf::Shader::loadFromFile()`. This parameter can have the type `sf::Shader::Type` or `const std::string&`. In order to cope with both types, we add a function template parameter. Our new `load()` function has the following declaration:

```
template <typename Parameter>
void load(Identifier id, const std::string& filename,
const Parameter& secondParam);
```

The function definition is listed in the following code. Do not confuse yourself by the two template parameter lists; the first one is required for the class template `ResourceHolder` and the second one for the function template `ResourceHolder::load()`. In the function body, only the `loadFromFile()` call is different from before.

```
template <typename Resource, typename Identifier>
template <typename Parameter>
void ResourceHolder<Resource, Identifier>::load(Identifier id,
const std::string& filename, const Parameter& secondParam)
{
    std::unique_ptr<Resource> resource(new Resource());
    if (!resource->loadFromFile(filename, secondParam))
        throw ...;

    ... // insertion like before
}
```

A nice side effect of this additional overload is that it enables other argument combinations for `loadFromFile()` too. The method of `sf::Texture` actually looks as shown in the following line of code:

```
bool loadFromFile(const std::string& filename,
const IntRect& area = IntRect())
```

The default parameter can be used if we want the texture to load only a rectangular area of the image. Usually, we do not specify it and load the whole file, but thanks to our second `load()` overload, we have now the possibility to use this parameter.

In our complete implementation, we have written a separate function that inserts resources into the map, in order to reduce code duplication.

Using the new `ResourceHolder` class template, we can visualize a possible in-game situation in the following diagram. On the left you see two resource holders, one for textures and one for fonts. Each one contains a map of enumerators to resources. The player's `Aircraft` class on the right stores a sprite that points to a texture, as well as a text that points to a font.

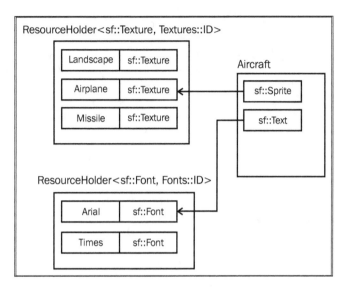

Summary

In this chapter, we have learned the important points about resource management. By now, we know the ideas behind resources and the facilities SFML provides to work with them. We have taken a look at a possible way resources are used in a bigger project, and implemented a generic resource holder that helps us with passing resources to different parts of the application. We also investigated possible error sources as well as techniques to handle them appropriately.

In the next chapter, we are going to develop the game world with a variety of objects in it. Most of these objects require different resources, which is a good opportunity to show our resource holder in a real-world example.

3
Forge of the Gods – Shaping Our World

In the previous chapter, we have covered loading, managing, and releasing of external resources. To sum up, we have investigated mechanisms to ensure that textures, fonts, or sounds are ready to be used as soon as we need them. This chapter attempts to bring knowledge around a few key topics:

- Entity systems in concept and practice
- The viewable area of our world and scrolling
- Tree-based scene graphs, rendering and updating of many entities
- Composition of all elements to shape the world

When writing a game, we invariably find the need to conceptualize our vision of the game into actual data structures. In other words, it is extremely important to have a clear idea of the scope of our vision. The world in our mind doesn't even have to scale remotely to what we consider our real world; it is a product of our own creation. It is well within our power, as game developers, to forge the whole world as a simple board game table, or an ant farm, or even scale up to a whole universe along with all the stars and planets.

The point is, it does not matter how our vision of the world looks, how small or big it is, or how realistic or abstract the concepts in it are, we will always want to represent that world in one or more data structures. For the reach of this book, we will apply these concepts directly to our own sample vision of a game, while leaving a solid background on the topic, for later implementation of new ideas and concepts.

Entities

An **entity** denotes a game element in the world. In our game, possible entities are friendly and enemy airplanes, bullets, missiles, or pickups that increase the player's strength. Entities interact with each other: enemy airplanes can fire missiles, the player's airplane may evade them, and the missiles may explode if they hit the player's plane, dealing damage to it. The player's aircraft can touch a pickup to collect it, as a result of which it gets a new ability. The possibilities are nearly unlimited, and they may occur between almost any pair of entity types.

In our code, we represent entities using the traditional approach of an entity hierarchy. We have a base class called `Entity`, which contains the data and functionality that all different kinds of entities have in common. We have multiple classes that derive from `Entity`, and that implement specific functionality. These derived classes could represent airplanes, projectiles (such as missiles), or pickups. One commonality between different entities is that they can move in our world with a certain velocity.

We implement the velocity attribute in the base class `Entity`, so each concrete entity has it. The velocity is represented using a two-dimensional vector. In addition to the member variable, we provide the `get` and `set` functions to access the velocity from outside the class. The `setVelocity()` method is overloaded to take either a vector or two separate floats. The header `Entity.hpp` contains the following class definition:

```
class Entity
{
    public:
        void                setVelocity(sf::Vector2f velocity);
        void                setVelocity(float vx, float vy);
        sf::Vector2f        getVelocity() const;

    private:
        sf::Vector2f        mVelocity;
};
```

After initialization, we want the velocity to be zero. Since the class `sf::Vector2f` has a default constructor, which initializes the vector to a zero vector, we need not define our own constructor; the compiler-generated one works fine.

The function definitions in the file `Entity.cpp` are not terribly surprising:

```
void Entity::setVelocity(sf::Vector2f velocity)
{
    mVelocity = velocity;
}

void Entity::setVelocity(float vx, float vy)
{
    mVelocity.x = vx;
    mVelocity.y = vy;
}

sf::Vector2f Entity::getVelocity() const
{
    return mVelocity;
}
```

Aircraft

Using the example of the aircraft, we need to define a concrete entity class. We derive it from `Entity`. Since we have different airplanes in our game, it would be nice to have a data type that can store them. An enumeration comes in handy; we call it `Type` and make it a member of the `Aircraft` class. Therefore, we can now refer to it as `Aircraft::Type`, which is quite expressive when we see it in the code. Up to now, we have two distinct airplanes, we call them `Eagle` and `Raptor`. Each type of aircraft corresponds to an enumerator in our enum.

Furthermore, we declare a constructor for the aircraft that takes its current type as parameter. We also declare a member variable for the type in the following code:

```
class Aircraft : public Entity
{
    public:
        enum Type
        {
            Eagle,
            Raptor,
        };

    public:
        explicit        Aircraft(Type type);

    private:
        Type            mType;
};
```

The constructor's definition is straightforward; we let it initialize our `mType` member variable:

```
Aircraft::Aircraft(Type type) : mType(type)
{
}
```

Now this is the fundament for our `Aircraft` class. During this book, we will continuously extend it and add new functionality.

Alternative entity designs

You should be aware that a class hierarchy is not the only option to model game entities. There are always different possibilities to design a piece of software, all of which have its own advantages and drawbacks.

The hierarchy-based approach gets to its limits when we introduce many, slightly different entity types. Imagine a complex game with different kinds of vehicles, such as tanks, ships, submarines, airplanes, and more. Every entity type has different capabilities, such as flying, transporting people, carrying weapons, and diving. It may be tempting to create corresponding base classes `TransportEntity`, `ArmedEntity`, `DivingEntity` that all derive from `Entity`. A submarine could then inherit `ArmedEntity` and `DivingEntity`; an armed freighter could inherit `TransportEntity` and `ArmedEntity`. On one hand, this design leads hand to the so-called diamond of death, where the base class `Entity` is indirectly inherited multiple times, requiring virtual inheritance. On the other hand, the hierarchy becomes very deep and rigid. In order to reuse functionality for different entities, it is moved to base classes. This makes classes towards the root of the hierarchy a lot heavier than they should be. This in turn results in derived classes which inherit a lot of functions and data they never need. Eventually, objects become overly large, hence slower to process and more difficult to maintain.

In such a case, **component-based design** would be an alternative, meaning that abilities are aggregated as components in the single entities, instead of base classes. Each entity would then hold the abilities as members. But as you might expect, this approach is not the silver bullet, either. Components often depend more on each other than theory would like them to, and they need an efficient and flexible way to communicate with each other. While component-based approaches are certainly an option to consider for large-scale games, they are rather complex for the first game to develop. In our basic aircraft shooter, the typical problems of entity hierarchies do not show, so we chose this approach for the sake of simplicity.

If you are interested in a more detailed explanation on the topic of component-based game design, we recommend reading the article series on the following website:

```
http://stefan.boxbox.org/game-development-design.
```

Rendering the scene

At one point, we have to reflect about how the game is rendered on the screen. How do we draw all the entities, the scenery, and interface elements (such as a health bar)? A simple option is to have different sequential containers through which we iterate. For each element, we call a possible `Entity::draw()` function to draw the corresponding entity on the screen. We only have to make sure that objects that appear behind others (such as the scenery background) are drawn first.

Relative coordinates

The sequential rendering approach works well for many cases, but makes it difficult to handle an entity relative to another one. Imagine we have a formation of airplanes, where one is the leader and the rest follows it. It would be nice if we could set the position of the following airplanes dependent on the leader, in the sense of "plane A is located 300 units behind (below on the screen) and 100 units right of the leader" instead of "plane A is located at position (x, y) in the world". We call (300, 100) a **relative position**, expressing where plane A is located with respect to the leader.

We can apply the principle of relative coordinates not only to position, but also to rotation and scale. In the mentioned example of a plane formation, we also want the planes to be headed towards the same direction as the leader. In other words, we want their rotation to be the same. If the followers' relative rotation is zero, all planes will face the same direction, namely the leader's one.

The advantage of relative coordinates consists of avoiding the need for manual synchronization of different entities. Using absolute coordinates, we have to recognize the leader and its followers, copy the leader's position to every follower, and add it to the follower's own position. This has to be done every time the position of the leader changes, which is cumbersome and error-prone (one can easily forget to update a single plane). Now compare that with the relative coordinate approach: we set the position of the leader, done. All followers adapt automatically.

This relationship is not limited to a single layer. An airplane that is following the leader can in turn have other followers that move relatively to it. Eventually, we build up a hierarchy of objects with relative transforms.

SFML and transforms

Now, the question is how we achieve the semantics of relative transforms in our game. Fortunately, SFML provides already the basic framework, on top of which we can build our own abstractions.

A geometrical **transform** specifies the way an object is represented on the screen. In mathematical terms, a transform maps a coordinate system onto another. **Translation** affects the position of an object, **rotation** affects its orientation, and **scale** affects its size. Although transforms are not limited to these three operations, we will focus on them, because they are the ones mostly used.

SFML provides an API to work with position, rotation, and scale in the class `sf::Transformable`. The class stores the three transforms separately and provides useful accessor functions such as `setPosition()`, `move()`, `rotate()`, `getScale()`, and many more. It can be used as a base class, such that the derived class automatically inherits those functions. The following diagram visualizes the three transforms you will encounter again and again:

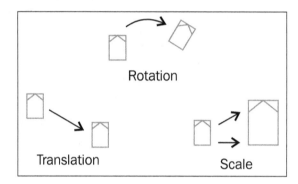

`sf::Transformable` also contains the methods `setOrigin()` and `getOrigin()`, which give access to the coordinate system's origin. The origin is the reference point for the three transforms—it determines, which point in the object is looked at to set/get the position, or around which point the object rotates, or which point the object uses as the center for scaling. The origin is specified in local coordinates (relative to the object). By default, it has the value (0, 0) and resides in the object's upper-left corner. Calling `setOrigin()` with the half object size places the origin to the object's center.

SFML provides another useful base class for graphical entities: the class `sf::Drawable` is a stateless interface and provides only a pure virtual function with the following signature:

```
virtual void Drawable::draw(sf::RenderTarget& target,
                            sf::RenderStates states) const = 0
```

The first parameter specifies, where the drawable object is drawn to. Mostly, this will be a `sf::RenderWindow`. The second parameter contains additional information for the rendering process, such as blend mode, transform, the used texture, or shader. SFML's high-level classes `Sprite`, `Text`, and `Shape` are all derived from `Transformable` and `Drawable`.

Scene graphs

In order to manage transform hierarchies in a user-friendly way, we develop a **scene graph**—a tree data structure consisting of multiple nodes, called **scene nodes**. Each scene node can store an object that is drawn on the screen, most often this is an entity.

Each node may have an arbitrary amount of child nodes, which adapt to the transform of their parent node when rendering. Children only store the position, rotation, and scale relative to their parent.

A scene graph contains a root scene node, which exists only once in a world. It resides above all other scene nodes in the hierarchy, thus it has no parent node.

Scene nodes

We represent the nodes in the scene graph with a class called `SceneNode`. Before we can implement it, we need to think about ownership semantics. The scene graph owns the scene nodes; therefore it is responsible for their lifetime and destruction. We want each node to store all its child nodes. If a node is destroyed, its children are destroyed with it. If the root is destroyed, the whole scene graph is torn down.

To store the children, we make use of the STL container `std::vector`. We cannot use `std::vector<SceneNode>`, since element types must be complete types (which they are only at the end of the `SceneNode` class definition, but not at the time of declaring the container as a member variable) and since our class is polymorphic (there will be derived classes overriding virtual functions of `SceneNode`). We could use `std::vector<SceneNode*>`, but then we would have to manage memory ourselves, so we take `std::vector<std::unique_ptr<SceneNode>>` instead. Since we are going to use the type `std::unique_ptr<SceneNode>` really often, we create a typedef for it, as a member inside the `SceneNode` class.

In addition to the children container, a pointer to the parent node is stored, so our class looks as follows:

```
class SceneNode
{
    public:
        typedef std::unique_ptr<SceneNode> Ptr;

    public:
                                SceneNode();

    private:
        std::vector<Ptr>        mChildren;
        SceneNode*              mParent;
};
```

The constructor initializes the parent pointer to `nullptr` and leaves the container empty.

> `nullptr` is a keyword introduced with C++11 and represents the value of a null pointer. The formerly used NULL is a macro for the integer value 0, which implies many problems. A function overloaded for `int` and `char*`, that is passed NULL as argument, would unexpectedly choose the `int` overload.
>
> For null pointer literals, `nullptr` should always be preferred over 0 or NULL. It is also convertible to the standard library smart pointers `std::unique_ptr` and `std::shared_ptr`.

Node insertion and removal

Now we write an interface to insert or remove child nodes into or from a scene node. We do this by adding the following two functions:

```
void        attachChild(Ptr child);
Ptr         detachChild(const SceneNode& node);
```

The first method takes a `unique_ptr<SceneNode>` by value, taking ownership of the scene node. The second method searches for an occurrence of the specified node, releases it from the container, and returns it to the caller, again wrapped in a `unique_ptr`. If the return value is ignored, the node will be destroyed.

The function to attach a child node is simple to implement. We set its parent pointer to the current node, and add the smart pointer to the container by moving its contents in the following code snippet:

```
void SceneNode::attachChild(Ptr child)
{
    child->mParent = this;
    mChildren.push_back(std::move(child));
}
```

The second method is slightly more complex. First, we search for the specified node in the container with the help of a lambda expression.

Lambda expressions are a C++11 language feature. They allow the definition of local functions inside other functions, and the direct usage in surrounding code.

A **lambda expression** creates an anonymous function object, similar to a named functor class with overloaded operator(). Its declaration consists of the following parts:

- The capture list specifies to which variables in the surrounding scope the lambda expression has access. [] captures no variables, [&] captures all variables by reference, [=] by value, [&node] and [node] capture only the listed variables by reference or value, respectively. The capture list is comparable to the arguments passed to a functor's constructor.
- The parameter list contains the parameters passed to the function. These correspond to the parameters of the functor's operator().
- The return type has the syntax -> type. If the function body consists of a single return statement, the return type can be omitted.
- The function body is enclosed in {} and contains the actual statements.

The lambda expression is invoked with each container element and returns true if the element's pointer p.get() is equal to the address of the wanted node. The STL algorithm std::find_if() returns an iterator to the found element, which we check for validity using assert.

```
SceneNode::Ptr SceneNode::detachChild(const SceneNode& node)
{
    auto found = std::find_if(mChildren.begin(), mChildren.end(),
    [&] (Ptr& p) -> bool { return p.get() == &node; });

    assert(found != mChildren.end());
```

In the second part of the function, we move the found node out of the container into the variable `result`. We set the node's parent pointer to `nullptr`, erase the empty element from the container, and return the smart pointer containing the detached node.

```
Ptr result = std::move(*found);
result->mParent = nullptr;
mChildren.erase(found);
return result;
}
```

Now that the basic tree operations of our scene graph are working, we can concentrate on the actual rendering.

Making scene nodes drawable

Our `SceneNode` class shall be rendered on the screen, thus we derive it from `sf::Drawable`. It shall store its current position, rotation, and scale as well as providing an interface to access them. Instead of re-inventing the wheel, we derive also from `sf::Transformable`, which gives us all that for free. In addition, we derive privately from `sf::NonCopyable` to state that our scene nodes cannot be copied (copy constructor and copy assignment operator are disabled).

We override the pure virtual `draw()` function of `sf::Drawable` to render the whole scene node. We also provide a new virtual function `drawCurrent()` which only draws the current object (but not the children). It can be overridden by classes deriving from `SceneNode`.

```
class SceneNode : public sf::Transformable, public sf::Drawable,
                  private sf::NonCopyable
{
    public:
        typedef std::unique_ptr<SceneNode> Ptr;

    public:
                                SceneNode();

        void                    attachChild(Ptr child);
        Ptr                     detachChild(const SceneNode& node);

    private:
        virtual void            draw(sf::RenderTarget& target,
                                    sf::RenderStates states) const;
```

```
virtual void        drawCurrent(sf::RenderTarget& target,
                        sf::RenderStates states) const;

private:
    std::vector<Ptr>  mChildren;
    SceneNode*        mParent;
};
```

The `draw()` function allows our class to be used as shown in the following
code snippet:

```
sf::RenderWindow window(...);
SceneNode::Ptr node(...);
window.draw(*node); // note: no node->draw(window) here!
```

The `window` class internally calls our `draw()` function. No other classes need access
to it, so we can make it private. If your compiler already supports this feature, you
can declare `draw()` with the `final` keyword, to prevent the function from being
overridden in classes derived from `SceneNode`.

Our function to draw the scene node has to deal with different transforms:

- The current node's transform that determines position, rotation, and scale
  relative to the parent node. It is retrieved via base class method `sf::Transfo
  rmable::getTransform()`.

- The parameter `states`, which is passed by value and has a member variable
  `transform` of type `sf::Transform`. This variable holds the information
  where to render the parent scene node.

Two transforms can be chained (applied one after other) using the overloaded
multiplication operators. Our expression with `operator*=` combines the parent's
absolute transform with the current node's relative one. The result is the absolute
transform of the current node, which stores where in the world our scene node
is placed.

```
void SceneNode::draw(sf::RenderTarget& target,
                    sf::RenderStates states) const
{
    states.transform *= getTransform();
```

Now, `states.transform` contains the absolute world transform. We can draw the
derived object with it by calling `drawCurrent()`. Both parameters are forwarded.

By the way, the `sf::Sprite` class handles transforms very similarly: it also combines
its own transform with the one passed in the render states. Thus, we effectively copy
SFML's behavior in `SceneNode`.

Eventually, we have to draw all the child nodes. We iterate through our container of smart pointers, and recursively invoke `draw()` on each element, again forwarding both parameters.

```
drawCurrent(target, states);

for (auto itr = mChildren.begin();
        itr != mChildren.end(); ++itr)
{
    (*itr)->draw(target, states);
}
}
```

In the code, we have factored out the last part into a function `drawChildren()`.

 In C++11, iteration through sequences can be achieved with the **range-based for** statement. It has the following syntax, which can be read as "for each `variable` in `sequence`":
```
for (Type variable : sequence)
```

If all current compilers supported range-based for, we could use the following code to iterate over all child nodes:

```
for (const Ptr& child : mChildren)
{
    child->draw(target, states);
}
```

Fortunately, C++ is a very powerful language. It allows us to emulate the range-based for loop with a few limitations, using a self-written macro FOREACH. We chose it to make code more readable, and to make porting to C++11 easier, when the feature is widely supported. Our loop then looks as follows:

```
FOREACH(const Ptr& child, mChildren)
{
    child->draw(target, states);
}
```

Note the increase in expressiveness and readability over the classical iterator loop.

Drawing entities

Meanwhile, our data structure for hierarchical rendering is operational, but nothing is actually rendered yet. In order to do so, the virtual method `drawCurrent()` must be overridden in derived classes. One of these derived classes is `Entity`; it inherits `SceneNode`, so that entities can be placed in the scene and rendered by SFML.

Since we want our plane to be rendered as an image on the screen, we use a `sf::Sprite` object. This sprite becomes a member of the `Aircraft` class.

```cpp
class Aircraft : public Entity // inherits indirectly SceneNode
{
    public:
        explicit        Aircraft(Type type);
        virtual void    drawCurrent(sf::RenderTarget& target,
                                    sf::RenderStates states) const;

    private:
        Type            mType;
        sf::Sprite      mSprite;
};
```

In `drawCurrent()`, we only draw the sprite. We call `sf::RenderTarget::draw()`, and pass `const sf::Drawable&` (our sprite) as first argument and the render states as second argument.

```cpp
void Aircraft::drawCurrent(sf::RenderTarget& target,
                           sf::RenderStates states) const
{
    target.draw(mSprite, states);
}
```

As you see, we needn't care about transforms anymore. Implementing rendering for a new entity has now become extremely simple! This is due to the fact that all the actual work is performed in our scene node and SFML.

Connecting entities with resources

There is one thing we have concealed: how our sprite is initialized. As you know, sprites need a texture to refer to, but where to get it from?

In *Chapter 2*, *Keeping Track of Your Textures – Resource Management*, we have developed the class template `ResourceHolder<Resource, Identifier>` which is able to store SFML resource objects such as textures. Now the time for its first application has come. We need to choose the template arguments with which we instantiate the template. Because we draw a sprite which needs a texture, the resource type will be `sf::Texture`.

Next, we ought to find a type for the resource identifier. For aircraft textures, we could use the enum `Aircraft::Type`. However, there might be other objects than airplanes that also require textures. The landscape is such an example. Therefore, we create a new enumeration `Textures::ID` with identifiers for the textures. So far, we only have two texture IDs, one for each of our aircraft types.

```
namespace Textures
{
    enum ID
    {
        Eagle,
        Raptor,
    };
}
```

Having defined the identifier type, we are ready to instantiate our resource holder for textures. Because it is used in several places, we create a type definition for it:

```
typedef ResourceHolder<sf::Texture, Textures::ID> TextureHolder;
```

We will now go back to our `Aircraft` class. In its constructor, we want to initialize the sprite with the correct texture. We could add a constructor parameter `const sf::Texture&`, but we directly pass a const reference to our texture holder instead. This has the advantage that the knowledge about the used texture stays local to our plane — the creator of the plane need not know what texture it uses. Also, if the plane suddenly requests more than one texture (for example, for an attached missile), we do not have to change the constructor signature and the code that invokes it.

Our constructor has now this declaration:

```
Aircraft(Type type, const TextureHolder& textures);
```

The `TextureHolder` class, which is an instantiation of the `ResourceHolder` class template, provides a function `const sf::Texture& get(Textures::ID id) const` which we can invoke with an identifier to get a texture back.

We do not have the identifier yet, but we have the plane type, stored in the constructor parameter type. We can map the aircraft type to the corresponding texture ID, for example, with a `switch` statement:

```
Textures::ID toTextureID(Aircraft::Type type)
{
    switch (type)
    {
        case Aircraft::Eagle:
            return Textures::Eagle;
```

```
            case Aircraft::Raptor:
                return Textures::Raptor;
        }
    }
```

We define this global function at the beginning of the `Aircraft.cpp` file, so it does not appear in the `Aircraft` interface. In our constructor, we then initialize our sprite with the texture:

```
Aircraft::Aircraft(Type type, const TextureHolder& textures):
mType(type), mSprite(textures.get(toTextureID(type)))

{
}
```

Instead of the `sf::Sprite` constructor which takes `const sf::Texture&`, it would also have been possible to call the method `sf::Sprite::setTexture()`.

Aligning the origin

By default, the origin of sprites is located in their upper-left corner. When we call `setPosition()`, we therefore always set the position of the sprite's upper-left corner. For various tasks such as object alignment or rotation, it is however more comfortable to work with the center. Therefore, we have to move the sprite's origin to its center.

For the center, we need the half size of the sprite. With `getLocalBounds()`, we get the local bounding rectangle (local means not taking any `sf::Sprite` transforms into account—as opposed to `getGlobalBounds()`). The rectangle is of type `sf::FloatRect`, which stores four float variables called `left`, `top`, `width`, and `height`. SFML also provides `sf::IntRect`, which stores four int varibles. Our local bounding rectangle's `left` and `top` coordinates are zero, while its `width` and `height` correspond to the sprite's texture size.

```
sf::FloatRect bounds = mSprite.getLocalBounds();
mSprite.setOrigin(bounds.width / 2.f, bounds.height / 2.f);
```

After all this work, our aircraft is finally drawable! When it is added to a scene graph, and somebody draws it, our plane will appear on the screen.

Scene layers

In the game, we often have different scene nodes that must be rendered in a certain order. Nodes with objects that are located "above" others (closer to the sky) must be drawn after them. For example, we might first draw a desert background, then an oasis and some buildings, above which we draw the planes, and eventually some health bars located in front of them. This is rather cumbersome to handle when we insert node by node to the scene graph, because we have to ensure the order manually.

Luckily, we can easily automate the ordering, even using the scene graph's current capabilities. We call a group of scene nodes that are rendered together a **layer**. Inside a layer, the rendering order is irrelevant—we just make sure we render the different layers in the right order. We represent a layer with an empty scene node, directly under the graph's root node. A layer node itself contains no graphics; it is only supposed to render its children. Since the scene graph is traversed node by node, we know that all children of layer one will be rendered before any children of layer two. We can assign a node to a certain layer by attaching it as a child to the corresponding layer node. As a result, we have an automatic ordering of different layers, without the need to manually sort objects.

Let us introduce two layers for now: one for the background, and one for entities in the air. We use an enum to have an appropriate type. The last enumerator `LayerCount` is not used to refer to a layer; instead it stores the total amount of layers.

```
enum Layer
{
    Background,
    Air,
    LayerCount
};
```

Updating the scene

In each frame, we update our world with all the entities inside. During an update, the whole game logic is computed: entities move and interact with each other, collisions are checked, and missiles are launched. Updating changes the state of our world and makes it progress over time, while rendering can be imagined as a snapshot of a part of the world at a given time point.

We can reuse our scene graph to reach all entities with our world updates. To achieve this, we implement a public `update()` member function in the `SceneNode` class. Analogous to the way we have proceeded for the `draw()` function, we split up `update()` into two parts: an update for the current node, and one for the child nodes. We thus write two private methods `updateCurrent()` and `updateChildren()`, of which the former is virtual.

All update functions take the frame time `dt` as a parameter of type `sf::Time` (the SFML class for time spans). This is the frame time we computed for the `Game` class in *Chapter 1*, *Making a Game Tick*. In our game, we work with fixed time steps, so `dt` will be constant. Nevertheless, we pass the frame time every time to the scene nodes and make entity behavior dependent on it. This leaves us the flexibility to change the frame rate or to experiment with other approaches to compute the frame time.

We add the following methods to our `SceneNode` class:

```
public:
    void            update(sf::Time dt);

private:
    virtual void    updateCurrent(sf::Time dt);
    void            updateChildren(sf::Time dt);
```

The implementation is the same as for rendering. The definition of `updateCurrent()` remains empty, by default we do nothing for a scene node.

```
void SceneNode::update(sf::Time dt)
{
    updateCurrent(dt);
    updateChildren(dt);
}


void SceneNode::updateCurrent(sf::Time)
{
}


void SceneNode::updateChildren(sf::Time dt)
{
    FOREACH(Ptr& child, mChildren)
        child->update(dt);
}
```

In derived classes, we can now implement specific update functionality, such as movement of each entity. In the `Entity` class, we override the virtual `updateCurrent()` method, in order to apply the current velocity. The class definition of `Entity` is expanded by the following lines of code:

```
private:
    virtual void            updateCurrent(sf::Time dt);
```

We offset the position by the velocity depending on the time step. A longer time step leads to a bigger offset, meaning that our entity is moved further over longer time.

```
void Entity::updateCurrent(sf::Time dt)
{
    move(mVelocity * dt.asSeconds());
}
```

Here, `move()` is a function of the indirect base class `sf::Transformable`. The expression `move(offset)` is a shortcut for `setPosition(getPosition() + offset)`.

Since `Aircraft` inherits `Entity`, the update functionality for it is also inherited. We thus do not need to re-define `updateCurrent()` in the `Aircraft` class, unless we want to execute further actions specifically for aircraft.

One step back – absolute transforms

Relative coordinates are nice and useful, but there are cases where we still want to access the absolute position of an object in the world. For example, to find out whether two entities collide, relative positions won't help us – we need to know where in the world the entities are located, not where in the local coordinate system.

To compute the absolute transforms, we can step upwards in the class hierarchy, and accumulate all relative transforms until we reach the root. This was also the reason why we introduced the parent pointer in the `SceneNode` class. In addition to the function `getPosition()`, which is inherited from `sf::Transformable` and returns the relative position, we add a new method `getWorldPosition()` to `SceneNode`, which returns the absolute position. First, we add a function `getWorldTransform()` that takes into account all the parent transforms. It multiplies all the `sf::Transform` objects from the root to the current node, its iterative implementation looks as follows. The position can be computed by transforming the origin `sf::Vector2f()` using the absolute transform.

```
sf::Transform SceneNode::getWorldTransform() const
{
    sf::Transform transform = sf::Transform::Identity;
```

```
    for (const SceneNode* node = this;
        node != nullptr; node = node->mParent)
    transform = node->getTransform() * transform;

  return transform;
}

sf::Vector2f SceneNode::getWorldPosition() const
{
    return getWorldTransform() * sf::Vector2f();
}
```

The constant `sf::Transform::Identity` represents the identity transform, which does not have any effect on the object. Strictly speaking, it is not necessary in this code, but it clarifies the way how transforms are applied from the beginning.

The view

A **view** is a concept that allows us to select the part of our world we want to see. You can imagine a view to work like an image recording device. Essentially, every game programmer needs to understand views in depth, simply because every graphical game will require that knowledge to be applied directly. Sometimes it is called view, camera, or differently. Be it a two-dimensional or three-dimensional simulation, this concept will always be present.

Talking about graphics in two dimensions, we can describe a view as a rectangle that represents the subset of our world that we want to see at a particular time.

Such a simple and yet powerful concept gives us the possibility to perform many interesting tasks, such as an animated camera following the player around, a spy camera that allows us to take a peek at a remote location, a combination of two views to create a split-screen multiplayer experience, as well as many other applications.

It is not hard to grasp the power of the view; you may begin by knowing SFML, which provides us this utility in the conveniently named class `sf::View`. This class acts as a viewing lens, which ensures that anything you attempt to draw to the screen that is outside the view's rectangle will remain unseen.

Besides the viewing rectangle, another parameter that defines the `sf::View` class is the viewport, which gives us control over how to map the viewing rectangle to the actual application window.

Viewport

It is very easy to visualize what a viewport does. It is no more than a rectangle, in unit-length coordinates, that defines what region of the application's window is going to be used. So, a viewport rectangle starting at (0, 0) and ending in (1, 1) means essentially that the entire window area will be used to render the world. This is the most common use of viewports.

Another special use case for this concept is to provide split-screen multiplayer support. In order to do that, one would only need to have two `sf::View` objects, one for the top half of the screen, and another for the bottom. Then, each view would be configured to take its respective portion of the screen, having their viewport rectangles defined as, respectively, (left=0, top=0, width=1, height=0.5) and (left=0, top=0.5, width=1, height=0.5).

This would immediately mean that we would have two distinct "eyes" looking at the world, and that they would only render in their own viewports. Each of these eyes may be looking at any region of the world without any conflicts. After having those two views configured, having a split-screen support would be as simple as activating the first view, rendering the world, then activating the second, and rendering it again. But always beware that rendering the world twice will effectively consume twice as much rendering power.

View optimizations

Requesting an object to draw itself to the screen, also known as a **draw call**, is one of the most expensive operations you can do in a game, therefore, for any game that goes beyond only a few sprites being drawn, we need to worry about rendering performance by reducing draw calls as much as we can.

One way to do this is to use **culling**, which is a term that encompasses a wide range of techniques. Using culling techniques is always a great optimization to do, and the benefits will almost always be worth the extra work. For example, checking if every object is within the viewing rectangle and only draw them if they are, is a very simple form of efficient culling.

Of course, for big scenes with lots of objects, the simple fact that we are iterating potentially thousands or millions of objects every frame will be a drag in the performance. Because of this, game developers usually implement some kind of spatial subdivision. A spatial subdivision system can be done in many ways, but it always consists on dividing the scene in multiple cells, which group all objects that reside within that given cell. This way it's possible to cull a group of objects altogether, avoiding expensive iterations and tests on those objects.

One of the most popular ways to subdivide space is to use a **quad tree**. A quad tree is a hierarchical tree of cells. Only leaf nodes can contain objects and they subdivide again when a predetermined number of objects are present. Every cell is at least big enough to contain all its children cells. The hierarchical approach allows us to stop iterating through every object and only perform tests down the tree if each cell passes the test. This effectively reduces the complexity of the algorithm from O(n) to O(log n), which is a very good optimization already. A quad tree is also much more efficient to find objects within the scene.

An alternative is a **circle tree**, which is similar to the quad tree, but instead each cell is a circle. This allows a different distribution of the objects and cheaper to compute tests. Whether to use one algorithm or the other depends on many factors. For each scene you may want to pick the most appropriate algorithm that will give you the most efficiency.

Resolution and aspect ratio

We have seen how viewports work, even though they are not always used explicitly. Now, it is very important to know how the viewing rectangle interacts with the specified viewport, and what pitfalls can we avoid by knowing that, along with what effects can we achieve by exploiting these notions to the limit. The **resolution** is the number of pixels a monitor or application window displays in each dimension. It is usually specified as width times height, for example, 1024 x 768. The **aspect ratio** is the ratio of the width to the height, for example, 1024:768 = 4:3.

The simplest possible use case of views is to have a window with a fixed size, and a view with the exact same dimensions, which implicitly means, the aspect ratio of view and window will be equal. This ratio is very important, because if the view rectangle is not proportional to the window size, we will experience a case of shrinking or stretching of our world.

Let's create an example by saying we have a window with size (640, 320) and a view with an equal rectangle. Then, we draw a circle in the middle of that screen, and when we verify, we see a perfect circle. However, as soon as we increase the view's rectangle height, without growing its width, as a result of trying to map more pixels to the very same space, we will notice that the circle is now shrunk vertically. It maintains the same width as before, but the height is smaller, turning the circle into an ellipse. This does not mean that we drew an incorrect circle, but rather that our view rectangle is not proportional and therefore shows distorted results.

It is very difficult to the programmer to predict view sizes that will fit perfectly to every screen, while keeping the same aspect ratio. There are tiny screens as well as very wide ones, and sometimes there is no perfect solution to this issue. However, there are tricks that can help handling this situation, to provide a better gaming experience to the audience, such as the "widescreen" technique, which leaves a bar on top of the screen and another on bottom without rendering, just so the remaining area is more alike the window size the programmer idealized. This kind of techniques is outside the scope of the book, but it is likely that after understanding the concept of viewports and the viewport rectangle, the reader is able to implement them by intuition.

This mapping of the view to the window can also be exploited beyond preventing graphical glitches. It can be used to apply effects to the world, by animating the view's rectangle, to create shrinking and stretching illusions in many ways.

View scrolling

Now that we covered the most important parameters of `sf::View`, we will talk about how we use it in the context of the chapter's sample game.

After knowing how to define the viewport, and mapping to it an arbitrary region of the world with `sf::View::setRect()` with correct aspect ratio, we now want to move the view around, to create movement along the game world.

Since our game's action occurs in a vertical corridor, with no horizontal movement apart from moving the plane inside the fixed width window we see, we don't need to consider the x axis.

In every step of the game loop, when updating the state of the world, we also scroll the view a little. We do this at a constant speed towards the negative y axis (up), so we see a little further at each time step. Of course, we also move the player's aircraft by the exact same distance, so it won't get left behind, but remains in action.

This incremental and automatic scrolling operation of the view is simply done in the update code, by doing:

```
mWorldView.move(0.f, mScrollSpeed * dt.asSeconds());
```

It is always important to multiply our values by the elapsed time in seconds, so we ensure that the speed of *n* pixels per second is guaranteed, independent of the simulation frame rate.

Zoom and rotation

The `sf::View` utility gives us another two precious features: zooming and rotating our view.

We can use the `sf::View::zoom(float factor)` function to easily approach or move away from the center of the view. The `factor` parameter means that the current view's rectangle will be multiplied by it. It is really that simple. A factor of one will have no effects on the zoom function. A factor bigger than one will grow the view's rectangle, which makes objects appear smaller and gives us the impression to watch from a more distant point of view. The opposite applies when using a factor less than one, which will make the world appear to be closer, just like when we zoom in a real camera.

About rotation, `sf::View` allows us to turn our view orientation to another angle than the default one, zero, in degrees. The easiest way to visualize the results of this operation is to picture how our world is seen under the default view orientation, and then imagine the whole content rotating relative to the center of the view.

This is a concept that is better understood by experimenting until the desired effect is reached. You can use `sf::View::rotate(float degrees)` to add a rotation angle to the current one, or `sf::View::setRotation(float degrees)` to set the rotation of the view to an absolute value.

Landscape rendering

As you can observe in the C++ sample for this chapter, our aircraft travels continuously over a desert. This continuity can be achieved in many ways and with many different levels of detail and complexity. However, we chose to go in a very simple and yet effective way of doing it, using a feature that SFML provides out of the box.

SpriteNode

In order to display our background sprite through the scene graph, we created a new `SceneNode` type, the `SpriteNode`, which acts as a simple `sf::Sprite` that can be plugged into our tree structure. Conveniently, this is all we need to make our landscape. We only have to create `SpriteNode` and attach it to our background layer of the scene graph.

To demonstrate the implementation of a new node type, there follows a small snippet of the `SpriteNode` declaration:

```
class SpriteNode : public SceneNode
{
    public:
        explicit            SpriteNode(const sf::Texture& texture);
                            SpriteNode(const sf::Texture& texture,
                                        const sf::IntRect& rect);

    private:
        virtual void        drawCurrent(sf::RenderTarget& target,
                                        sf::RenderStates states) const;

    private:
        sf::Sprite          mSprite;
};
```

The `sf::Sprite` class is constructed and prepared at startup and not touched again in the future. This is a proof of the scene graph's power, showing us that the relative transforms work very well because we can manipulate the positioning, rotation, and scale of `SpriteNode`, and these transforms are inherently applied to the `sf::Sprite` object as well.

With the sprite node, we have also introduced the last piece in our scene graph for the moment. The following diagram should give you an impression of the current inheritance hierarchy. The grey classes at the top are part of SFML, the black ones are ours.

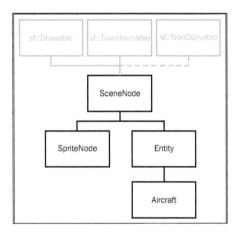

Landscape texture

In order to have a good landscape, without wasting too much memory having multiple images to represent it along the whole level, we used a tileable texture.

A tileable texture is no more than an image that can be put together continuously, without letting the player notice that we actually have one single image repeating itself. This is possible because the seam between every two instances of the image is not noticeable. The image's beginning fits perfectly into its ending, creating an illusion of infinity, with just one texture. As you can see in the following figure, multiple desert images can be put together without creating a hard seam, giving the illusion that it's only one image.

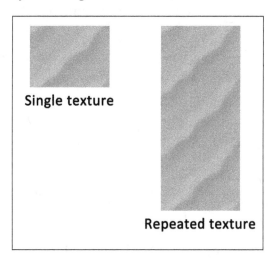

That is exactly what we did. We made a desert "tile", which is only big enough to fill one screen. Using the following technique, we made it look infinite, repeating itself along the whole level.

Texture repeating

The key to our tiling effect is exactly the texture repeating feature that SFML provides us. Every `sf::Texture` comes along with the option to enable repeating along both axis with the `sf::Texture::setRepeated(bool)` function.

When repeating is enabled for a texture, it means that it will be theoretically infinite, tiling itself continuously as much as required. When a `sf::Sprite` object links to a texture in this mode, it will behave normally until the sprite requests a texture rectangle that is larger than the texture's real dimensions. In that moment, the sprite will display the texture along its whole size.

As a practical case, we can picture a texture that is only a square, such as a floor's tile. Using this texture with a `sf::Sprite` object would normally allow us to see only one tile, no matter how big dimensions we have set with `sf::Sprite::setTextureRect()`. However, as soon as the texture activates its repeating mode, `sf::Sprite` would now render a nice tiled floor, without any extra effort!

Composing our world

Up to now, we have taken a look at entities and the scene graph, we know how to render and update objects in the world, and we have seen how views and scrolling work. We have a concrete knowledge about many building blocks, now it is time to assemble them to shape a model of our fictional world.

Completely unforeseen, we create a new class called `World`. On one side, our `World` class must contain all the data related to rendering:

- A reference to the render window
- The world's current view
- A texture holder with all the textures needed inside the world
- The scene graph
- Some pointers to access the scene graph's layer nodes

On the other hand, we store some logical data:

- The bounding rectangle of the world, storing its dimensions
- The position where the player's plane appears in the beginning
- The speed with which the world is scrolled
- A pointer to the player's aircraft

Concerning functionality, we implement public functions to update and draw the world. We also add two private functions to load the texture and to build up the scene. Since we only have one world and we don't want it to be copied, the class derives privately from `sf::NonCopyable`.

```cpp
class World : private sf::NonCopyable
{
    public:
        explicit        World(sf::RenderWindow& window);
        void            update(sf::Time dt);
        void            draw();
```

```
private:
    void            loadTextures();
    void            buildScene();

private:
    enum Layer
    {
        Background,
        Air,
        LayerCount
    };

private:
    sf::RenderWindow&                       mWindow;
    sf::View                                mWorldView;
    TextureHolder                           mTextures;
    SceneNode                               mSceneGraph;
    std::array<SceneNode*, LayerCount>      mSceneLayers;

    sf::FloatRect                           mWorldBounds;
    sf::Vector2f                            mSpawnPosition;
    float                                   mScrollSpeed;
    Aircraft*                               mPlayerAircraft;
};
```

For the scene layers, we use an array of pointers with the size `LayerCount`.

 std::array is a C++11 class template for fixed-size static arrays. It offers the same functionality and performance as C arrays, but has many advantages. It provides value semantics, which allow copies, assignments, and passing or returning objects from functions. There is no implicit conversion to pointers, and index access is checked in debug mode. Additionally, an STL-conforming interface with useful methods such as size(), begin(), or end() is provided. Because of the additional safety and features, std::array should always be preferred over C arrays.

World initialization

In the constructor, we build up the world. The following figure can help to imagine the dimensions of our world:

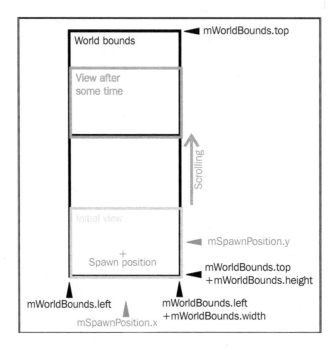

The constructor initializes the important attributes. The `mWorldBounds` rectangle is initialized so that the upper-left corner lies at position (0, 0). Its width equals the window's width, and for its height we take an arbitrary value, here `2000`. This is rather small value, but it shows already after a short time that the desert texture ceases to repeat any longer, leaving behind a black background.

The `mSpawnPosition` vector is initialized depending on the world bounds and the window. According to the previous figure, the vector's x coordinate is assigned the middle of the screen, and its y coordinate is the same as the bottom of the world minus a half screen height.

```
:  mWindow(window)
,  mWorldView(window.getDefaultView())
,  mWorldBounds(
       0.f,                                    // left X position
       0.f,                                    // top Y position
       mWorldView.getSize().x,                 // width
       2000.f)                                 // height
,  mSpawnPosition(
       mWorldView.getSize().x / 2.f,                        // X
       mWorldBounds.height - mWorldView.getSize()
,  mPlayerAircraft(nullptr)                                 // Y
{
    loadTextures();
    buildScene();

    mWorldView.setCenter(mSpawnPosition);
}
```

For the scroll speed, we choose a negative value, since we scroll upwards and the y axis points downwards. The aircraft pointer is initialized with a null pointer literal. In the constructor body, we call our two private functions that are in charge of further initialization. Finally, we move the view to the correct start position. As you see in the figure, its center initially matches the player's spawn position.

Loading the textures

Now, let's have a look at texture loading. Thanks to our ResourceHolder class, this part could not be simpler:

```
void World::loadTextures()
{
    mTextures.load(Textures::Eagle,  "Media/Textures/Eagle.png");
    mTextures.load(Textures::Raptor, "Media/Textures/Raptor.png");
    mTextures.load(Textures::Desert, "Media/Textures/Desert.png");
}
```

We do not handle exceptions here, since the World class cannot react to them. Without the textures, we are not able to construct our world meaningfully, thus it is reasonable that we let possible exceptions abort the constructor.

But if we handle exceptions nowhere, the program will crash. We put an exception handler into the `main()` function, giving the user a meaningful error description:

```
int main()
{
    try
    {
        Game game;
        game.run();
    }
    catch (std::exception& e)
    {
        std::cout << "\nEXCEPTION: " << e.what() << std::endl;
    }
}
```

Building the scene

Now comes the interesting part: building up the scene, which is done in the `World::buildScene()` method. First, we initialize the different scene layers. We iterate through our array of layer node pointers and initialize each element. `std::unique_ptr::get()` returns a raw pointer to the stored object, we do not transfer ownership to the array. Finally, we attach the new node to the scene graph's root node as shown in the following code:

```
for (std::size_t i = 0; i < LayerCount; ++i)
{
    SceneNode::Ptr layer(new SceneNode());
    mSceneLayers[i] = layer.get();

    mSceneGraph.attachChild(std::move(layer));
}
```

After the background texture for the desert is loaded, we configure it to repeat itself. We also create a texture rect (with int coordinates) using the conversion from the world bounds (which have the type `sf::FloatRect` and thus store float coordinates).

```
sf::Texture& texture = mTextures.get(Textures::Desert);
sf::IntRect textureRect(mWorldBounds);
texture.setRepeated(true);
```

Then, we create our `SpriteNode` class that links to the desert texture. We pass to its constructor the texture rectangle. This grants that our sprite is as big as the whole world. While the desert image is only one screen wide, it is tiled along the whole level in -y direction.

```
std::unique_ptr<SpriteNode> backgroundSprite(
    new SpriteNode(texture, textureRect));
backgroundSprite->setPosition(
    mWorldBounds.left,
    mWorldBounds.top);
mSceneLayers[Background]
    ->attachChild(std::move(backgroundSprite));
```

Finally, we have come to the point where we add the airplanes! First, we create the player's airplane. We set the world's pointer `mPlayerAircraft` to the newly created scene node. Then, we specify an initial position (the spawn position) and velocity. The forward velocity equals the scroll speed. We also introduce a sideward velocity with value `40`, to show a more interesting movement pattern. At last, we attach the plane to the `Air` scene layer.

```
std::unique_ptr<Aircraft> leader(
    new Aircraft(Aircraft::Eagle, mTextures));
mPlayerAircraft = leader.get();
mPlayerAircraft->setPosition(mSpawnPosition);
mPlayerAircraft->setVelocity(40.f, mScrollSpeed);
mSceneLayers[Air]->attachChild(std::move(leader));
```

Since single planes are boring, we give our leader an escort of two other airplanes, one on each side. After construction, we set a position and attach the escort to the leader's scene node. The specified position is thus interpreted relative to the leader. In the following example, the first escort plane is located `80` units to the left and `50` units behind the leader:

```
std::unique_ptr<Aircraft> leftEscort(
    new Aircraft(Aircraft::Raptor, mTextures));
leftEscort->setPosition(-80.f, 50.f);
mPlayerAircraft->attachChild(std::move(leftEscort));
```

For the second escort, the code is almost the same, except that the relative x position is now positive, meaning that this plane is located to the right.

```
std::unique_ptr<Aircraft> rightEscort(
    new Aircraft(Aircraft::Raptor, mTextures));
rightEscort->setPosition(80.f, 50.f);
mPlayerAircraft->attachChild(std::move(rightEscort));
```

That was it, now our scene is ready! Now, our scene graph looks as shown in the following diagram. Below the description of each node, you see the most derived class type.

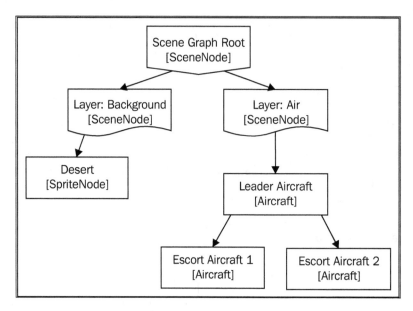

Update and draw

The update() and draw() methods bring the encapsulated scene graph functionality to the API of the World class.

The function to draw sets the current view and delegates the work to the scene graph:

```
void World::draw()
{
    mWindow.setView(mWorldView);
    mWindow.draw(mSceneGraph);
}
```

The update function controls world scrolling and entity movement. First, the view is scrolled according to the passed time. Next, we check if the player's aircraft reaches a certain distance (150) from the world's borders, and flip its x velocity in this case. This results in the plane moving back, until it reaches the other border, and the procedure repeats. Eventually, we forward the update to the scene graph, which actually applies the velocities.

```
void World::update(sf::Time dt)
{
    mWorldView.move(0.f, mScrollSpeed * dt.asSeconds());

    sf::Vector2f position = mPlayerAircraft->getPosition();
    sf::Vector2f velocity = mPlayerAircraft->getVelocity();

    if (position.x <= mWorldBounds.left + 150
    || position.x >= mWorldBounds.left + mWorldBounds.width - 150)
    {
        velocity.x = -velocity.x;
        mPlayerAircraft->setVelocity(velocity);
    }

    mSceneGraph.update(dt);
}
```

Integrating the Game class

By now we already know how the Game class works, what a game loop is for, and how to take advantage of it. For this chapter, we take the previously used Game class, and plug into it our newcomer World class.

Because we obeyed a few principles, this integration is very easy and it's just a matter of having a World object inside the Game class, and then letting it update and draw itself in the appropriate times.

The run() method

Our application's main() function has a simple job. It allocates a Game object, and lets it run itself through the run() method. When the run() method exits, the program releases its resources and closes.

Therefore, it is within the run() method that the magic happens! It is responsible for managing the famous game loop, fetching input from the window system, updating the world, and ordering the rendering of the game.

In the next chapter, events and input will be covered in depth. For now, it is only important to understand how the drawing sequence happens inside the `run()` method:

```
mWindow.clear();
mWorld.draw();

mWindow.setView(mWindow.getDefaultView());
mWindow.draw(mStatisticsText);
mWindow.display();
```

This code closely resembles the high-level drawing of a frame for any game. The function call `mWindow.clear()` ensures that our frame buffer, the canvas where the frame will be drawn, is cleaned up before we start drawing. Then, we let the world draw itself, where it defines its own view and orders the scene graph to render itself. Finally, because we want to display some text in the corner of the screen for statistical purposes, we activate the default view, which is always the same so the text always appears fixed on the screen.

On the `mWindow.display()` call, we tell SFML we are done drawing the frame and it proceeds to upload it to our screen right away.

From this moment, you should be able to better dissect a game's mechanics and visualize its structure in your mind, mapping it directly to a data structure in C++. We can use the mental toolbox learned in this chapter to help us lay out our thoughts into actual computational data. This hypothetical toolbox contains many tools: managing entities and their transformations, scene graphs, views as cameras, graphical tricks, and others. But more importantly, we have started to understand how to properly glue all these elements together in a harmonious simulation. Furthermore, you have also seen many smaller techniques, which you may or may not have known, for example, practical use cases of C++11 features. So far, our result looks as shown in the following screenshot:

Summary

This chapter has moved away from the typical minimal examples, and has given you deeper insights to a possible game architecture. As always, keep in mind that we have chosen one of many design options—not every game needs a scene graph, sometimes a list of entities is enough.

In the next chapter you can expect information about handling both input events and real-time state of the keyboard and mouse. Also, you will learn about command systems to deliver input to game entities as well as dynamic key binding mechanisms, which allow you to configure the set of controls of a game in runtime.

4
Command and Control – Input Handling

In the previous chapter, we talked about how to implement the world our game takes place in and the different objects that the world is made up of. In this chapter, we will focus on how to give the player the power to manipulate this world.

In this chapter we aim to learn:

- SFML events and their purpose as input
- SFML real-time input and its difference from events
- A command-based communication system to deliver events in our world
- How to dynamically bind keys at runtime

In the previous chapters, we have used events to manage input, but we have not really delved into what they are or what they are meant to be used for. That is the first point of this chapter. After that, we will look at more concepts of input than just simply events.

Polling events

Generally speaking, **events** are objects that are triggered when something happens; mostly related to the user input. Events are a construct in the underlying operating system. On top of them, SFML provides a nice abstraction layer that is easier to use and cross-platform. SFML goes with a polling design to have you work with events. When an input occurs, the operating system reports it to the application. SFML processes this input, converts it into the corresponding SFML event type, and puts it into a queue of waiting events. In your actual application code, you extract events from this queue using the `sf::Window::pollEvent()` function (note that `sf::Window` is the base class of `sf::RenderWindow`, without the rendering functionality). The `pollEvent()` function signature is a bit interesting:

```
bool sf::Window::pollEvent(sf::Event& event);
```

Now this is a bit special and might not be self-explanatory. The problem with `pollEvent()` is that we want to receive two different values. We want to receive the actual event and a value affirming that we got it from the list. If the second value is false, we will not receive anything.

SFML uses a common approach to a polling system, which allows us to retrieve one event instance at a time by continuously calling `pollEvent()` until the function returns a false value, which means there are no more events to poll. In the meanwhile, for every positive return value, we know that our `sf::Event` variable has been filled with important event information.

That is why in all our examples up to now, we have received events in this following fashion:

```
sf::Event event;
while (window.pollEvent(event))
{
    // Handle the event
}
```

Here we poll events from the window until its internal list becomes empty. There is a `waitEvent()` function as well, that waits until it receives an event, but that is pretty redundant for our case, so we will not dig into that.

The event structure we have used so much already is built up of an enum and a union of different event structures. As a short reminder, a union is similar to struct, with the main difference that all the member variables occupy the same memory location. Therefore, only one member can be actively used at a time. Applied to sf::Event, the very nature of union grants that an event will never be two things at the same time. Depending on the value of the sf::Event::type member variable, a different union member is filled with useful data. When we receive an event, we first check the type of it, and depending on it we access the specific data. We have to be careful to access the correct union members, otherwise we risk undefined behavior.

We can group the different events to four different categories: **window**, **joystick**, **keyboard**, and **mouse**. We will try to cover each and every one of the events, but it will be near to impossible to go into too much detail, otherwise this chapter would be huge. I urge you to check out SFML's documentation for more information, in case anything is unclear on the events.

Window events

In this section, we have the window-based events which are the events that concern windows directly. I have listed them as follows, with their intended purposes and the conditions under which they are generated:

- sf::Event::Closed: This event occurs when the users somehow request that they want the window closed. Mostly, this amounts to pressing the **[X]** button in the window, or a shortcut such as *Alt + F4* on Windows. This event does not have any data associated with itself. We have already used it plenty and your application should always handle this event.

- sf::Event::Resized: This event is triggered when the window is resized. Most often this is when the user drags on the edges of the window to manually resize it. The data type associated with this is sf::Event::SizeEvent and can be accessed through the member event.size. Of course, resizing the window is only possible if you have enabled it to be resized.

- sf::Event::LostFocus and sf::Event::GainedFocus: These events come from the window when it gains or loses focus. Focus here means that this window is the one that the user has chosen right now and it will receive the user input. No data apart from the event type is associated with these events. These events are of interest when you want to pause the game if the user clicks outside the window or switches to another application.

Joystick events

Now we have to cover the joystick-based events. These events are fired whenever a connected joystick or gamepad changes its state. Every joystick event has a data structure associated with it. A common member they all have is the ID number for the joystick. The ID is required in order to keep track of which joystick generated the event, since there can be more than one joystick. We have the following joystick events that can be generated:

- Joysticks have buttons, for button-related events we have the event types `sf::Event::JoystickButtonPressed` and `sf::Event::JoystickButtonReleased`. These are triggered when a button on the joystick is pressed or released. The data structure associated with this is `sf::Event::JoystickButtonEvent` with the member `event. joystickButton`. You should keep in mind that the buttons can be of a variable amount.

- The `sf::Event::JoystickMoved` event is generated when the analog stick or digital cross moves; it has the structure `sf::Event::JoystickMoveEvent` for its data. It is accessible through the member `event.joystickMove`. A thing to note here is that joysticks work in axes, so the movement is measured in an axis as well. It is not guaranteed that the joysticks support all axes.

- Last we have the event of when a joystick is connected or disconnected, allowing you to handle hot-plugging joysticks. The event types are `sf::Event::JoystickConnected` and `sf::Event::JoystickDisconnected`. The data type is `sf::Event::JoystickConnectEvent` and is accessible through the member `event.joystickConnect`.

Keyboard events

Now the defining feature of a PC, the keyboard. The keyboard generates events as the primary input device available to computers:

- For the event when the user presses down a key, we have the event type `sf::Event::KeyPressed`. The data structure for this event is `sf::Event::KeyEvent`, which is accessed through `event.key`. It holds all the data of the current state of the keyboard associated with that key press. The member variable `event.key.code` contains the actual key, while other members such as `event.key.control` are Booleans that state whether a modifier is pressed. If you hold a key for a while, multiple `KeyPressed` events will be triggered. This key repetition option can be deactivated using `sf::Window::setKeyRepeatEnabled()`.

- The event `sf::Event::KeyReleased` is the counterpart to `KeyPressed`; it is triggered when you release a key. To retrieve information about the key release, you can also access the structure `sf::Event::KeyEvent` via `event.key`—just like when a key was pressed.

- Last, we have a little special event that SFML creates for your convenience. It is called `sf::Event::TextEntered` and is designed for receiving formatted text from the user. Using the normal key event for this is a very tedious task, so this event helps out a lot. The data structure is `sf::Event::TextEvent` and it is accessible through `event.text`.

Mouse events

Last, but not the least, we have the mouse-based events. These are generated when the state of the cursor, the mouse buttons or the mouse wheel changes:

- First we have the `sf::Event::MouseEntered` and `sf::Event::MouseLeft` events. These are triggered when the mouse cursor enters or leaves the window.

- Next we consider when the cursor moves inside the window. The type for this is `sf::Event::MouseMoved` and its associated structure is `sf::MouseMoveEvent`. You can access the data from the `event.mouseMove` member. The coordinates in the data structure are measured in window pixels and they are unaffected by scaling or any other transformation from your window's current view. Please notice how the Y coordinate increases as we go down. The origin of the window is always at the top-left corner and then grows up to the size of the window:

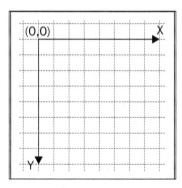

- Then, we have the buttons of the mouse. For them we have the `sf::Event::MouseButtonPressed` and `sf::Event::MouseButtonReleased` types. They come associated with the `sf::Event::MouseButtonEvent` structure and its data can be accessed through the `event.mouseButton` member.

- Last is the mouse wheel on the mouse. When its state changes, it generates an event of type `sf::Event::MouseWheelMoved`. Attached with this is the data structure `sf::Event::MouseWheelEvent` that you can access via the member `event.mouseWheel`.

> Always remember, the mouse wheel doesn't have a global state. This means that we will be notified that the mouse wheel is being moved by some unit, but this information doesn't constitute an actual rotation value, just an offset corresponding to the movement we performed with the physical mouse.

Getting the input state in real time

Now, we have gone through many varieties of events. A problem with events is that they report once when the state changes, but you cannot continuously ask them how the state of the input devices look right now.

You can solve this by book keeping yourself, which we have done in the examples preceding this chapter. But SFML, in an effort to make input management easier, has implemented classes that let you access these states in **real time** whenever you want from wherever you want. We will use the notion of real-time input to denote this alternative method of handling user input.

The three classes `sf::Joystick`, `sf::Keyboard`, and `sf::Mouse` can provide almost the same information that the event-based counterparts do, but with some minor variations. They are summarized here and their difference to the events is shown; we recommend visiting the SFML documentation for more details on them. The three classes contain only static functions, so they are not designed to be instantiated. Instead, you can access the real-time input state globally from any place:

- `sf::Joystick`: This class provides same tools that are similar to the joystick-based events. They are based on ID numbers for the joystick, they can state if a joystick is connected or disconnected or get the current input state of the joystick. You can also ask how many buttons the joystick has and if the joystick supports a specific axis.

- `sf::Keyboard`: This is a really small class. It has one function `isKeyPressed()`, you can ask if a key is pressed and it returns either `true` or `false`. Nothing fancy.

- `sf::Mouse`: This class is a bit tricky. It behaves normally with the buttons, the function `isButtonPressed()` tells you if a button is being pressed or not. The part that differs from the events is the position. Previously, you polled the event from a window so you always knew what window you wanted the mouse to be relative to. Now you don't know that anymore. So if you ask `sf::Mouse::getPosition()` for the mouse position, you will get the screen coordinates. Luckily there is an overload that takes a window. It will calculate the relative position from the provided window and the result is as you first expected.

Now let's look at a real example where we would want to use this. Do you remember when we had that circle that we moved by pressing keys on the keyboard? We polled events from the window and pushed them to `Game::handlePlayerInput()` and then we did the movement in `Game::update()`:

```
void Game::handlePlayerInput(sf::Keyboard::Key key,
bool isPressed)
{
    if (key == sf::Keyboard::W)
        mIsMovingUp = isPressed;
        else if (key == sf::Keyboard::S)
    mIsMovingDown = isPressed;
        else if (key == sf::Keyboard::A)
    mIsMovingLeft = isPressed;
        else if (key == sf::Keyboard::D)
    mIsMovingRight = isPressed;
}

void Game::update()
{
    sf::Vector2f movement(0.f, 0.f);
    if (mIsMovingUp)
        movement.y -= 1.f;
    if (mIsMovingDown)
        movement.y += 1.f;
    if (mIsMovingLeft)
        movement.x -= 1.f;
    if (mIsMovingRight)
        movement.x += 1.f;

    mPlayer.move(movement);
}
```

If you look closely, you can see that we are book keeping what key has been pressed down. But now we have got the real-time functions, so now we can minimize this by asking `sf::Keyboard` if a button has been pressed down, instead of checking a couple of Boolean values. The exact same functionality but using real-time input instead will be significantly smaller. We do not even need the `handlePlayerInput()` function anymore because everything will be handled in `update()` instead:

```
void Game::update(sf::Time elapsedTime)
{
    sf::Vector2f movement(0.f, 0.f);
    if (sf::Keyboard::isKeyPressed(sf::Keyboard::W))
        movement.y -= PlayerSpeed;
    if (sf::Keyboard::isKeyPressed(sf::Keyboard::S))
        movement.y += PlayerSpeed;
    if (sf::Keyboard::isKeyPressed(sf::Keyboard::A))
        movement.x -= PlayerSpeed;
    if (sf::Keyboard::isKeyPressed(sf::Keyboard::D))
        movement.x += PlayerSpeed;

    mPlayer.move(movement * elapsedTime.asSeconds());
}
```

This is all that we need now. Every frame, we query SFML if the appropriate keys are being pressed. This removes our need of book keeping the events, making our life much easier and our code much simpler to read and follow.

Although, even if we have this powerful tool provided to us, it is not a golden hammer. Events are still very much needed and have their own purposes as we will explore now.

Events and real-time input – when to use which

It depends on the context. A rule of thumb is: if you are interested, if a state has changed, you should use events. If you want to know the current state, then you use the real-time functions. Here is an example:

```
if (sf::Mouse::isButtonPressed(sf::Mouse::Left))
    // WHILE the left mouse button is being pressed, do something
if (event.type == sf::Event::MouseButtonPressed)
    // WHEN the left mouse button has been pressed, do something
```

In the first `if` statement we do something during the time that the mouse is being pressed down, while in the second version we only do something once after we have pressed the button down.

Delta movement from the mouse

A common thing that you want in your game is to get the delta movement of the cursor. For the game we are making here in this book, it won't be needed but it's such a common functionality that we should still go through what it is.

The delta movement is the difference of the cursor position between two frames; that is, it is the distance that the cursor has traveled:

```
sf::Vector2i mousePosition = sf::Mouse::getPosition(mWindow);
sf::Vector2i delta = mLastMousePosition - mousePosition;
mLastMousePosition = mousePosition;
```

A little book keeping is needed here but nothing major. The delta vector contains the data we need for anything relative. Now we are not making a first person shooter, but in that scenario you would like this data in order to perform the rotation of the camera. There are uses in 2D as well of course! Delta mouse movement can be used for dragging the view of a map and lots more.

In some cases this naive method can become a problem eventually. What if you are constantly moving more and more to the left? Eventually you will move outside the window and reach the end of the screen. What then? The mouse will stop and the delta will stay at a solid zero until you start moving back. This is no good, if we go back to a first person shooter example, it would make the game totally unplayable. But thanks to SFML this problem is easy to solve.

In the `sf::Mouse` class we have a `setPosition()` function pair. It works exactly the same as the `sf::Mouse::getPosition()` functions, but it sets the mouse position on the window instead of querying for it. And, you can use the basic version that sets it in the screen coordinates or you can set it relative to your window:

```
sf::Vector2i windowCenter(mWindow.getSize() / 2u);
sf::Vector2i mousePosition = sf::Mouse::getPosition(mWindow);
sf::Vector2i delta = windowCenter - mousePosition;
sf::Mouse::setPosition(windowCenter, mWindow);
```

In this example, we reset the mouse to the center of the window, after we have calculated the delta. And since we always know that the mouse starts from the center of the screen, we don't have to book keep it anymore and can just use the half size of the window.

Playing nice with your application neighborhood

Now what we learned in the last part is indeed handy, but it has got its problem. What if the user tabs out and tries to interact with the other applications that are running in the background? We would be constantly forcing the mouse back to the center of our window, making it impossible to do anything else than playing our game.

Believe it or not, this is actually very annoying for a lot of people, including ourselves. When we are debugging our application, this behavior will make it impossible to work with the IDE in the background. We have to detect when the user doesn't want to interact with us anymore and behave properly.

This is where events come in again. If you remember, we had the event types `sf::Event::GainedFocus` and `sf::Event::LostFocus` that notify the application as soon as the window gains or loses focus:

```
void Game::processEvents()
{
    sf::Event event;
    while(mWindow.pollEvent(event))
    {
        if (event.type == sf::Event::GainedFocus)
            mIsPaused = false;
        else if (event.type == sf::Event::LostFocus)
            mIsPaused = true;
    }
}

void Game::run()
{
    while (mWindow.isOpen())
    {
        if (!mIsPaused)
            update();

        render();
        processEvents();
    }
}
```

In this example, we keep track of the focus of our application. We toggle a Boolean value depending on the focus that tells us if the game should be paused or not. Then, how do we prevent the game from changing if we are paused? That is simple with our current architecture; we just branch out the update call to only be called if the game is not paused. That way the game will keep rendering, registering events, and be responsive to the user and the OS. But it won't change its state over time.

A command-based communication system

Up to now, you have seen how events and real-time inputs are handled. In our game, we might handle them as follows (the aircraft methods are fictional to show the principle):

```
// One-time events
sf::Event event;
while (window.pollEvent(event))
{
    if (event.type == sf::Event::KeyPressed
      && event.key.code == sf::Keyboard::X)
        mPlayerAircraft->launchMissile();
}

// Real-time input
if (sf::Keyboard::isKeyPressed(sf::Keyboard::Left))
    mPlayerAircraft->moveLeft();
else if (sf::Keyboard::isKeyPressed(sf::Keyboard::Right))
    mPlayerAircraft->moveRight();
```

There are several problems with this approach. On one side, we have hardcoded keys, so a user cannot choose WASD instead of arrow keys for movement. On the other side, we gather input and logic code in one place. The game logic code grows as we implement more features, and makes the originally simple code complicated.

For example, imagine that we want to keep the airplane inside the screen bounds. So we could only move the airplanes to the left if it is currently inside the screen, which can be verified using an `if` condition. In case of the missiles, we want to check whether enough ammunition is available before firing, leading to another `if` statement. Maybe, we want to limit the fire interval, so that the player must wait at least one second between two launched missiles. For this, we need a timer and further logic, and we already have plenty of game-logic code mixed with the input-handling code. Sure, we could outsource the code into functions, but there is still a problem.

Sometimes, we do not know whom to affect when the user input occurs. Imagine a guided missile which is steered by the player. The missile itself may be stored somewhere in the depths of the world's scene graph, we do not have access to it at the time we handle input. To gain access, a pointer would have to be passed from the scene graph via the `World` to the `Game` class. The same thoughts apply to many other entities in the game, eventually we would duplicate the information about the world at the place where input is handled.

This is of course not what we want. Instead, we aim to separate input handling and game logics. A possible approach to achieve this goal is discussed in the following sections.

Introducing commands

Here after, commands denote messages that are sent to various game objects. A command is able to alter the object and to issue orders such as moving an entity, firing a weapon, and triggering an explosion.

We design a structure Command that contains a function object, which can be called on any game object represented by a scene node:

```
struct Command
{
    std::function<void(SceneNode&, sf::Time)>    action;
};
```

> std::function is a C++11 class template to implements callback mechanisms. It treats functions as objects and makes it possible to copy functions or to store them in containers. The std::function class is compatible with function pointers, member function pointers, functors, and lambda expressions. The template parameter represents the signature of the function being stored.

The following example shows std::function in action. First, we assign a function pointer to it, then we assign a lambda expression:

```
int add(int a, int b) { return a + b };
std::function<int(int, int)> adder1 = &add;
std::function<int(int, int)> adder2
    = [] (int a, int b) { return a + b; };
```

The std::function object can be called using its overloaded operator():

```
int sum = adder1(3, 5);            // same as add(3, 5)
```

> Using the standard function template std::bind(), the function arguments can be bound to the given values. The std::bind() function returns a new function object that can be stored inside std::function.

In the earlier example, we can fix the second argument to 1 and thus have a new function that takes only one argument. The placeholder _1 expresses that the first argument is forwarded, while the second argument is bound to the constant 1:

```
std::function<int(int)> increaser = std::bind(&add, _1, 1);
int increased = increaser(5);     // same as add(5, 1)
```

For more detailed information, consult a standard library documentation such as www.cppreference.com. Coming back to our game, the Command structure's member variable action contains the function that implements the order issued to an object. The first parameter is a reference to a scene node, which is affected by the command. The second parameter denotes the delta time of the current frame. For example, we can instantiate a command as follows:

```
void moveLeft(SceneNode& node, sf::Time dt)
{
    node.move(-30.f * dt.asSeconds(), 0.f);
}

Command c;
c.action = &moveLeft;
```

Using the lambda expressions, the equivalent functionality can be written as follows:

```
c.action = [] (SceneNode& node, sf::Time dt)
{
    node.move(-30.f * dt.asSeconds(), 0.f);
};
```

In short, we can now define any operation on a scene node inside a Command object. The advantage of a command over a direct function call is abstraction: We do not need to know on which scene node to invoke the function; we only specify the action that is performed on it. The message passing system is responsible to deliver the commands to the correct recipients.

Receiver categories

In order to ensure the correct delivery, we divide our game objects into different categories. Each category is a group of one or multiple game objects, which are likely to receive similar commands. For example, the player's aircraft is an own category, the enemies are one, the projectiles launched by the enemies are one, and so on.

We define an enum to refer to the different categories. Each category except None is initialized with an integer that has one bit set to 1, and the rest are set to 0:

```
namespace Category
{
    enum Type
    {
        None            = 0,
        Scene           = 1 << 0,
        PlayerAircraft  = 1 << 1,
        AlliedAircraft  = 1 << 2,
        EnemyAircraft   = 1 << 3,
    };
}
```

This makes it possible to combine different categories with the bitwise OR operator. When we want to send a command to all available airplanes, we can create a combined category as follows:

```
unsigned int anyAircraft = Category::PlayerAircraft
                         | Category::AlliedAircraft
                         | Category::EnemyAircraft;
```

The SceneNode class gets a new virtual method that returns the category of the game object. In the base class, we return Category::Scene by default:

```
unsigned int SceneNode::getCategory() const
{
    return Category::Scene;
}
```

In a derived class, we can override `getCategory()` to return a specific category. For example, we can say that an aircraft belongs to the player if it is of type `Eagle`, and that it is an enemy otherwise:

```
unsigned int Aircraft::getCategory() const
{
    switch (mType)
    {
        case Eagle:
            return Category::PlayerAircraft;

        default:
            return Category::EnemyAircraft;
    }
}
```

Of course, this is just a simple demonstration of how categories work. You can implement a much more complex logic to determine a game object's category. An object may also be part of multiple categories, where operator | is used to combine categories. This is the reason why the return type of `getCategory()` is `unsigned int` and not `Category::Type`.

In our game, categories are stored as `unsigned int` variables. This implies a small issue that you should be aware of: Integer flags are not type-safe. Meaningless numbers can be assigned to category variables, not only enumerators in the `Category` namespace. A bigger problem is however the confusion between different enum types:

```
Command command;
command.category = Aircraft::Eagle; // only Eagles receive command
```

Accidentally, the enums `Category::Type` and `Aircraft::Type` were mistaken, but the code still compiles, leading to nasty bugs. Type safety could be achieved by overloading bitwise operators for the enum, a dedicated class template `Flags<Enum>` could store flag combinations.

Getting back to commands, we give our `Command` class another member variable that stores the recipients of the command in a category:

```
struct Command
{                                            Command();

    std::function<void(SceneNode&, sf::Time)>    action;
    unsigned int                                 category;
};
```

The default constructor initializes the category to `Category::None`. By assigning a different value to it, we can specify exactly who receives the command. If we want a command to be executed for all airplanes except the player's one, the category can be set accordingly:

```
Command command;
command.action = ...;
command.category = Category::AlliedAircraft
                 | Category::EnemyAircraft;
```

Command execution

We have discussed how to construct commands with a function and a receiver category. In order to execute them, the function must be invoked on the receivers.

In our world, commands are passed to the scene graph, inside which they are distributed to all scene nodes with the corresponding game objects. Each scene node is responsible for forwarding a command to its children.

We write a non-virtual method `SceneNode::onCommand()` which is called every time a command is passed to the scene graph. First, we check if the current scene node is a receiver of the command, that is, if it is listed in the command's receiver category. The check is performed using the bitwise AND operator. If a bit is set in both the command's and the current node's category, then we know that the node receives the command. In this case, we can execute the command by invoking the `action` member of type `std::function` on the current node, and with the current frame time. The second part of `onCommand()` forwards the command to all the child nodes:

```
void SceneNode::onCommand(const Command& command, sf::Time dt)
{
    if (command.category & getCategory())
        command.action(*this, dt);

    FOREACH(Ptr& child, mChildren)
        child->onCommand(command, dt);
}
```

Command queues

Now that the interface to distribute a command inside the scene graph is ready, we need a way to transport commands to the world and the scene graph. For this purpose, we write a new class `CommandQueue`. This class is a very thin wrapper around a queue of commands. A queue is a **FIFO (first in, first out)** data structure that ensures that elements, which are inserted first, are also removed first. Only the front element can be accessed. The standard library already provides the container adapter `std::queue`, which implements a queue interface on top of a full-featured STL container such as `std::deque`.

Our class looks similar to the following:

```cpp
class CommandQueue
{
    public:
        void        push(const Command& command);
        Command     pop();
        bool        isEmpty() const;

    private:
        std::queue<Command> mQueue;
};
```

It only provides three methods, which directly forward their calls to the underlying `std::queue`. Their definitions are straightforward, and hence they are omitted here.

The `World` class holds an instance of `CommandQueue`. In the `World::update()` function, all commands that have been triggered since the last frame are forwarded to the scene graph:

```cpp
void World::update(sf::Time dt)
{
    ...

    // Forward commands to the scene graph
    while (!mCommandQueue.isEmpty())
        mSceneGraph.onCommand(mCommandQueue.pop(), dt);

    // Regular update step
    mSceneGraph.update(dt);
}
```

As explained earlier, `SceneNode::onCommand()` distributes a command across all scene nodes. We also provide a getter function to access the command queue from outside the world:

```
CommandQueue& World::getCommandQueue()
{
    return mCommandQueue;
}
```

Handling player input

Since this chapter is about input, it would be interesting to see how the commands can be exploited to react to the SFML events and real-time input. Up to now, player input has been handled in the `Game` class. But it deserves an own class, we call it `Player`.

The `Player` class contains two methods to react to the SFML events and real-time input, respectively:

```
class Player
{
    public:
        void        handleEvent(const sf::Event& event,
                                CommandQueue& commands);
        void        handleRealtimeInput(CommandQueue& commands);
};
```

These methods are invoked from the `Game` class, inside the `processInput()` member function. Only the `sf::Event::Closed` event is still handled inside `Game`, all other events are delegated to the `Player` class:

```
void Game::processInput()
{
    CommandQueue& commands = mWorld.getCommandQueue();

    sf::Event event;
    while (mWindow.pollEvent(event))
    {
        mPlayer.handleEvent(event, commands);

        if (event.type == sf::Event::Closed)
            mWindow.close();
    }

    mPlayer.handleRealtimeInput(commands);
}
```

Now let's see how input is handled inside the `Player` class. We treat the example of the arrow keys and real-time input with `sf::Keyboard`. What we want to do is change the aircraft's velocity if an arrow key is pressed. For our command, we need an action function, we design it as a function object (functor) similar to the following:

```
struct AircraftMover
{
    AircraftMover(float vx, float vy)
    : velocity(vx, vy)
    {
    }

    void operator() (SceneNode& node, sf::Time) const
    {
        Aircraft& aircraft = static_cast<Aircraft&>(node);
        aircraft.accelerate(velocity);
    }

    sf::Vector2f velocity;
};
```

When the functor is invoked, `operator()` is called, which adds `(vx, vy)` to the current aircraft velocity. `aircraft.accelerate(velocity)` is a utility function that acts equivalently to `aircraft.setVelocity(aircraft.getVelocity() + velocity)`. In other words, the variable `velocity` is added to the aircraft's current velocity. The downcast is required because the command stores a function which is invoked on `SceneNode&`, but we need `Aircraft&`. It is safe as long as we guarantee with the receiver category that only correct types receive the command. We can now construct a command as follows:

```
Command moveLeft;
moveLeft.category = Category::PlayerAircraft;
moveLeft.action = AircraftMover(-playerSpeed, 0.f);
```

Since we often work on entities that are classes derived from `SceneNode`, the constant need for downcasts is annoying. It would be much more user friendly if we could directly create a function with the signature `void(Aircraft& aircraft, sf::Time dt)` instead. This is possible, if we provide a small adapter `derivedAction()` that takes a function on a derived class such as `Aircraft` and converts it to a function on the `SceneNode` base class. We create a lambda expression, inside which we invoke the original function `fn` on the derived class, passing a downcast argument to it. An additional assertion checks in the debug mode that the conversion is safe, which is extremely helpful to avoid bugs. The lambda expression uses a `[=]` capture list, meaning that variables referenced from its body (such as the variable `fn`) are copied from the surrounding scope:

```cpp
template <typename GameObject, typename Function>
std::function<void(SceneNode&, sf::Time)>
    derivedAction(Function fn)
{
    return [=] (SceneNode& node, sf::Time dt)
    {
        // Check if cast is safe
        assert(dynamic_cast<GameObject*>(&node) != nullptr);

        // Downcast node and invoke function on it
        fn(static_cast<GameObject&>(node), dt);
    };
}
```

Given this adapter, we can change our `AircraftMover` to take `Aircraft&` instead of `SceneNode&`:

```cpp
struct AircraftMover
{
    ...

    void operator() (Aircraft& aircraft, sf::Time) const
    {
        aircraft.accelerate(velocity);
    }
};
```

A command would then be constructed as follows:

```cpp
Command moveLeft;
moveLeft.category = Category::PlayerAircraft;
moveLeft.action
    = derivedAction<Aircraft>(AircraftMover(-playerSpeed, 0));
```

To be honest, our adapter does not have the simplest implementation, but it should be worth the advantage that after writing it once, we can create actions in a much cleaner way, without the need to downcast again and again.

Let's get back to the interesting part. Let's finally define `Player::handleRealtimeInput()`, which creates a command every frame an arrow key is held down:

```
void Player::handleRealtimeInput(CommandQueue& commands)
{
    const float playerSpeed = 30.f;

    if (sf::Keyboard::isKeyPressed(sf::Keyboard::Up))
    {
        Command moveLeft;
        moveLeft.category = Category::PlayerAircraft;
        moveLeft.action = derivedAction<Aircraft>(
            AircraftMover(-playerSpeed, 0.f));
        commands.push(moveLeft);
    }
}
```

For one-time events, the handling is quite similar. As a simple example, we write a lambda expression that outputs the position of the player's aircraft every time the user presses the *P* key:

```
void Player::handleEvent(const sf::Event& event,
                         CommandQueue& commands)
{
    if (event.type == sf::Event::KeyPressed
     && event.key.code == sf::Keyboard::P)
    {
        Command output;
        output.category = Category::PlayerAircraft;
        output.action = [] (SceneNode& s, sf::Time)
        {
            std::cout << s.getPosition().x << ","
                      << s.getPosition().y << "\n";
        };
        commands.push(output);
    }
}
```

Simple, isn't it? Once you have understood the concepts of functions and lambda expressions, you can quickly build complex functionalities. Note that you don't have to use lambda expressions, you can still stick to functors such as `AircraftMover`. But in some situations, lambdas allow you to express semantics far more compactly.

Now that was it, our command system is complete!

Commands in a nutshell

We have discussed many components in our command-based system; easy for someone to get lost. The following diagram should give you an overview about the whole functionality. Basically, the system is split into an input handling and a game logic side. SFML events are polled in `Game` and forwarded to `Player`, which transforms the events to commands and feeds `CommandQueue` with them. The same process is followed for the real-time input, `Player` checks the current input state and pushes corresponding commands to the queue. The `CommandQueue` class stores a queue of commands and acts as the bridge between input handling and game logic. On the game logic side, the `World` class pops commands from the `CommandQueue` class and sends them to the root of the scene graph, inside which the commands are distributed depending on their receiver categories. Eventually, the functions stored in each command are applied to the correct game objects. The following diagram gives an overview of the command system and the way it is integrated into our game architecture:

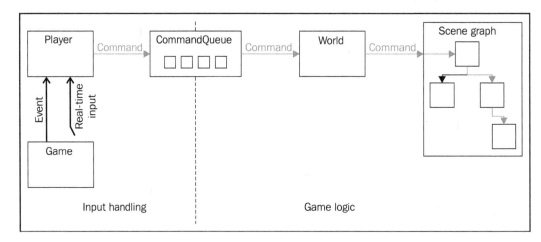

Implementing the game logic

You certainly remember the basic example of the aircraft floating from left to right and back from *Chapter 3, Forge of the Gods – Shaping Our World*. As we now use player input, we do not need that code any more. However, we write some new code; for example we want to ensure that the player's plane remains inside the view, now that it can move freely.

All this is done in the function `World::update()`. In the following paragraphs, we advance through it step by step, explaining each piece of code. We begin with scrolling the view and setting the player's velocity to zero. Note that we really use zero, not the scrolling speed, so that the player falls behind relative to the moving view. The scrolling speed is addressed later in this function:

```
void World::update(sf::Time dt)
{
    mWorldView.move(0.f, mScrollSpeed * dt.asSeconds());
    mPlayerAircraft->setVelocity(0.f, 0.f);
```

Next, all commands from the queue are forwarded to the scene graph. This makes our plane react to the user input. When an arrow key is held down, the plane's velocity will be changed:

```
    while (!mCommandQueue.isEmpty())
        mSceneGraph.onCommand(mCommandQueue.pop(), dt);
```

Now, the basic velocity has been set. If right and top arrow keys are both held down, the plane will fly diagonally to the upper-right corner, but the velocity will be faster than the velocity when either the right or top key is pressed. To correct diagonal velocities, we divide the velocity by the square root of two. We also add the scroll speed. Now it is evident why we have not done this before; we could not have checked for diagonal movements if the velocity had not been zero:

```
    sf::Vector2f velocity = mPlayerAircraft->getVelocity();

    if (velocity.x != 0.f && velocity.y != 0.f)
        mPlayerAircraft->setVelocity(velocity / std::sqrt(2.f));

    mPlayerAircraft->accelerate(0.f, mScrollSpeed);
```

In the next step, the regular update step of the scene is performed:

```
    mSceneGraph.update(dt);
```

The only thing left to do is to handle the case where the plane leaves the visible area of the screen. First, we compute the rectangle of the current view, and then we keep all X and Y coordinates inside the boundaries, given some distance to the screen's border. Last, we call `Aircraft::setPosition()` to apply the corrected position:

```
sf::FloatRect viewBounds(
    mWorldView.getCenter() - mWorldView.getSize() / 2.f,
    mWorldView.getSize());
const float borderDistance = 40.f;

sf::Vector2f position = mPlayerAircraft->getPosition();
position.x = std::max(position.x,
    viewBounds.left + borderDistance);
position.x = std::min(position.x,
    viewBounds.left + viewBounds.width - borderDistance);
position.y = std::max(position.y,
    viewBounds.top + borderDistance);
position.y = std::min(position.y,
    viewBounds.top + viewBounds.height - borderDistance);
mPlayerAircraft->setPosition(position);
}
```

A general-purpose communication mechanism

What you have seen in the previous sections are commands—how they are used for input. Note that during the design process of our message-passing system, we have paid attention to encapsulate input handling and to make the other components generic and reusable. Only the `Player` class is directly coupled to the input; the classes `Command` and `CommandQueue` can deal with any functions that affect scene nodes for a given amount of time.

This genericity will be a great advantage, as it makes it possible to use our command system for other sources of control, like the network or artificial intelligence. We can even use the command system for in-game events, to notify entities about happenings in the world. All we need to do is to set up the corresponding command, push it to the queue, and it will be automatically delivered to the related scene nodes.

Customizing key bindings

A big part with input management in a game is allowing the user to customize how he interacts with it, like the keys. Most of the time, you can find the most popular key bindings and see them written directly in the code. But there will always be people that want to do stuff their way.

We have to provide tools in order to dynamically bind the keys to specific actions. With the command queue introduced in the previous sections, this becomes a much easier task to accomplish.

With the command queue, we already define specific actions for a specific key. The difference is that right now, we have it hardcoded as follows:

```
if (sf::Keyboard::isKeyPressed(sf::Keyboard::Left))
    commands.push(moveLeft);
if (sf::Keyboard::isKeyPressed(sf::Keyboard::Right))
    commands.push(moveRight);
```

The problem with this code is that it is very inflexible. We have to change a lot in order to allow any key to respond to any action. We have two clearly separate sets of data that we want to link together. We have the actual action that we want to perform, such as moving left or right. Then, we have the input key, the key that is to trigger the action.

Now the keys in `sf::Keyboard` are just part of an enum. So on top of this, we create an enum in our `Player` class that represents the different kinds of actions we associate with the pressed keys:

```
class Player
{
    public:
        enum Action
        {
            MoveLeft,
            MoveRight,
            ...
        };

        void              assignKey(Action action,
                                    sf::Keyboard::Key key);
        sf::Keyboard::Key getAssignedKey(Action action) const;
        ...
```

```
        private:
            static bool             isRealtimeAction(Action action);

        private:
            std::map<sf::Keyboard::Key, Action> mKeyBinding;
            std::map<Action, Command>           mActionBinding;
    };
```

Here, we have divided the input into two abstractions. We have the key binding to a specific action, and we have the binding of an action to a specific command. This is all we need to remove any hardcoded segments of input.

Next step is actually using this to translate an input to a command, which will essentially be our key bindings. We do this best by iterating through our key bindings map and just performing a simple check if the key is being pressed. If it is, we tell the command queue to insert our command we provide it with. The function `Player::isRealtimeAction()` returns if the specified action is triggered by the real-time input (as opposed to events).

```
    void Player::handleRealtimeInput(CommandQueue& commands)
    {
        FOREACH(auto pair, mKeyBinding)
        {
            if (sf::Keyboard::isKeyPressed(pair.first)
            && isRealtimeAction(pair.second))
                commands.push(mActionBinding[pair.second]);
        }
    }
```

Just remember that this function has to be called once every frame, otherwise nothing will happen.

The two functions `assignKey()` and `getAssignedKey()` set and get the key mapped to a specific action. Their implementations perform map operations as expected, the only notable thing is that `assignKey()` checks that no two keys map to the same action.

The command stored under an action in `mActionBinding` knows exactly what it is supposed to do, so you don't have to provide any extra code to handle the key press, since it has been abstracted out into its own entity. You have already done this previously in the chapter. The difference now is that we store the commands in the map together instead of unique variables.

The following is the constructor, where we set the default settings that you expect and prepare everything to work:

```
Player::Player()
{
    mKeyBinding[sf::Keyboard::Left] = MoveLeft;
    mKeyBinding[sf::Keyboard::Right] = MoveRight;

    mActionBinding[MoveLeft].action =
    [] (SceneNode& node, sf::Time dt)
    {
        node.move(-playerSpeed * dt.asSeconds(), 0.f);
    };

    mActionBinding[MoveRight].action =
    [] (SceneNode& node, sf::Time dt)
    {
        node.move(playerSpeed * dt.asSeconds(), 0.f);
    };

    FOREACH(auto& pair, mActionBinding)
        pair.second.category = Category::PlayerAircraft;
}
```

We assign the actions to the keys and achieve our initial key binding. After that we create the commands and implement the lambda function to be executed. The last iteration is just to ensure that the commands are only applied on the player aircraft. It should all look familiar.

Now this itself is not really dynamic. All we have provided is the possibility to make it dynamic. We don't have a setting screen where you can manipulate the bindings or a way to parse the data from a `config` file. We will actually create a settings screen later in the book in the GUI chapter. This would have been a way too big topic to cover in this chapter as well.

Why a player is not an entity

Well, the `Player` class can very much be considered as an entity, but in our case it is just a controller of entities. The class represents the player's input in the world of the game. In our gameplay, this entails only to manipulating a node in our scene graph.

Take this with a grain of salt. This is something that people do differently, we could have created a player entity and a player controller or have everything in the player entity.

Our opinion while writing was that this is a much cleaner way to do it and gives a nice separation of the external input signals from the player and the game logic. We felt much more comfortable working like this, instead of potentially having a giant blob inside the hierarchy of entities.

Summary

Reading through this chapter, you learned a whole new mechanism to handle input and deliver it correctly to the game's entities. It may not be the simplest concept you will come across, but it certainly pays off later, when you see it under heavier action. Not only have we played with event delivering systems, but we also paid a lot of attention on how to capture input and handle every detail about it. This is essential for every game, after all, who would like to play a game that plays itself?

After having a basic world scene with robust behaviors and features, it is now time to start looking at other phases of a game's development. In other words, the next chapter will cover mechanisms which are not directly related to the game's mechanics and systems, but that instead allow a coherent flow between multiple parts of a game, such as the pause and main menu, the game itself and others that you will encounter. Therefore, expect a lot of interesting information on handling this kind of management that you see in games so often.

5
Diverting the Game Flow – State Stack

In the earlier chapters of this book, you have learned how to make an efficient program structure for a game, modern game loops, and data structures to contain a world with rich graphics. You also learned how to deal with user input, making it an interactive simulation. With the combination of all those pieces of knowledge, we can already make an interesting game experience. However, a game is usually more than that. A full blown product doesn't just open and let you play without an explanation, a menu, or a title screen. That is what is going to be covered in this chapter, the ability to make the game richer by adding different states and screens to it.

The main bits of knowledge to acquire throughout the chapter are as follows:

- The state and the stack
- Navigating between states
- Moving our game into a state
- The title screen as the entry point of the game
- Our old friend, the main menu
- Implementing an overlay pause screen
- A simple example of a concurrent loading state

Defining a state

While it is a bit difficult to define correctly what a state actually is, and because that also depends on the implementation we choose to go with, we will try to pass our own idea of what states are and how they should behave.

We can look at a state as an independent screen in the gaming software, an object that encapsulates the logic and graphics of a determined group of functionality and information.

Nothing stops us from creating a state that behaves in any way we'd like; however, there are some usual guidelines into what belongs to the same state. Let's try to prove this shallowly by looking at the commercial games of our time. We will often see most games showing introduction videos, from the trailer of the game to company brand logos. We can look at each of these screens as states. In fact, having a `VideoState` that would simply playback a video and proceed to the next state would fit this model perfectly!

Then, we usually see a title screen, which is all about fancy artwork and minor information. That would be another state. Usually, by pressing a key, we would enter into the main menu, which itself is another effective state. If we look closely at any game, we can more or less define what belongs to each state, and that is the exact point so you can understand the concept better. There are countless ways you can separate your game into multiple states, but practicing always makes you achieve cleaner and more efficient designs!

Using such a system is of extreme importance. The combination of all these screens working together as one final product always makes a game feel more professional and rich in features.

However, not all the states are the same. While some states take over the whole screen and are running individually, others will work together, in parallel, rendering to the same screen, to achieve a variety of effects such as the very common pause screen, which still shows the game in background without motion.

To manage states efficiently and in an easy way, we create the stack!

The state stack

One way to visualize the flow of the game screens would be to picture a finite state machine of all the screens and how they trigger each other's appearance. However, while that works and is logically accurate, we broaden the concept of the active state into a stack.

Finite State Machine (FSM): While this is a well known concept across the world of computation, we will shortly describe the state machine as a collection of states that ensures that only one state is active at any given time. The transition of the current state into a new one is always triggered by a condition or a timer. So, for any state of the FSM, there will be a determined set of triggers that will activate new states when appropriate.

Now, turning the active state into a stack essentially means that the current state is not an individual piece anymore, but rather a stacked group of pieces, when necessary. Usually, the state mechanism will only have one state active at a time, and while this is true, we effectively have a finite state machine as it is known by the computer science community. In other situations, however, such as the infamous pause screen, we will break the concept of FSM a little and have states on top of states, representing the active state all together.

As you can see in the following figure, a usual game flow can be represented like this:

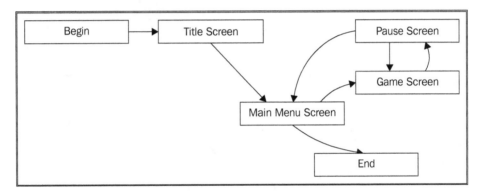

To manage all these screens and transitions, we create the `StateStack` class:

```cpp
class StateStack : private sf::NonCopyable
{
    public:
        enum Action
        {
            Push,
            Pop,
            Clear,
        };

    public:
        explicit            StateStack(State::Context context);

        template <typename T>
        void                registerState(States::ID stateID);

        void                update(sf::Time dt);
        void                draw();
        void                handleEvent(const sf::Event& event);

        void                pushState(States::ID stateID);
        void                popState();
        void                clearStates();

        bool                isEmpty() const;

    private:
        State::Ptr          createState(States::ID stateID);
        void                applyPendingChanges();

    private:
        struct PendingChange
        {
            ...
            Action              action;
            States::ID          stateID;
        };

    private:
        std::vector<State::Ptr>             mStack;
        std::vector<PendingChange>          mPendingList;
        State::Context                      mContext;
        std::map<States::ID,
            std::function<State::Ptr()>>    mFactories;
};
```

We also create the so called `State` class:

```
class State
{
    public:
        typedef std::unique_ptr<State> Ptr;
        struct Context { ... };

    public:
                             State(StateStack& stack, Context context);
        virtual              ~State();

        virtual void         draw() = 0;
        virtual bool         update(sf::Time dt) = 0;
        virtual bool         handleEvent(const sf::Event& event) = 0;

    protected:
        void                 requestStackPush(States::ID stateID);
        void                 requestStackPop();
        void                 requestStateClear();

        Context              getContext() const;

    private:
        StateStack*          mStack;
        Context              mContext;
};
```

Adding states to StateStack

All states in the game have a unique identifier declared in an enum `States`, located in the `StateIdentifiers.hpp` file. For example, ID `States::Game` refers to the `GameState` class.

Initially, we register inside the stack all the states we may use. We do not create all the state objects from the beginning, since some of them may never exist, therefore we avoid loading resources of never-used states. Instead, we have factory functions that create a new state on-demand, represented by `std::function`. The member variable `StateStack::mFactories` maps state IDs to those factory functions.

A member function `StateStack::registerState()` inserts such mappings. The template parameter `T` is the derived state class we want to register. A lambda expression acts as a factory for the state: It creates an object of the derived class `T` by passing the stack and context to its constructor. This object is wrapped into a unique pointer and returned as a base class pointer. The lambda expression is assigned to the corresponding state ID in the map:

```
template <typename T>
void StateStack::registerState(States::ID stateID)
{
    mFactories[stateID] = [this] ()
    {
        return State::Ptr(new T(*this, mContext));
    };
}
```

This approach has the advantage that the `StateStack` class need not know the concrete state classes, we thus keep dependencies low. For state classes that take more than two parameters, we can write an overload to pass an additional argument (which will be done in later chapters). If your compiler supports variadic templates, a single function template will handle all these cases.

The `createState()` method takes an ID of a state, and returns a smart pointer to a newly created object of the corresponding state class. It does so by looking up the ID in the map and invoking the stored `std::function` factory, which returns the `std::unique_ptr` to the `State` base class:

```
State::Ptr StateStack::createState(States::ID stateID)
{
    auto found = mFactories.find(stateID);
    assert(found != mFactories.end());

    return found->second();
}
```

Handling updates, input, and drawing

Until this point, we taught the concept of the stack and the states it holds. Now it is time to feed our `StateStack` and consequently our active `State` objects with events, update, and drawing orders.

Input

Every polled event is fed to the state stack. Then, internally, the stack will deliver that event to the active states:

```
void StateStack::handleEvent(const sf::Event& event)
{
    for (auto itr = mStack.rbegin(); itr != mStack.rend(); ++itr)
    {
        if (!(*itr)->handleEvent(event))
            return;
    }

    applyPendingChanges();
}
```

In this `for` loop, you can verify that we iterate the active stack from the end to the beginning, in other words, from the highest state to the lowest. And, if any of the states returns false in its `handleEvent()` method, the loop is immediately ended. This gives the control to the states that may not want to let input flow to other states than itself!

Update

The updating happens under the same guidelines of event handling, both the delivery order and the stopping of update propagation to lower states, if desired.

Draw

Drawing is straightforward; the `StateStack` class will order every active state to render itself.

The first state to be drawn is the lowest and oldest on the stack, and only then come the others, in order. This grants that the states are transparent, and you will be able to see the underlying screens. Anyway, if you don't desire to see pixels from the lower states, you can use `sf::RectangleShape` to draw a colored rectangle over the whole screen, blocking the undesired graphics, as you will see later in this chapter.

Delayed pop/push operations

As you can see in the source, the StateStack class provides the pushState() and popState() functions to let us add and remove states from the active stack.

However, in the middle of an event or update iteration by the stack, it is not possible to alter the active state stack because it would generate a conflict when adding/ removing objects to a container that is being iterated.

Because of this, those functions don't immediately push or pop states into the stack, but rather register these actions in a pending action list, so they can be processed later, when it's safe.

Then, inside your own state logic code, you call requestStackPush() and requestStackPop(), allowing the states to alter the stack from within their own code, without risking the safety of the program, thanks to the delayed processing of push and pop operations.

A special kind of pop operation is also provided, allowing a state to call requestStackClear(), which will completely empty the active stack.

These delayed processing operations are done in the following function:

```
void StateStack::applyPendingChanges()
{
    FOREACH(PendingChange change, mPendingList)
    {
        switch (change.action)
        {
            case Push:
                mStack.push_back(createState(change.stateID));
                break;

            case Pop:
                mStack.pop_back();
                break;

            case Clear:
                mStack.clear();
                break;
        }
    }

    mPendingList.clear();
}
```

The state context

In general, every screen will need to display some text or sprites, draw to the screen, among other common things. Due to this fact, and to avoid unnecessary memory wasting by loading the same texture or font to memory in multiple places, we introduced the `State::Context` structure. It works as a holder of shared objects between all states of our game.

Essentially, every state will now have access to the `getContext()` method, which itself contains the pointer to the window used to draw its objects and resource holders such as font and texture managers. Here's the declaration of the structure:

```
struct Context
{
                    Context(sf::RenderWindow& window,
                        TextureHolder& textures,
                        FontHolder& fonts,
                        Player& player);

    sf::RenderWindow*   window;
    TextureHolder*      textures;
    FontHolder*         fonts;
    Player*             player;
};
```

The usefulness of the state context is undeniable. It will save system memory by reusing the same fonts and textures for every state. It will also provide access to the window's view at all times, which is a necessity when positioning and resizing our objects relatively to the view's dimensions.

Integrating the stack in the Application class

Since we have now more states than the game itself, we create a new class `Application` that controls input, logic updates, and rendering. Having a ready `StateStack` implementation waiting to be used, it is time to promote it into the `Application` class. We will plug our new state architecture into our `Application` class and then start using it!

First, we add the `mStateStack` member variable to `Application`. We register all the states in an own method:

```
void Application::registerStates()
{
    mStateStack.registerState<TitleState>(States::Title);
    mStateStack.registerState<MenuState>(States::Menu);
    mStateStack.registerState<GameState>(States::Game);
    mStateStack.registerState<PauseState>(States::Pause);
}
```

Now there are a few more things we must care about for a full integration of our state architecture:

- Feeding it with events in the `Application::processInput()` function:

```
while (mWindow.pollEvent(event))
{
    mStateStack.handleEvent(event);
}
```

- Updating with the elapsed time:

```
void Application::update(sf::Time dt)
{
    mStateStack.update(dt);
}
```

- Rendering of the stack, in the middle of the frame draw:

```
mStateStack.draw();
```

- Closing the game when no more states are left:

```
if (mStateStack.isEmpty())
    mWindow.close();
```

And now that everything is plugged in and ready to go, in the end of our constructor we make the machine start with the title screen!

```
mStateStack.pushState(States::Title);
```

Navigating between states

So far we have our state machine in place and running smoothly, the title screen starts up the program, but how to make the title screen call another state to its place when someone hits a key?

That is exactly what the StateStack class's delayed push and pop mechanism is for. Inside a state handleEvent() and update(), you are given three methods to control the execution and transitions of states: requestStackPush(), requestStackPop(), and requestStackClear().

It is appropriate to use these methods to request new states to be pushed, or to show and replace the current one, as you will verify that our example states do throughout this chapter.

Creating the game state

So far we have covered the theory and practice for inserting the state stack into our sample game. It is fully functional but yet empty, so, it is finally time to create our first state, the game state.

For this, we create a class named GameState and we proceed to relocate the code that could be found in the Game class related to the actual aircraft gameplay to its new home:

```cpp
class GameState : public State
{
    public:
                            GameState(StateStack& stack,
                                    Context context);

        virtual void        draw();
        virtual bool        update(sf::Time dt);
        virtual bool        handleEvent(const sf::Event& event);

    private:
        World               mWorld;
        Player&             mPlayer;
};
```

The title screen

Because a good place to start is always the beginning, we are about to create the title screen; that initial screen you sometimes see in games. Before you enter the main menu of the game, it asks you to press any key.

We decided to go with the name `TitleState`, and define it as follows:

```cpp
class TitleState : public State
{
    public:
                                TitleState(StateStack& stack,
                                        Context context);

        virtual void            draw();
        virtual bool            update(sf::Time dt);
        virtual bool            handleEvent(const sf::Event& event);

    private:
        sf::Sprite              mBackgroundSprite;
        sf::Text                mText;

        bool                    mShowText;
        sf::Time                mTextEffectTime;
};
```

Our implementation of this screen is not very different from what you are used to see. It shows a background with a little information about the game, besides its title and then blinks a big old **Press any key to continue** message.

Here's how we detect the key stroke and use our state system to trigger a new state:

```cpp
bool TitleState::handleEvent(const sf::Event& event)
{
    if (event.type == sf::Event::KeyPressed)
    {
        requestStackPop();
        requestStackPush(States::Menu);
    }

    return true;
}
```

The background is merely an image covering the whole window and the blinking effect on the `sf::Text` object is achieved through this little trick:

```
bool TitleState::update(sf::Time dt)
{
    mTextEffectTime += dt;

    if (mTextEffectTime >= sf::seconds(0.5f))
    {
        mShowText = !mShowText;
        mTextEffectTime = sf::Time::Zero;
    }

    return true;
}
```

The magic happening here is simple. The variable `mShowText` determines the visibility of the `sf::Text` object, so we toggle it every half second, achieving the blinking effect.

Every time the state updates, we have a time counter `mTextEffectTime` that increments with the elapsed time. Then, when that elapsed time is greater than half a second, we just toggle the `mShowText` variable and restart the counter.

Main menu

Okay, our title screen just finished, the user pressed a key and it is time to launch another screen, the famous main menu!

This is probably the most common state you will find in virtually every game, it is responsible for presenting the user its options and what can be done with the game. This is usually the point where you change settings, start or continue your game, watch videos and artwork, or simply exit the game.

For simplicity, we created the most basic main menu possible. It only presents two options: play and exit. Then, you can select which one you want by pressing the return key or alternate between the options with the up and down arrow keys.

Please notice this is a basic form of graphical user interface, which is the topic in the next chapter, therefore you can expect interesting improvements to it when we introduce the user interfaces in more depth!

This state is not so different from the title screen but it does implement the option selection, and here is how we did it:

```
enum OptionNames
{
    Play,
    Exit,
};


std::vector<sf::Text>    mOptions;
std::size_t              mOptionIndex;
```

First we declare the containers of our options in the `MenuState` class, as well as the enumerator of the available options.

Then, we setup and push to the `mOptions` array the `sf::Text` objects, in the constructor, as follows:

```
sf::Text playOption;
playOption.setFont(font);
playOption.setString("Play");
centerOrigin(playOption);
playOption.setPosition(context.window->getView().getSize() / 2.f);
mOptions.push_back(playOption);
```

The `mOptionIndex` integer variable is present so that we can track which is the currently selected option between all those in the `mOptions` array; it will have a value between `0` and `n-1`, `n` being the number of options in the menu, which is two in our example.

Finally, we define the most important function that helps controlling this menu:

```
void MenuState::updateOptionText()
{
    if (mOptions.empty())
        return;

    // White all texts
    FOREACH(sf::Text& text, mOptions)
        text.setColor(sf::Color::White);

    // Red the selected text
    mOptions[mOptionIndex].setColor(sf::Color::Red);
}
```

This function is called once after constructing `mOptions` and again every time the `mOptionIndex` value changes. It ensures that only the selected option is highlighted in red, and the remaining is in white.

About what makes the `mOptionIndex` value actually change, it is merely simple handling of key presses in the `handleEvent()` function:

```
if (event.key.code == sf::Keyboard::Up)
{
    if (mOptionIndex > 0)
        mOptionIndex--;
    else
        mOptionIndex = mOptions.size() - 1;

    updateOptionText();
}

else if (event.key.code == sf::Keyboard::Down)
{
    if (mOptionIndex < mOptions.size() - 1)
        mOptionIndex++;
    else
        mOptionIndex = 0;

    updateOptionText();
}
```

Now that we handled the selection of an action between multiple options, it is time to actually make them push their own states and give the game continuity:

```
if (event.key.code == sf::Keyboard::Return)
{
    if (mOptionIndex == Play)
    {
        requestStackPop();
        requestStackPush(States::Game);
    }
    else if (mOptionIndex == Exit)
    {
        requestStackPop();
    }
}
```

We have seen how to push states before so it is not a big deal anymore. However, the Exit option applies something new; it only requests to pop itself without pushing anything else in its place.

In consequence, after the MenuState class is popped, the state stack is left empty. This is exactly the condition that is checked in the Application class in order to exit its loop, so the game closes naturally when the user selects this option.

Of course, if there would be another state present in the stack at this moment, it would not really be empty, and the game could not close. A good way to prevent this would be to request a clearing of the whole stack, instead of just popping the menu state. However, by doing it this way we can detect possible programming errors faster by not concealing the presence of a state that shouldn't be there in the first place.

Pausing the game

After having a cute menu that allows the game to start playing, we find ourselves locked again inside GameState. Indeed, we can play, but what about when we get tired of it or just want to take a break? That's when the pause screen comes into the scene!

We make use of the PauseState class not only as a way to rest and go have a coffee, but also as a gateway for going back to the main menu.

The implementation of this screen follows the line of the previous ones although it has some remarks and little things that make it special. To begin with, it is a state that is not meant to work by itself, but rather on the top of the state stack, living simultaneously with GameState, at least.

Because of this, we apply directly the concepts we implemented in the StateStack mechanism. The screen of PauseState is transparent and we can see the game in the background:

```
void PauseState::draw()
{
    sf::RenderWindow& window = *getContext().window;
    window.setView(window.getDefaultView());

    sf::RectangleShape backgroundShape;
    backgroundShape.setFillColor(sf::Color(0, 0, 0, 150));
    backgroundShape.setSize(sf::Vector2f(window.getSize()));

    window.draw(backgroundShape);
    window.draw(mPausedText);
    window.draw(mInstructionText);
}
```

When we are drawing this screen, we can assume that the game has been already drawn. The backgroundShape rectangle fits the whole screen as a way to darken what we see on the background. If we wanted an opaque screen and cease to see the game we could simply set the fill color of backgroundShape with full alpha (255).

On the event handling topic, we simply define PauseState to pop it again and return to game if *Escape* is pressed again. Besides that, we also return to the main menu when *Backspace* is pressed:

```
if (event.key.code == sf::Keyboard::BackSpace)
{
    requestStateClear();
    requestStackPush(States::Menu);
}
```

So, why call requestStateClear() instead of requestStatePop()? Easy! The PauseState class has no idea how many states are lying underneath it in the stack.

Even though usually there will be only GameState living under it, this may not be a truth quite easily. GameState might have pushed other game play states on its top, like tutorial states or information displayers.

Therefore, to be safe, we request a complete clearing of the stack and only then a push of the main menu.

The last thing that is very important to notice about PauseState is the return false; statement in the end of handleEvent() and update() functions.

If you were paying close attention earlier this chapter, it will be obvious to you what those mean in this context; nevertheless, returning false in those functions works as a smooth trick to automatically pause our GameState. Because PauseState is the top screen and it doesn't let any underlying states update or handle events, all those are inherently paused by absence of input or discrete time updates.

For convenience, we could have a pause method in the GameState class but we don't even need it thanks to the state system!

The loading screen – sample

While our example game does not use a loading screen up to this point, we have decided to provide a possible implementation of such a state. You can find its source code together with the sources of this chapter, as well as guide yourself through the following paragraphs into understanding it.

A loading screen is a state like any other, except for one thing; it performs a task in the background, using a parallel thread of execution. Using threads and understanding them in full is out of the scope of this book; however, SFML does provide `sf::Thread`, a cross-platform implementation for launching and managing multiple branches of execution in a program. Because of this, we will briefly introduce the use of `sf::Thread` and apply it directly into our loading screen.

But why do we need to use threads? Simply because a loading screen will most often be passing a number of resources from the hard drive into memory and this will be a lengthy process, and even worse, a blocking process.

We need to ensure that our state remains fluid in its execution, that all calls are finished as fast as they can, and the game has a solid frame rate. Having our loading screen stuck in a method loading a huge list of resources would defeat this purpose, as while a resource loading operation is being executed, the state couldn't display a smooth progress bar. Due to this issue, we let the loading operation happen in a parallel thread, while the loading state keeps running without interruption!

In order to implement such a state we create two classes, `LoadingState` and `ParallelTask`. `LoadingState` is responsible for displaying information of what is being loaded and a progress bar so the user has some perception of how much time is left to begin playing. The `ParallelTask` class will manage the actual loading operation and give some feedback to the `LoadingState` class.

Please note that while these two classes are not integrated in the chapter's sample application, you can find their sources in `LoadingState.hpp`, `LoadingState.cpp`, `ParallelTask.hpp`, and `ParallelTask.cpp` in the source directory of the chapter.

Progress bar

To better understand the implementation of `LoadingState` which is not that different from the other screens, lets take a look at its members:

```
sf::Text              mLoadingText;
sf::RectangleShape    mProgressBarBackground;
sf::RectangleShape    mProgressBar;
ParallelTask          mLoadingTask;
```

We have `sf::Text` to display our `Loading Resources` string, two `sf::RectangleShape` objects for the progress bar background and fill, and a `ParallelTask` object.

First things first, constructing the objects happens as follows:

```
mLoadingText.setFont(font);
mLoadingText.setString("Loading Resources");
centerOrigin(mLoadingText);
mLoadingText.setPosition(window.getSize().x / 2u, window.getSize().y /
2u + 50);

mProgressBarBackground.setFillColor(sf::Color::White);
mProgressBarBackground.setSize(sf::Vector2f(window.getSize().x - 20,
10));
mProgressBarBackground.setPosition(10, mLoadingText.getPosition().y +
40);

mProgressBar.setFillColor(sf::Color(100,100,100));
mProgressBar.setSize(sf::Vector2f(200, 10));
mProgressBar.setPosition(10, mLoadingText.getPosition().y + 40);

setCompletion(0.f);

mLoadingTask.execute();
```

The `mLoadingText` function is configured with position, font, and string. Then, the background of the progress bar is initialized with a white color and a size that fits the window horizontally except for a 20 pixel wide margin, split between each side.

Both `mProgressBar` and `mProgressBarBackground` are at the exact same position, so that `mProgressBar` can grow inside the background correctly. The progress bar is set with a grey color, so it can be seen over its background.

To finalize, we simply ensure the progress bar is at 0 percent completion, with a width of 100 pixels and then launch the parallel task.

The `setCompletion()` method is nothing more than the following:

```
void LoadingState::setCompletion(float percent)
{
    if (percent > 1.f)
        percent = 1.f; // clamp

    mProgressBar.setSize(sf::Vector2f(
        mProgressBarBackground.getSize().x * percent,
        mProgressBar.getSize().y));
}
```

It merely resets the width of the progress bar fill color to a percent of the background width, as you can see.

This is enough to provide us a static progress bar, while a parallel task is already executing in the background; now it is important to go fetch data from the task to update the state:

```
bool LoadingState::update(sf::Time)
{
    // Update the progress bar from the remote task or finish it
    if (mLoadingTask.isFinished())
    {
        requestStackPop();
        requestStackPush(States::Game);
    }
    else
    {
        setCompletion(mLoadingTask.getCompletion());
    }
    return true;
}
```

This method's body is just as simple as it looks, if the parallel task has finished already, it is time to spawn the game state, because in theory it already has the needed resources to run. Otherwise, if the task is still executing, we will only update the progress bar.

ParallelTask

So far we have been able to see that a `ParallelTask` object runs in the background and allows querying some information about the task's progress.

To remain as simple as possible explaining the concept of a task executed in a parallel thread, we decided to implement the sample class as a dummy operation that does not do any actual loading, but rather just waits ten seconds for a timer to expire and finalize the task.

But, before explaining our implementation, let's approach a couple of concepts rapidly.

Thread

A thread is essentially a function that runs in another branch of execution. You know the mandatory `main()` function, right? That is the entry point of every application, when it is called by the operating system, it creates one thread: the main one. You can visualize it as a sequential stream of commands that flows until the `main()` function is over and exits the program.

We can conclude from this that one thread is one function call. The same way `main()` is a thread function, there can be others. So, if inside the main function, we spawn a new thread by "calling" its function, the only difference between that and a normal call is that the program doesn't wait until that function ends, but rather continues execution while another stream of commands starts running in parallel.

This is the essence of multi-threading and there isn't a lot to add to it. To do this branching in execution, SFML provides `sf::Thread`. This class implies that you have to link a `sf::Thread` object to a function on its constructor, such as `sf::Thread(&myFunc)` for a global function or `sf::Thread(&MyClass::myFunc, myClassObject)` for a member function of a class.

When you call `sf::Thread::launch()`, all it does is to call the linked function in a separate thread.

Once that function returns, the thread is also shut down automatically. Destroying the `sf::Thread` object while its thread is still running results in an abrupt termination of the thread.

Seems easy, right? Well, there are some more things to have in consideration. Using threads is very straightforward but there are concerns we must always have in mind when working with them.

Concurrency

When two threads are running in parallel, everything will go smoothly if they don't touch the same data at the same time. Anyway, it is very normal that two or more threads want to read/write to the same variables, if not for more, to communicate between them.

It probably goes without saying that if the processor is reading and writing to the same memory address at the same time, we are going to have a nice crash or an undefined behavior in our program, which can be troublesome to debug and correct.

But then, how to guarantee that multiple threads operate on shared data at turns, with proper synchronization? This is a very delicate topic that must not be taken lightly; however, there are mechanisms in SFML that help us achieve this!

Here, we introduce you to sf::Mutex and sf::Lock. These are incredible tools to protect shared data when working with multi-threading. We won't be explaining in depth how they work internally, but rather try to apply it directly and understand it by example, by looking at the ParallelTask class implementation.

Task implementation

The code for this implementation is as follows:

```
class ParallelTask
{
    public:
                            ParallelTask();
        void                execute();
        bool                isFinished();
        float               getCompletion();

    private:
        void                runTask();

    private:
        sf::Thread          mThread;
        bool                mFinished;
        sf::Clock           mElapsedTime;
        sf::Mutex           mMutex;
};
```

By taking a look at the ParallelTask declaration, you can see that the API used by LoadingState exposed. Besides that, you can see the runTask() function, which is the actual thread function that is launched in parallel execution.

Then, in its members, we can see the expected sf::Thread, the sf::Clock to count the elapsed time, and a Boolean variable to check if the task is done yet or not. The sf::Mutex object is meant to protect both the mClock and mFinished variables from concurrent access, as you will see in the following sample:

```
bool ParallelTask::isFinished()
{
    sf::Lock lock(mMutex);
    return mFinished;
}
```

The first line in the function's body is what we call locking variables. If you noticed, isFinished() is called by LoadingState::update(), which is the main thread while mFinished can be changed by the task thread as well, immediately when it finishes. This could randomly cause a simultaneous read and write by two threads, which would result in bad luck for us as programmers. We say randomly because there is nothing controlling the synchronization of the two threads, the simultaneous access can either happen or not.

By locking the sf::Mutex object before touching sensitive data, we ensure that if a thread tries to lock an already locked resource, it will wait until the other thread unlocks it. This creates synchronization between threads because they will wait in line to access shared data one at a time.

Because sf::Lock is a RAII compliant class, as soon as it goes out of scope and is destructed, the sf::Mutex object automatically unlocks.

To finalize, here is the actual thread function of our task:

```
void ParallelTask::runTask()
{
    // Dummy task - stall 10 seconds
    bool ended = false;
    while (!ended)
    {
        sf::Lock lock(mMutex); // Protect the clock
        if (mElapsedTime.getElapsedTime().asSeconds() >= 10.f)
            ended = true;
    }

    { // mFinished may be accessed from multiple threads, protect
        sf::Lock lock(mMutex);
        mFinished = true;
    }
}
```

You may have noticed that there is a lock in every read or write of the shared variables. The extra brackets are just a way of releasing that same lock as soon as possible, so the variable is then available for other threads to access.

All this function does is it remains in a while loop until the clock has ticked for ten seconds and then lets the thread finish after setting mFinished to true.

Summary

Here we conclude the fifth chapter of the book. Through its pages, we tried to pass on a lot of useful information about state managing and game flow. We talked about states and stacks of states, both in concept and in implementation. Also, we saw how to implement a handful of screens that we usually see in games, using our StateStack system to our advantage. Navigation between states was also covered and we even talked about functionality we don't use in the game, but that will certainly come handy in the future! Better to know and not need it, than to need it and not know about it!

As you noticed, this chapter is of extreme importance not only to this game, but every game you might make. All the code written from this chapter and on will be compliant with the state architecture which makes it a good reason to grasp these concepts the best you can!

The next chapter will concern the graphical user interface of the game. We will discuss how to implement a basic version of a widget hierarchy containing buttons and labels.

6
Waiting and Maintenance Area – Menus

Most games have menus and it's something the player expects when opening up a new game. Even in its simplest form, there is a user interface that responds to the user, and gives him the information he needs to enjoy the game. You might have noticed that we implemented a simple menu in the previous chapter, but it's a prime example where you should refactor and extract into its own class. This is what we will do in this chapter:

- Design a user interface components hierarchy
- Implement the base component class
- Implement containers, labels, and buttons
- Create a proper title screen
- Create a settings screen

What we aim in this chapter is to give you a fundamental understanding of creating a **graphical user interface (GUI)**. GUI design is a huge topic that deserves its own book, but we will do a crash course together.

Normally, in a GUI you use the mouse as an input source; you click on a button and something happens. But for our examples we keep it simple by having you navigate by the keyboard. The difference lies in complexity of the methods: one does not exclude the other. But the focus of this chapter is the components of the hierarchy.

The GUI hierarchy, the Java way

The architecture for the GUI framework will resemble a lot of other toolkits such as Java's Swing/AWT library as it's a well working concept. Note that it is not exactly reproduced, rather is used as a source of inspiration. In the end, what we aim to achieve is a working menu state based on this design, but without pumping the state full of boilerplate GUI code.

We create a namespace GUI in order to make the distinction clear to other parts of our game, since a lot of the names such as "component" are generic, and can be misinterpreted easily. We start with one core base class, which the entire hierarchy rests on. We call it Component and in our case it is quite small. It defines the interface that we will be using regularly besides setting up the objects. The class defines a couple of virtual functions, one of which is the handleEvent() function. We let the Component class inherit from sf::Drawable for the same reason as the scene nodes. To have an interface for drawing to an SFML window:

```
namespace GUI
{
class Component : public sf::Drawable
                , public sf::Transformable
                , private sf::NonCopyable
{
    public:
        typedef std::shared_ptr<Component> Ptr;
    public:
                            Component();
        virtual             ~Component();
        virtual bool        isSelectable() const = 0;
        bool                isSelected() const;
        virtual void        select();
        virtual void        deselect();
        virtual bool        isActive() const;
        virtual void        activate();
        virtual void        deactivate();
        virtual void        handleEvent(const sf::Event& event) = 0;
    private:
        bool                mIsSelected;
        bool                mIsActive;
};
}
```

You might be wondering about the pure virtual `isSelectable()` function and the other virtual ones. They exist for buttons and containers. For the moment, you can just assume that `isSelectable()` returns false, and that the virtual ones are based on the two variables with similar names. The core for the GUI is the `Component::handleEvent()` function because this is where the magic happens. The typedef of a shared pointer of `Component` to the name `Component::Ptr` is for convenience purposes. You don't need it, but it makes code more readable, by simplifying the name we use.

The class template `std::shared_ptr` is a C++11 smart pointer. In contrast to `std::unique_ptr`, multiple pointers share an object. Reference counting ensures that the object remains alive as long as any `shared_ptr` points to it. If an object is not referenced anymore, it will be destroyed.

While unique pointers result in zero performance and memory overhead, shared pointers are rather expensive because of reference counting semantics and thread safety. Therefore, they should be used with care — shared ownership is rarely required.

The function template `std::make_shared()` allows construction of shared pointer objects. Instead of the first statement with the `new` operator, you can use the second. This enables an internal optimization (object and reference counter are stored together).

```
std::shared_ptr<T> s(new T(a, b));
auto s = std::make_shared<T>(a, b);
```

The reason for using a shared pointer, instead of the unique pointer we have been so diligent in using before, is because it is more flexible. We want to give you a bare-bones setup for developing GUI on which you can extend upon. On one hand, `std::shared_ptr` allows users of GUI components to hold a `std::weak_ptr` which becomes invalid as soon as the `Component` is destroyed. But more importantly, a component can be shared in different places. If two different containers (maybe in different application states) use exactly the same component with the same attributes, they can share it.

The function for handling events is virtual because its implementation is different for every class inheriting from `Component`. Further classes we define are `GUI::Container`, `GUI::Button`, and `GUI::Label`. These are the most basic components that you will need, and it will be easy to expand the system with more components later.

So we start with containers. What is the purpose of a container? Well, obviously to bind other components together logically. But remember, since we are using a shared pointer, it doesn't mean that the container owns the components. It is also responsible for selecting one of the components inside its list, in order to highlight it. This is to know when you try to activate a button, which button should it activate. So let's look at the implementation of the `Container` class. We start with the public interface which consists of the following functions:

```
Container::Container()
: mChildren()
, mSelectedChild(-1)
{
}
```

```
void Container::pack(Component::Ptr component)
{
    mChildren.push_back(component);
    if (!hasSelection() && component->isSelectable())
        select(mChildren.size() - 1);
}
bool Container::isSelectable() const
{
    return false;
}
```

Nothing is really exciting here. We have our list with children, and we can pack a new component into this list. The only special thing is that we check if we have a currently selected child. If not, we check if the incoming child is selectable, and if it is, we select it. Lastly, a container is not a selectable component.

Now to the exciting part:

```
void Container::handleEvent(const sf::Event& event)
{
    if (hasSelection() && mChildren[mSelectedChild]->isActive())
    {
        mChildren[mSelectedChild]->handleEvent(event);
    }
    else if (event.type == sf::Event::KeyReleased)
    {
        if (event.key.code == sf::Keyboard::W
          || event.key.code == sf::Keyboard::Up)
        {
            selectPrevious();
        }
        else if (event.key.code == sf::Keyboard::S
                || event.key.code == sf::Keyboard::Down)
        {
            selectNext();
        }
        else if (event.key.code == sf::Keyboard::Return
                || event.key.code == sf::Keyboard::Space)
        {
            if (hasSelection())
                mChildren[mSelectedChild]->activate();
        }
    }
}
```

Now this is, as said before, where the magic happens. Depending on the current state of the container and what input we get from the events, the action that is performed is different. Let's go through the function.

First we check if we have a valid selection through the helper function `hasSelection()`, and whether the component is active. All the helper function does is; check if the `mSelectedChild` variable is a valid index, zero, or more. If both conditions are true, then the active component is the one that should receive the events instead of the container managing it. This gives a possibility to have a composite hierarchy in the GUI. In our simple example, this feature is not used, but it would be extremely useful when you implement an input box, or any kind of component that needs to capture input.

So, what if the container is the one in focus for the input? Then we provide ways for the user to simply navigate the container and activate any selected component. In order to make the code easier to read, we use helper functions instead of having a large function with a lot of logic in it.

```cpp
void Container::select(std::size_t index)
{
    if (mChildren[index]->isSelectable())
    {
        if (hasSelection())
            mChildren[mSelectedChild]->deselect();
        mChildren[index]->select();
        mSelectedChild = index;
    }
}

void Container::selectNext()
{
    if (!hasSelection())
        return;
    // Search next component that is selectable
    int next = mSelectedChild;
    do
        next = (next + 1) % mChildren.size();
    while (!mChildren[next]->isSelectable());
    // Select that component
    select(next);
}
void Container::selectPrevious()
{
    if (!hasSelection())
        return;
```

```
    // Search previous component that is selectable
    int prev = mSelectedChild;
    do
        prev = (prev + mChildren.size() - 1) % mChildren.size();
    while (!mChildren[prev]->isSelectable());
    // Select that component
    select(prev);
}
```

The helper functions don't have too much logic in it, and thus aren't so complex. The first one takes care of the book-keeping needed with the selection, to make sure only one component is marked as selected. The `selectPrevious()` and `selectNext()` functions only implement the stepping to find the next selectable component and the looping of the menu selection.

The `Container` acts as the root for the GUI we want to show. You create a GUI object at the top in your state, and then you pack other components into it. Here is a demonstration using labels:

```
auto demoLabel = std::make_shared<GUI::Label>(
    "This is a demonstration!", *getContext().fonts);
mGUIContainer.pack(demoLabel);

// Later in code...
mWindow.draw(mGUIContainer);
while(mWindow.pollEvent(event))

mGUIContainer.handleEvent(event);
```

You see in the states code how this simplifies a lot of problems, and makes the code a lot cleaner and nicer to read. `Label` is a very small class, as all it does is simply show some text on the screen.

```
Label::Label(const std::string& text, const FontHolder& fonts)
: mText(text, fonts.get(Fonts::Label), 16)
{
}

bool Label::isSelectable() const
{
    return false;
}
void Label::draw(sf::RenderTarget& target, sf::RenderStates states)
const
{
```

```
        states.transform *= getTransform();
        target.draw(mText, states);
}
void Label::setText(const std::string& text)
{
        mText.setString(text);
}
```

The only thing to note is that labels are not selectable. They are just a bunch of text, so there is no reason to be able to select them.

Let's get to the interesting part that we want in the GUI buttons. Fortunately, together with the logic already implemented in containers and components, buttons themselves don't need a lot of logic, other than the data they require for rendering and execution on activation.

So what do buttons add to their class? First we have the sprite and the text that a button renders. But most often, we want a button to execute something when it is pressed. Instead of querying the button if it has been pressed, we go with callbacks using the handy `std::function` class. When the button is activated by the GUI container, we execute the callback.

However, the callback functionality is not favorable in every scenario, so we also support the poll method where you ask the button if it is held down. In our system, we call it toggle, that is, the button remains in a pressed state until explicitly told to change. Normally, the button deactivates itself after the callback has been fired. If the button can be toggled on the other hand, it will not deactivate; this must be explicitly done by the user.

In the context of a button, the terms "activate" and "deactivate" refer to the two states pressed and released. We call them "activate" and "deactivate" because these are generalized terms for GUI design. Another case when we would like to activate but are not pressing the actual object could be, for instance, a selected item in a list box.

```
Button::Button(const FontHolder& fonts, const TextureHolder& textures)
// ...
{
        mSprite.setTexture(mNormalTexture);
        mText.setPosition(sf::Vector2f(mNormalTexture.getSize() / 2u));
}

bool Button::isSelectable() const
{
        return true;
}
```

```
void Button::select()
{
    Component::select();
    mSprite.setTexture(mSelectedTexture);
}

void Button::deselect()
{
    Component::deselect();
    mSprite.setTexture(mNormalTexture);
}

void Button::activate()
{
    Component::activate();
    if (mIsToggle)
        mSprite.setTexture(mPressedTexture);
    if (mCallback)
        mCallback();
    if (!mIsToggle)
        deactivate();
}

void Button::deactivate()
{
    Component::deactivate();
    if (mIsToggle)
    {
        if (isSelected())
            mSprite.setTexture(mSelectedTexture);
        else
            mSprite.setTexture(mNormalTexture);
    }
}
```

We only have to book-keep the current texture of the sprite and its activation/ deactivation scheme, thanks to the code we have written in the previous classes. And the callback makes it very easy to hook in your own code to be run.

Updating the menu

So, let's see our code in actual use. Do you remember `MenuState` from the previous chapter? There we implemented some menu logic, so you could choose between two options. Now this can be cleaned up a lot; as a result the menu state shrinks drastically.

```
MenuState::MenuState(StateStack& stack, Context context)
: State(stack, context)
, mGUIContainer()
{
    ...
    auto playButton = std::make_shared<GUI::Button>(
        *context.fonts, *context.textures);
    playButton->setPosition(100, 250);
    playButton->setText("Play");
    playButton->setCallback([this] ()
    {
        requestStackPop();
        requestStackPush(States::Game);
    });
    mGUIContainer.pack(playButton);
}
```

The constructor initializes the buttons and packs them into the `Container`. As you can see, the lambda expression we give to the `Button` is the place where we actually describe the action we want the button to do. The rest of the functions are changed to use the GUI container to render and handle events.

```
void MenuState::draw()
{
    sf::RenderWindow& window = *getContext().window;
    window.setView(window.getDefaultView());
    window.draw(mBackgroundSprite);
    window.draw(mGUIContainer);
}
bool MenuState::update(sf::Time)
{
    return true;
}
bool MenuState::handleEvent(const sf::Event& event)
{
    mGUIContainer.handleEvent(event);
    return false;
}
```

This gives us much cleaner code than what we had in the previous chapter. Now we also don't have any risk of code duplication if we would like to have a menu in another place, such as the pause state. The pause menu looks very similar to this code, so we won't go through that as well.

The promised key bindings

We implement a new state; the `SettingsState` which you access through a button on the menu. What is the purpose for the `SettingsState` in our example? Currentlywe have the key bindings inside there. Everything we need has already been implemented with the GUI, so we only have to define the actual state.

The constructor of the `SettingsState` class one is pretty big so we snip it.

```
SettingsState::SettingsState(StateStack& stack, Context context)
: State(stack, context)
, mGUIContainer()
{
    mBackgroundSprite.setTexture(
        context.textures->get(Textures::TitleScreen));
    mBindingButtons[Player::MoveLeft] =
        std::make_shared<GUI::Button>(...);
    mBindingLabels[Player::MoveLeft] =
        std::make_shared<GUI::Label>(...);
    ... // More buttons and labels
    updateLabels();
    auto backButton = std::make_shared<GUI::Button>(...);
    backButton->setPosition(100, 375);
    backButton->setText("Back");
    backButton->setCallback([this] ()
    {
        requestStackPop();
    });
    mGUIContainer.pack(mBindingButtons[Player::MoveLeft]);
    mGUIContainer.pack(mBindingLabels[Player::MoveLeft]);
    ...
    mGUIContainer.pack(backButton);
}
```

We have put all the binding buttons and the associated labels in a static array, and associate to them the action they bind for. This means we don't have to duplicate a lot of callbacks, which you may have notice are missing. Instead, we have marked the button as one that toggles. We also have an `updateLabels()` function call. It's a helper function to make sure the labels are writing out the correct name for the key.

```
void SettingsState::updateLabels()
{
    Player& player = *getContext().player;
    for (std::size_t i = 0; i < Player::ActionCount; ++i)
    {
        sf::Keyboard::Key key =
            player.getAssignedKey(static_cast<Player::Action>(i));
        mBindingLabels[i]->setText(toString(key));
    }
}
```

Thanks to having it in an array, it's easy to loop through the labels and update them. Now moving on to the `handleEvent()` function, where we actually do something with the buttons.

```
bool SettingsState::handleEvent(const sf::Event& event)
{
    bool isKeyBinding = false;
    for (std::size_t action = 0; action < Player::ActionCount;
++action)
    {
        if (mBindingButtons[action]->isActive())
        {
            isKeyBinding = true;
            if (event.type == sf::Event::KeyReleased)
            {
                getContext().player->assignKey
(static_cast<Player::Action>(action), event.key.code);
                mBindingButtons[action]->deactivate();
            }
            break;
        }
    }

    if (isKeyBinding)
        updateLabels();
    else
        mGUIContainer.handleEvent(event);
    return false;
}
```

So how do we do this? If a button is pressed, then it will be activated, and since it's a button that toggles, it will stay active until we tell it to deactivate. So we loop through the array of buttons and check if anyone of them is active. If they are, then we are currently binding a key. When we get a key released event, then we change that binding on the player to the new key with the specified action before we deactivate the button again. After the loop, we update the labels, such that they have the correct name for everything. If no button is active, then we are not currently trying to bind a key, and should pass the event to the GUI container instead.

When we are done, the result should look like, as shown in the following screenshot:

Summary

So, in this chapter we implemented the foundation for a GUI library that can easily be extended upon. Even without extending the classes, it provided a functional user interface.

Implementing a nice and simple composite GUI library, along with handling its events and rendering were some of the skills attained in the chapter. Also, we have shown how to integrate such a system into what we already had, making the menu and the settings state richer than ever.

Now it is time to keep going into the next chapter, where we will handle gameplay mechanics. This means adding a fun factor to the game we are making, by adding enemies, projectiles, and other gameplay rules, which define a game's quality more prominently than other systems do. After all, who would want to play the best graphically accurate game if it weren't fun?

7
Warfare Unleashed – Implementing Gameplay

In *Chapter 5, Diverting the Game Flow – State Stack* and *Chapter 6, Waiting and Maintenance Area – Menus*, you have seen how to handle menus and states, now it is time to return to the actual game. Up till now, we have built a world that can contain various entities, and implemented the basic interaction mechanisms through updates, drawing, and commands. However, this is not particularly interesting as long as the world is empty.

In this chapter, we are going to populate the world, and implement the core part of the game; the actual gameplay with enemies, weapons, battles, and goodies. We are going to cover the following topics:

- Enemy aircraft controlled by a simple artificial intelligence
- Projectiles such as a machine gun or missiles
- Pickups that improve the player's equipment
- Collision detection and response between entities in the scene graph
- The world's update cycle and automatic removal of entities

Equipping the entities

You have heard about entities for the first time in *Chapter 3, Forge of the Gods – Shaping Our World*, where we built the World class and the scene graph. As a quick reminder, the SceneNode base class was inherited by the Entity class. Entities are the central part of this chapter. It's all about the interaction between entities of different kinds. Before starting to implement all those interactions, it is reasonable to think about crucial properties our entities need to have.

Introducing hitpoints

Since, we are preparing our airplanes for the battlefield, we need to provide them with new specific attributes. To our class definition of Entity, we add a new member variable that memorizes the current hitpoints. **Hitpoints (HP)** are a measure for the hull integrity of an entity; the entity is destroyed as soon as the hitpoints reach or fall below zero.

In addition to the member variable, we provide member functions that allow the modification of the hitpoints. We do not provide direct write access, however, the hitpoints can be decreased (the plane is damaged) or increased (the plane is repaired). Also, a destroy() function instantly destroys the entity.

```
class Entity : public SceneNode
{
    public:
        explicit    Entity(int hitpoints);
        void        repair(int points);
        void        damage(int points);
        void        destroy();

        int         getHitpoints() const;
        bool        isDestroyed() const;

        ...
    private:
        int         mHitpoints;
        ...
};
```

The implementation is as expected: repair() adds the specified hitpoints, damage() subtracts them, and destroy() sets them to zero.

Storing entity attributes in data tables

In our game, there are already two different airplanes with different attributes. For this chapter, we introduce a third one to make the game more interesting. With an increasing amount of new aircraft types, attributes such as speed, hitpoints, used texture, or fire rate may vary strongly among them. We need to think of a way to store those properties in a central place, allowing easy access to them.

What we clearly want to avoid are case differentiations in every Aircraft method, since this makes the local logic code less readable, and spreads the attributes across different functions. Instead of if/else cascades or switch statements, we can store the attributes in a central table, and just access the table every time we need an attribute.

Let's define the type of such a table entry in the case of an airplane. We choose the simplest way, and have a structure `AircraftData` with all members public. This type is defined in the file `DataTables.hpp`.

```
struct AircraftData
{
    int             hitpoints;
    float           speed;
    Textures::ID    texture;
};
```

While `AircraftData` is a single table entry, the whole table is represented as a sequence of entries, namely `std::vector<AircraftData>`.

Next, we write a function that initializes the table for different aircraft types. We begin to define a vector of the correct size (`Aircraft::TypeCount` is the last enumerator of the enum `Aircraft::Type`, it contains the number of different aircraft types). Since the enumerators are consecutive and begin at zero, we can use them as indices in our STL container. We thus initialize all the attributes for different airplanes, and eventually return the filled table.

```
std::vector<AircraftData> initializeAircraftData()
{
    std::vector<AircraftData> data(Aircraft::TypeCount);

    data[Aircraft::Eagle].hitpoints = 100;
    data[Aircraft::Eagle].speed = 200.f;
    data[Aircraft::Eagle].texture = Textures::Eagle;

    data[Aircraft::Raptor].hitpoints = 20;
    data[Aircraft::Raptor].speed = 80.f;
    data[Aircraft::Raptor].texture = Textures::Raptor;
    ...

    return data;
}
```

The global function `initializeAircraftData()` is declared in `DataTables.hpp` and defined in `DataTables.cpp`. It is used inside `Aircraft.cpp`, to initialize a global constant `Table`. This constant is declared locally in the `.cpp` file, so only the `Aircraft` internals can access it. In order to avoid name collisions in other files, we use an anonymous namespace.

```
namespace
{
const std::vector<AircraftData> Table = initializeAircraftData();
}
```

Inside the `Aircraft` methods, we can access a constant attribute of the own plane type using the member variable `mType` as index. For example, `Table[mType].hitpoints` denotes the maximal hitpoints of the current aircraft.

Data tables are only the first step of storing gameplay constants. For more flexibility, and to avoid recompiling the application, you can also store these constants externally, for example, in a simple text file or using a specific file format. The application initially loads these files, parses the values, and fills the data tables accordingly.

Nowadays, it is very common to load gameplay information from external resources. There are text-based formats such as YAML or XML, as well as, many application-specific text and binary formats. There are also well-known C++ libraries such as Boost.Serialize (`www.boost.org`) that help with loading and saving data structures from C++.

One possibility that has recently gained popularity consists of using script languages, most notably Lua (`www.lua.org`), in addition to C++. This has the advantage that not only constant data, but dynamic functionality can be outsourced and loaded during runtime.

Displaying text

We would like to add some text on the display, for example, to show the hitpoints or ammunition of different entities. Since this text information is supposed to be shown next to the entity, it stands to reason to attach it to the corresponding scene node. We therefore, create a `TextNode` class which inherits `SceneNode` as shown in the following code:

```
class TextNode : public SceneNode
{
    public:
        explicit            TextNode(const FontHolder& fonts,
                            const std::string& text);
        void                setString(const std::string& text);

    private:
        virtual void        drawCurrent(sf::RenderTarget& target,
                            sf::RenderStates states) const;

    private:
        sf::Text            mText;
};
```

The implementation of the functions is not complicated. The SFML class `sf::Text` provides most of what we need. In the `TextNode` constructor, we retrieve the font from the resource holder and assign it to the text.

```
TextNode::TextNode(const FontHolder& fonts, const std::string& text)
{
    mText.setFont(fonts.get(Fonts::Main));
    mText.setCharacterSize(20);
    setString(text);
}
```

The function to draw the text nodes just forwards the call to the SFML render target, as you know it from sprites.

```
void TextNode::drawCurrent(sf::RenderTarget& target, sf::RenderStates
states) const
{
    target.draw(mText, states);
}
```

For the interface, mainly the following method is interesting. It assigns a new string to the text node, and automatically adapts to its size. centerOrigin() is a utility function we wrote; it sets the object's origin to its center, which simplifies positioning a lot.

```
void TextNode::setString(const std::string& text)
{
    mText.setString(text);
    centerOrigin(mText);
}
```

In the Aircraft constructor, we create a text node and attach it to the aircraft itself. We keep a pointer mHealthDisplay as a member variable and let it point to the attached node.

```
std::unique_ptr<TextNode> healthDisplay(new TextNode(fonts, ""));
mHealthDisplay = healthDisplay.get();
attachChild(std::move(healthDisplay));
```

In the method Aircraft::update(), we check for the current hitpoints, and convert them to a string, using our custom toString() function. The text node's string and relative position are set. Additionally, we set the text node's rotation to the negative aircraft rotation, which compensates the rotation in total. We do this in order to have the text always upright, independent of the aircraft's orientation.

```
mHealthDisplay->setString(toString(getHitpoints()) + " HP");
mHealthDisplay->setPosition(0.f, 50.f);
mHealthDisplay->setRotation(-getRotation());
```

Creating enemies

Enemies are other instances of the `Aircraft` class. They appear at the top of the screen and move downwards, until they fly past the bottom of the screen. Most properties are the same for the player and enemies, so we only explain the new aircraft functionality.

Movement patterns

By default, enemies fly downwards in a straight line. But it would be nice if different enemies moved differently, giving the feeling of a very basic **artificial intelligence (AI)**. Thus, we introduce specific movement patterns. Such a pattern can be described as a sequence of directions to which the enemy airplane heads. A direction consists of an angle and a distance.

```
struct Direction
{
                                Direction(float angle, float distance);
    float                       angle;
    float                       distance;
};
```

Our data table for aircraft gets a new entry for the sequence of directions as shown in following code:

```
struct AircraftData
{
    int                     hitpoints;
    float                   speed;
    Textures::ID            texture;
    std::vector<Direction>  directions;
};
```

Let's implement a zigzag movement pattern for the Raptor plane. First, it steers for 80 units in 45 degrees direction. Then, the angle changes to -45 degrees, and the plane traverses 160 units back. Last, it moves again 80 units in +45 degrees direction, until it arrives at its original x position.

```
data[Aircraft::Raptor].directions.push_back(Direction( 45, 80));
data[Aircraft::Raptor].directions.push_back(Direction(-45, 160));
data[Aircraft::Raptor].directions.push_back(Direction( 45, 80));
```

For the Avenger plane, we use a slightly more complex pattern: it is essentially a zigzag, but between the two diagonal movements, the plane moves straight for 50 units.

```
data[Aircraft::Avenger].directions.push_back(Direction(+45,   50));
data[Aircraft::Avenger].directions.push_back(Direction(  0,   50));
data[Aircraft::Avenger].directions.push_back(Direction(-45,  100));
data[Aircraft::Avenger].directions.push_back(Direction(  0,   50));
data[Aircraft::Avenger].directions.push_back(Direction(+45,   50));
```

The following figure shows the sequence of directions for both planes; the Raptor plane is located on the left, Avenger on the right:

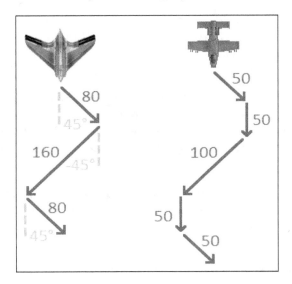

This way of defining movement is very simple, yet it enables a lot of possibilities. You can let the planes fly in any direction (also sideward or backwards); you can even approximate curves when using small intervals.

Now, we look at the logic we have to implement to follow these movement patterns. To the `Aircraft` class, we add two member variables: `mTravelledDistance`, which denotes the distance already travelled for each direction, and `mDirectionIndex`, to know which direction the plane is currently taking.

First, we retrieve the aircraft's movement pattern and store it as a reference to `const` named `directions`. We only proceed if there are movement patterns for the current type (otherwise the plane flies straight down).

```
void Aircraft::updateMovementPattern(sf::Time dt)
{
    const std::vector<Direction>& directions
    = Table[mType].directions;
    if (!directions.empty())
    {
```

Second, we check if the current direction has already been passed by the plane (that is, the travelled distance is higher than the direction's distance). If so, the index is advanced to the next direction. The modulo operator allows a cycle; after finishing the last direction, the plane begins again with the first one.

```
float distanceToTravel
= directions[mDirectionIndex].distance;
if (mTravelledDistance > distanceToTravel)
{
    mDirectionIndex
    = (mDirectionIndex + 1) % directions.size();
    mTravelledDistance = 0.f;
}
```

Now, we have to get a velocity vector out of the angle. First, we turn the angle by 90 degrees (by default, 0 degrees points to the right), but since our planes fly downwards, we work in a rotated coordinate system, such that we can use a minus to toggle between left/right. We also have to convert degrees to radians, using our function `toRadian()`.

The velocity's x component is computed using the cosine of the angle multiplied with the maximal speed; analogue for the y component, where the sine is used. Eventually, the travelled distance is updated:

```
float radians
= toRadian(directions[mDirectionIndex].angle + 90.f);
float vx = getMaxSpeed() * std::cos(radians);
float vy = getMaxSpeed() * std::sin(radians);
setVelocity(vx, vy);
mTravelledDistance += getMaxSpeed() * dt.asSeconds();
    }
}
```

 Note that if the distance to travel is no multiple of the aircraft speed, the plane will fly further than intended. This error is usually small, because there are many logic frames per second, and hardly noticeable, since each enemy will only be in the view for a short time.

Spawning enemies

It would be good if enemies were initially inactive, and the world created them as soon as they come closer to the player. By doing so, we do not need to process enemies that are relevant in the distant future; the scene graph can concentrate on updating and drawing active enemies.

We create a structure nested inside the `World` class that represents a spawn point for an enemy.

```
struct SpawnPoint
{
    SpawnPoint(Aircraft::Type type, float x, float y);

    Aircraft::Type type;
    float          x;
    float          y;
};
```

A member variable `World::mEnemySpawnPoints` of type `std::vector<SpawnPoint>` holds all future spawn points. As soon as an enemy position enters the battlefield, the corresponding enemy is created and inserted to the scene graph, and the spawn point is removed.

The `World` class member function `getBattlefieldBounds()`, returns `sf::FloatRect` to the battlefield area, similar to `getViewBounds()`. The battlefield area extends the view area by a small rectangle at the top, inside which new enemies spawn before they enter the view. If an enemy's y coordinate lies below the battlefield's `top` member, the enemy will be created at its spawn point. Since enemies face downwards, they are rotated by 180 degrees.

```
void World::spawnEnemies()
{
    while (!mEnemySpawnPoints.empty()
        && mEnemySpawnPoints.back().y
         > getBattlefieldBounds().top)
    {
        SpawnPoint spawn = mEnemySpawnPoints.back();

        std::unique_ptr<Aircraft> enemy(
            new Aircraft(spawn.type, mTextures, mFonts));
        enemy->setPosition(spawn.x, spawn.y);
        enemy->setRotation(180.f);

        mSceneLayers[Air]->attachChild(std::move(enemy));

        mEnemySpawnPoints.pop_back();
    }
}
```

Now, let's insert the spawn points. `addEnemy()` effectively calls `mEnemySpawnPoints.push_back()`, and interprets the passed coordinates relative to the player's spawn position. After inserting all spawn points, we sort them by their y coordinates. By doing so, `spawnEnemies()` needs to check only the elements at the end of the sequence instead of iterating through it every time.

```
void World::addEnemies()
{
    addEnemy(Aircraft::Raptor,    0.f,   500.f);
    addEnemy(Aircraft::Avenger, -70.f,  1400.f);
    ...

    std::sort(mEnemySpawnPoints.begin(), mEnemySpawnPoints.end(),
    [] (SpawnPoint lhs, SpawnPoint rhs)
    {
        return lhs.y < rhs.y;
    });
}
```

Here is an example of the player facing four Avenger enemies. Above each, you see how many hitpoints it has left.

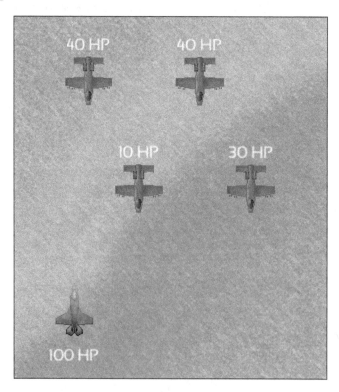

Adding projectiles

Finally, time to add what makes a game fun. Shooting down stuff is essential for our game. The code to interact with the World class is already defined, thanks to the actions in Player and to the existing Entity base class. All that's left is to define the projectiles themselves.

We start with the Projectile class. We have normal machine gun bullets and homing missiles represented by the same class. This class inherits from the Entity class and is quite small, since it doesn't have anything special that differentiates it from other entities apart from collision tests, which we will talk about later.

```cpp
class Projectile : public Entity
{
    public:
        enum Type
        {
            AlliedBullet,
            EnemyBullet,
            Missile,
            TypeCount
        };

    public:
                            Projectile(Type type,
                            const TextureHolder& textures);

        void                guideTowards(sf::Vector2f position);
        bool                isGuided() const;

        virtual unsigned int    getCategory() const;
        virtual sf::FloatRect   getBoundingRect() const;
        float                   getMaxSpeed() const;
        int                     getDamage() const;


    private:
        virtual void        updateCurrent(sf::Time dt,
                            CommandQueue& commands);
        virtual void        drawCurrent(sf::RenderTarget& target,
                            sf::RenderStates states) const;
```

```
    private:
        Type                mType;
        sf::Sprite          mSprite;
        sf::Vector2f        mTargetDirection;
};
```

Nothing fun or exciting here; we add some new helper functions such as the one to guide the missile towards a target. So let's have a quick look at the implementation. You might notice, we use the same data tables that we used in the `Aircraft` class to store data.

```
Projectile::Projectile(Type type, const TextureHolder& textures)
: Entity(1)
, mType(type)
, mSprite(textures.get(Table[type].texture))
{
    centerOrigin(mSprite);
}
```

The constructor simply creates a sprite with the texture we want for the projectile. We will check out the guide function when we actually implement the behavior of missiles. The rest of the functions don't hold anything particularly interesting. Draw the sprite and return a category for the commands and other data needed.

To get an overview of the class hierarchy in the scene graph, here is an inheritance diagram of the current scene node types. The data table structures which are directly related to their corresponding entities are shown at the bottom of the following diagram:

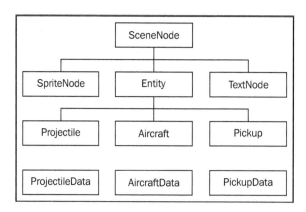

Firing bullets and missiles

So let's try and shoot some bullets in the game. We start with adding two new actions in the `Player` class: `Fire` and `LaunchMissile`. We define the default key bindings for these to be the Space bar and *M* keys.

```
Player::Player()
{
    // Set initial key bindings
    mKeyBinding[sf::Keyboard::Left] = MoveLeft;
    mKeyBinding[sf::Keyboard::Right] = MoveRight;
    mKeyBinding[sf::Keyboard::Up] = MoveUp;
    mKeyBinding[sf::Keyboard::Down] = MoveDown;
    mKeyBinding[sf::Keyboard::Space] = Fire;
    mKeyBinding[sf::Keyboard::M] = LaunchMissile;

    // ...
}

void Player::initializeActions()
{
    // ...
    mActionBinding[Fire].action = derivedAction<Aircraft>(
    std::bind(&Aircraft::fire, _1));
    mActionBinding[LaunchMissile].action =derivedAction<Aircraft>(
    std::bind(&Aircraft::launchMissile, _1));
}
```

So when we press the keys bound to those two actions, a command will be fired which calls the aircraft's `fire()` and `launchMissile()` functions. However, we cannot put the actual code that fires the bullet or missile in those two functions. The reason is, because if we could, we would have no concept of how much time has elapsed. We don't want to fire a projectile for every frame. We want there to be some cool down until the next time we fire a bullet, to accomplish that we need to use the delta time passed in the aircraft's `update()` function.

Instead, we mark what we want to fire by setting the Boolean flags `mIsFiring` or `mIsLaunchingMissile` to true in the `Aircraft::fire()` and the `Aircraft::launchMissile()` functions, respectively. Then we perform the actual logic in the `update()` function using commands. In order to make the code clearer to read, we have extracted it to its own function.

```
void Aircraft::checkProjectileLaunch(sf::Time dt, CommandQueue&
commands)
{
    if (mIsFiring && mFireCountdown <= sf::Time::Zero)
```

```
    {
        commands.push(mFireCommand);
        mFireCountdown += sf::seconds(1.f / (mFireRateLevel+1));
        mIsFiring = false;
    }
    else if (mFireCountdown > sf::Time::Zero)
    {
        mFireCountdown -= dt;
    }

    if (mIsLaunchingMissile)
    {
        commands.push(mMissileCommand);
        mIsLaunchingMissile = false;
    }
}
```

We have a cool down for the bullets. When enough time has elapsed since the last bullet was fired, we can fire another bullet. The actual creation of the bullet is done using a command which we will look at later. After we spawn the bullet, we reset the countdown. Here, we use += instead of =; with a simple assignment, we would discard a little time remainder in each frame, generating a bigger error as time goes by. The time of the countdown is calculated using a member variable mFireCountdown in Aircraft. Like that, we can improve the aircraft's fire rate easily. So if the fire rate level is one, then we can fire a bullet every half a second, increase it to level two, and we get every third of a second. We also have to remember to keep ticking down the countdown member, even if the user is not trying to fire. Otherwise, the countdown would get stuck when the user released the Space bar.

Next is the missile launch. We don't need a countdown here, because in the Player class, we made the input an event-based (not real-time based) input.

```
bool Player::isRealtimeAction(Action action)
{
    switch (action)
    {
        case MoveLeft:
        case MoveRight:
        case MoveDown:
        case MoveUp:
        case Fire:
            return true;
```

```
        default:
            return false;
    }
}
```

Since the `switch` statement does not identify `LaunchMissile` as a real-time input, the user has to release the *M* key before he can shoot another missile. The user wants to save his missiles for the moment he needs them.

So, let's look at the commands that we perform, in order to actually shoot the projectiles. We define them in the constructor in order to have access to the texture holder. This shows one of the strengths of lambda expressions in C++11.

```
Aircraft::Aircraft(Type type, const TextureHolder& textures)
{
    mFireCommand.category = Category::SceneAirLayer;
    mFireCommand.action =
    [this, &textures] (SceneNode& node, sf::Time)
    {
        createBullets(node, textures);
    };

    mMissileCommand.category = Category::SceneAirLayer;
    mMissileCommand.action =
    [this, &textures] (SceneNode& node, sf::Time)
    {
        createProjectile(node, Projectile::Missile, 0.f, 0.5f,
        textures);
    };
}
```

Now, we can pass the texture holder to the projectiles without any extra difficulty, and we don't even have to keep an explicit reference to the resources. This makes the `Aircraft` class and our code a lot simpler, since the reference does not need to exist in the `update()` function.

The commands are sent to the air layer in the scene graph. This is the node where we want to create our projectiles. The missile is a bit simpler to create than bullets, that's why we call directly `Aircraft::createProjectile()`. So how do we create bullets then?

```
void Aircraft::createBullets(SceneNode& node, const TextureHolder&
textures) const
{
    Projectile::Type type = isAllied()
    ? Projectile::AlliedBullet : Projectile::EnemyBullet;
```

```
switch (mSpreadLevel)
{
    case 1:
        createProjectile(node, type, 0.0f, 0.5f, textures);
        break;

    case 2:
        createProjectile(node, type, -0.33f, 0.33f, textures);
        createProjectile(node, type, +0.33f, 0.33f, textures);
        break;

    case 3:
        createProjectile(node, type, -0.5f, 0.33f, textures);
        createProjectile(node, type,  0.0f, 0.5f, textures);
        createProjectile(node, type, +0.5f, 0.33f, textures);
        break;
    }
}
```

For projectiles, we provide different levels of fire spread in order to make the game more interesting. The player can feel that progress is made, and that his aircraft becomes more powerful as he is playing. The function calls createProjectile() just as it was done for the missile.

So how do we actually create the projectile and attach it to the scene graph?

```
void Aircraft::createProjectile(SceneNode& node,
Projectile::Type type, float xOffset, float yOffset,
const TextureHolder& textures) const
{
    std::unique_ptr<Projectile> projectile(
        new Projectile(type, textures));

    sf::Vector2f offset(
        xOffset * mSprite.getGlobalBounds().width,
        yOffset * mSprite.getGlobalBounds().height);
    sf::Vector2f velocity(0, projectile->getMaxSpeed());

    float sign = isAllied() ? -1.f : +1.f;
    projectile->setPosition(getWorldPosition() + offset * sign);
    projectile->setVelocity(velocity * sign);
    node.attachChild(std::move(projectile));
}
```

We create the projectile with an offset from the player and a velocity required by the projectile type. Also, depending on if this projectile is shot by an enemy or the player, we will have different directions. We do not want the enemy bullets to go upwards like the player's bullets or the other way around.

Implementing gunfire for enemies is now a tiny step; instead of calling `fire()` when keys are pressed, we just call it always. We do this by adding the following code to the beginning of the `checkProjectileLaunch()` function:

```
if (!isAllied())
    fire();
```

Now we have bullets that fly and split the sky.

Homing missiles

What would a modern aircraft be if it hadn't got an arsenal of homing missiles? This is where we start to add intelligence to our missiles; they should be capable of seeking enemies autonomously.

Let's first look at what we need to implement on the projectile site. For homing missiles, the functions `guideTowards()` and `isGuided()`, as well as the variable `mTargetDirection` are important. Their implementation looks as follows:

```
bool Projectile::isGuided() const
{
    return mType == Missile;
}

void Projectile::guideTowards(sf::Vector2f position)
{
    assert(isGuided());
    mTargetDirection = unitVector(position - getWorldPosition());
}
```

The function `unitVector()` is a helper we have written. It divides a vector by its length, thus, always returns a vector of length one. The target direction is therefore a unit vector headed towards the target.

In the function `updateCurrent()`, we steer our missile. We change the current missile's velocity by adding small contributions of the target direction vector to it. By doing so, the velocity vector continuously approaches the target direction, having the effect that the missile flies along a curve towards the target.

`approachRate` is a constant that determines, to what extent the target direction contributes to the velocity. `newVelocity`, which is the weighted sum of the two vectors, is scaled to the maximum speed of the missile. It is assigned to the missile's velocity, and its angle is assigned to the missile's rotation. We use +90 here, because the missile texture points upwards (instead of right).

```cpp
void Projectile::updateCurrent(sf::Time dt,
CommandQueue& commands)
{
    if (isGuided())
    {
        const float approachRate = 200.f;

        sf::Vector2f newVelocity = unitVector(approachRate
        * dt.asSeconds() * mTargetDirection + getVelocity());

        newVelocity *= getMaxSpeed();
        float angle = std::atan2(newVelocity.y, newVelocity.x);

        setRotation(toDegree(angle) + 90.f);
        setVelocity(newVelocity);
    }

    Entity::updateCurrent(dt, commands);
}
```

> Note that there are many possibilities to guide a missile. **Steering behaviors** define a whole field of AI; they incorporate advanced mechanisms such as evasion, interception, and group behavior. Don't hesitate to search on the internet if you're interested.

Now, we have guided the missile to a certain position, but how to retrieve that position? We want our missile to pursuit the closest enemy. For this, we switch from `Projectile` to the `World` class, where we write a new function. First, we store all currently active (that is, already spawned and not yet destroyed) enemies in the member variable `mActiveEnemies`. With the command facility, this task is almost trivial:

```cpp
void World::guideMissiles()
{
    Command enemyCollector;
    enemyCollector.category = Category::EnemyAircraft;
    enemyCollector.action = derivedAction<Aircraft>(
    [this] (Aircraft& enemy, sf::Time)
```

```
{
    if (!enemy.isDestroyed())
        mActiveEnemies.push_back(&enemy);
});
```

Next, we have to find the nearest enemy for each missile. We set up another command, now for projectiles, that iterates through the active enemies to find the closest one. Here, `distance()` is a helper function that returns the distance between the centers of two scene nodes.

```
Command missileGuider;
missileGuider.category = Category::AlliedProjectile;
missileGuider.action = derivedAction<Projectile>(
[this] (Projectile& missile, sf::Time)
{
    // Ignore unguided bullets
    if (!missile.isGuided())
        return;

    float minDistance = std::numeric_limits<float>::max();
    Aircraft* closestEnemy = nullptr;

    FOREACH(Aircraft* enemy, mActiveEnemies)
    {
        float enemyDistance = distance(missile, *enemy);

        if (enemyDistance < minDistance)
        {
            closestEnemy = enemy;
            minDistance = enemyDistance;
        }
    }
```

In case we found a closest enemy, we let the missile chase it.

```
    if (closestEnemy)
        missile.guideTowards(
        closestEnemy->getWorldPosition());
});
```

After defining the second command, we push both to our queue, and reset the container of active enemies. Remember that the commands are not yet executed, they wait in the queue until they are invoked on the scene graph in `World::update()`.

```
mCommandQueue.push(enemyCollector);
mCommandQueue.push(missileGuider);
```

```
        mActiveEnemies.clear();
    }
```

That's it, now we are able to fire and forget!

The result looks as follows:

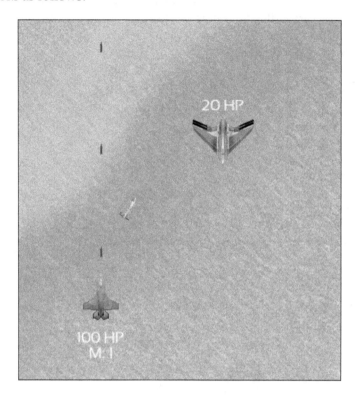

Picking up some goodies

Now we have implemented enemies and projectiles. But even if the player shot enemy airplanes down, and had exciting battles, he wouldn't remark that his success changes anything. You want to give the player the feeling that he is progressing in the game. Usual for this game genre are power-ups that the enemies drop when they are killed. So let's go ahead and implement that in our game.

Now this is the same story as with the projectile. Most of the things we need have already been implemented; therefore, this will be quite easy to add. What we want is only an entity that, when the player touches it, applies an effect to the player and disappears. Not much work with our current framework.

```cpp
class Pickup : public Entity
{
    public:
        enum Type
        {
            HealthRefill,
            MissileRefill,
            FireSpread,
            FireRate,
            TypeCount
        };

    public:
                                    Pickup(Type type,
                                    const TextureHolder& textures);

        virtual unsigned int    getCategory() const;
        virtual sf::FloatRect   getBoundingRect() const;

        void                    apply(Aircraft& player) const;

    protected:
        virtual void            drawCurrent(sf::RenderTarget& target,
                                    sf::RenderStates states) const;

    private:
        Type                    mType;
        sf::Sprite              mSprite;
};
```

So, let's start looking at a few interesting parts. As usual, we have a data table, create a sprite and center it, so the constructor looks just as you would expect it. Let's investigate the `apply()` function, and how the data table is created. In `apply()`, a function object stored in the table is invoked with `player` as argument. The `initializePickupData()` function initializes the function objects, using `std::bind()` that redirects to the `Aircraft` member functions.

```cpp
void Pickup::apply(Aircraft& player) const
{
    Table[mType].action(player);
}
```

```cpp
std::vector<PickupData> initializePickupData()
{
    std::vector<PickupData> data(Pickup::TypeCount);

    data[Pickup::HealthRefill].texture = Textures::HealthRefill;
    data[Pickup::HealthRefill].action
    = std::bind(&Aircraft::repair, _1, 25);

    data[Pickup::MissileRefill].texture = Textures::MissileRefill;
    data[Pickup::MissileRefill].action
    = std::bind(&Aircraft::collectMissiles, _1, 3);

    data[Pickup::FireSpread].texture = Textures::FireSpread;
    data[Pickup::FireSpread].action
    = std::bind(&Aircraft::increaseSpread, _1);

    data[Pickup::FireRate].texture = Textures::FireRate;
    data[Pickup::FireRate].action
    = std::bind(&Aircraft::increaseFireRate, _1);

    return data;
}
```

The pickups call already defined functions on the player aircraft that let us modify its state. These functions may repair it, refill it with missiles, or improve its firepower. It's nice when things just work out of the box.

That's how the scene looks when two pickups (health and fire rate) are floating in the air. You may notice that the player's Eagle plane shoots two bullets at once, which is the result of a previously collected fire spread pickup.

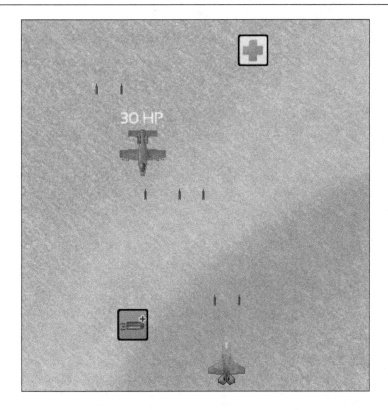

Collision detection and response

Now that our world is full of entities, let's implement interactions between them. Most interactions occur in the form of a collision; two airplanes collide and explode, projectiles of the player's Gatling gun perforate an enemy, and a pickup is collected by the player, and so on.

First, we write a function that computes the **bounding rectangle** of an entity. This is the smallest possible rectangle that completely contains the entity. As such, it represents an approximation of the entity's shape, which makes computations simpler. Here is an example implementation: `getWorldTransform()` multiplies the `sf::Transform` objects from the scene root to the leaf. `sf::Transform::transformRect()` transforms a rectangle, and may enlarge it if there is a rotation (since the rectangle has to remain axis-aligned). `sf::Sprite::getGlobalBounds()` returns the sprite's bounding rectangle relative to the aircraft.

```
sf::FloatRect Aircraft::getBoundingRect() const
{
    return getWorldTransform()
            .transformRect(mSprite.getGlobalBounds());
}
```

To get a better imagination of the bounding rectangle, take a look at `SceneNode.cpp` in the online code base. You can uncomment the call to `drawBoundingRect()` inside `SceneNode::draw()`.

For our collision, we write a function that checks whether a collision between two entities occurs. Here, we simply check bounding rectangles of the entities for an overlap. This approach is not extremely accurate, but easily implemented, and good enough for many purposes.

> There is a wide range of more elaborated collision detection algorithms. A popular algorithm is the **Separating Axis Theorem**, which checks for collisions between two convex polygons. You can read more about it at www.metanetsoftware.com/technique/tutorialA.html.

Our function is implemented using the SFML method `sf::FloatRect::intersects()` which checks for rectangle intersection.

```
bool collision(const SceneNode& lhs, const SceneNode& rhs)
{
    return lhs.getBoundingRect()
            .intersects(rhs.getBoundingRect());
}
```

> Note that we wrote the function for `SceneNode` and not `Entity`. This is because collision occurs inside the scene graph, so we avoid the downcasts. Scene nodes that do not have a physical representation have an empty bounding rectangle, which does not intersect with others.

Finding the collision pairs

Given the `collision()` function, we can determine in each frame, which pairs of entities collide. We store the pointers to the entities in `std::pair<SceneNode*, SceneNode*>`, for which we have created the `SceneNode::Pair` typedef. All collision pairs are stored in a `std::set` instance.

Basically, we need to compare every scene node with every other scene node to determine if a collision between the two occurs. To do this in a recursive way, we use two methods. The first one, `checkNodeCollision()`, evaluates a collision between `*this` with its children, and the function argument `node`.

The first three lines check if a collision occurs, and if the nodes are not identical (we do not want an entity to collide with itself). By calling `isDestroyed()`, we exclude entities that have already been destroyed, and that are no longer part of the gameplay. If the four conditions are true, we insert the pair to our set. The STL algorithm `std::minmax()` takes two arguments and returns a pair with `first` being the smaller, and `second` being the greater of the two arguments (where smaller means lower address in this case). Thus, `std::minmax(a,b)` and `std::minmax(b,a)` return always the same pair. This comes in very handy in our case—together with the sorted set, we automatically ensure that a collision between entities A and B is inserted only once (and not twice as A-B and B-A pairs).

```
void SceneNode::checkNodeCollision(SceneNode& node, std::set<Pair>&
collisionPairs)
{
    if (this != &node && collision(*this, node)
     && !isDestroyed() && !node.isDestroyed())
        collisionPairs.insert(std::minmax(this, &node));

    FOREACH(Ptr& child, mChildren)
        child->checkNodeCollision(node, collisionPairs);
}
```

The second part invokes the function recursively for all children of `*this`.

Now, we have checked the whole scene graph against one node, but we want to check the whole scene graph against all nodes. This is where our second function `checkSceneCollision()` comes into play. For the argument and all its children, a collision between the current node `*this` and the argument node `sceneGraph` is evaluated.

```
void SceneNode::checkSceneCollision(SceneNode& sceneGraph,
std::set<Pair>& collisionPairs)
{
    checkNodeCollision(sceneGraph, collisionPairs);

    FOREACH(Ptr& child, sceneGraph.mChildren)
        checkSceneCollision(*child, collisionPairs);
}
```

Reacting to collisions

What we have seen now is how collision detection works. The other part is collision response, where collisions result in gameplay actions.

For every frame, we store all collided scene nodes in a set. Now we can iterate through this set of `SceneNode*` pairs, and dispatch on the categories of each collision partner. First, we write a helper function that returns true if a given pair matches two assumed categories. For example, we want to check if a pair represents a collision between the player aircraft and a dropped pickup. We do not want the order of the parameters `type1` and `type2` to influence the result, that's why we check if the first node matches the first category and the second node the second category, as well as vice versa. In the vice versa case, we swap the node pointers so that their order is the same as the arguments' order. Because the first parameter `colliders` is passed by reference, the caller will then have a consistent ordering (`colliders.first` matches `type1` and `colliders.second` matches `type2`).

```
bool matchesCategories(SceneNode::Pair& colliders,
                       Category::Type type1, Category::Type type2)
{
    unsigned int category1 = colliders.first->getCategory();
    unsigned int category2 = colliders.second->getCategory();

    if (type1 & category1 && type2 & category2)
    {
        return true;
    }
    else if (type1 & category2 && type2 & category1)
    {
        std::swap(colliders.first, colliders.second);
        return true;
    }
    else
    {
        return false;
    }
}
```

Our actual dispatch function is now rather simple. We check the whole scene graph for collisions, and fill the set with collision pairs. Then, we iterate through the set and differentiate between the collisions categories.

```
void World::handleCollisions()
{
    std::set<SceneNode::Pair> collisionPairs;
    mSceneGraph.checkSceneCollision(mSceneGraph, collisionPairs);

    FOREACH(SceneNode::Pair pair, collisionPairs)
    {
        if (matchesCategories(pair,
            Category::PlayerAircraft, Category::EnemyAircraft))
        {
            ... // React to player-enemy collision
        }
    }
}
```

We have four combinations of categories which trigger a collision, as shown in the following diagram:

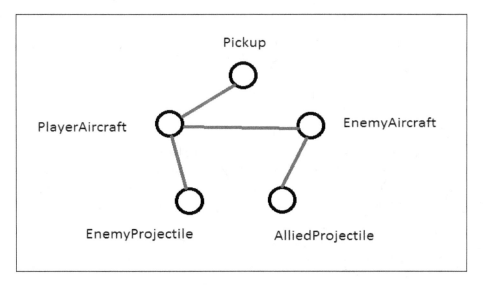

Correspondingly, we need four calls to matchesCategories() in order to react to all possible combinations. Note that the argument pair is passed by reference—possibly its members are swapped to match the category order. Therefore, we can be sure about the pointer's categories, and safely downcast from SceneNode* to the concrete entity.

We begin with the collision between the two airplanes. In this case, we always destroy the enemy, and deal damage to the player, depending on the enemy's current hitpoints.

```
if (matchesCategories(pair,
    Category::PlayerAircraft, Category::EnemyAircraft))
{
    auto& player = static_cast<Aircraft&>(*pair.first);
    auto& enemy = static_cast<Aircraft&>(*pair.second);

    player.damage(enemy.getHitpoints());
    enemy.destroy();
}
```

Next, we handle the case where the player's aircraft collects a pickup by touching it. We apply the effect to the player and destroy the pickup.

```
else if (matchesCategories(pair,
    Category::PlayerAircraft, Category::Pickup))
{
    auto& player = static_cast<Aircraft&>(*pair.first);
    auto& pickup = static_cast<Pickup&>(*pair.second);

    pickup.apply(player);
    pickup.destroy();
}
```

Last, we react to the collision between projectiles and aircraft. We only consider player projectiles that hit the enemy airplanes, and enemy projectiles that hit the player's airplane. Since the reaction is the same for both cases, we can unify them. We destroy the projectile, and deal the corresponding damage to the aircraft.

```
else if (matchesCategories(pair,
    Category::EnemyAircraft, Category::AlliedProjectile)
  || matchesCategories(pair,
    Category::PlayerAircraft, Category::EnemyProjectile))
{
    auto& aircraft = static_cast<Aircraft&>(*pair.first);
    auto& projectile = static_cast<Projectile&>(*pair.second);

    aircraft.damage(projectile.getDamage());
    projectile.destroy();
}
```

Very straightforward, isn't it? You can easily implement new interactions by adding another `if` clause. Want to intercept enemy missiles? No problem; add a case for `Category::AlliedProjectile` and `Category::EnemyProjectile`. Allow friendly fire, and see enemy planes taking each other down? Just write a collision for two entities of category `Category::EnemyAircraft`.

An outlook on optimizations

Since we test all possible scene node combinations, the number of collision checks increases quadratically (by a power of two) with the number of scene nodes. This can become a performance bottleneck if we have very many entities. There are several ways to cope with this issue.

First, needless comparisons can be reduced. Recursion can be replaced with iteration; one possible solution is to write an iterator class that traverses scene graphs. This would avoid checking each combination twice, and checking a scene node for collision with itself.

```
for (SceneNode::iterator left = mSceneGraph.begin();
     left != mSceneGraph.end(); ++left)
{
    for (SceneNode::iterator right = std::next(left);
         right != mSceneGraph.end(); ++right)
    {
        ... // Collision detection
    }
}
```

By storing pointers to entities that are interesting for collisions (instead of all scene nodes) in a separate container, we would reduce unnecessary checks too. We could even go further and directly store the entities with their full type. For example, we might have `std::vector<Aircraft*>` for the enemies and `std::vector<Projectile*>` for the allied bullets, so there would be no need for category dispatching.

Those approaches are a good start, but the time complexity is still quadratic. In a big world, it is clearly meaningless to check every possible pair of entities for collisions, since most of them are too far away. An optimization would base on locality. We only check entities that are close to each other. In order to achieve this, the world could be divided into a grid of equally sized cells. Each entity is assigned to a cell. For collision detection, only entities inside the same cell and the neighbor cells are checked, which drastically reduces the amount of required comparisons. Going this way further would lead to data structures such as quadtrees.

Concerning collision response, if there are many cases to consider, the dispatching could be done using a two-dimensional lookup table. The categories of both partners would serve as indices, and the table entries are function objects that implement the collision response for a concrete collider pair.

As nice as these optimizations sound, there is a price to pay — the implementation becomes more complicated. A decent amount of book keeping is required to keep everything synchronous, for example, the grid. Each time an entity moves, it might move to another cell, so we have to keep track of it. Newly created entities must be inserted, and destroyed entities must be removed from the right cell.

In conclusion, such optimizations are not only nice to have, but a bare necessity when the world and the number of entities grow. However, the implied book-keeping overhead does not pay off for smaller scenarios, which is a reason why we kept things simple in our game.

An interacting world

A lot of game logic has been implemented in the different entities, now we look at functionality that is defined in the `World` class. You have already seen the collision in the last section.

Cleaning everything up

During the game, entities are destroyed in battle, and have to be removed from the scene graph. We do not remove them instantly. Once in a frame, we iterate through the scene graph, check which nodes have been destroyed, and detach them from their parents. To find out whether a node has been destroyed, we write the virtual function `SceneNode::isDestroyed()`. By default, it returns false. A derived entity may specify a condition under which it returns true. Usually, this will be the case when the hitpoints are zero or less (that is, the entity is destroyed).

```
bool Entity::isDestroyed() const
{
    return mHitpoints <= 0;
}
```

In addition, we add a virtual function that checks if a scene node should be removed from the scene graph. By default, this is true as soon as the node is destroyed.

```
bool SceneNode::isMarkedForRemoval() const
{
    return isDestroyed();
}
```

However, this need not always be the case. Imagine an entity that has been destroyed, but still needs to reside for some time in the world, in order to drop a pickup, show an explosion animation, or similar. While `isDestroyed()` tells whether entities are logically dead and therefore, don't interact with the world anymore, `isMarkedForRemoval()` tells whether the scene node can be removed from the scene graph. The `Aircraft` class itself delays removal after destruction, to let enemies drop their pickups in the `update()` function. There, a special flag determines the return value.

```
bool Aircraft::isMarkedForRemoval() const
{
    return mIsMarkedForRemoval;
}
```

The removal is performed by the following method. In the first part, `std::remove_if()` rearranges the children container, so that all active nodes are at the beginning, and the ones to remove at the end. The call to `erase()` actually destroys these `SceneNode::Ptr` objects. In the second part, the function is recursively called for all child nodes. `std::mem_fn()` creates a function object which returns true, if and only if, the member function passed as argument returns true.

```
void SceneNode::removeWrecks()
{
    auto wreckfieldBegin = std::remove_if(mChildren.begin(),
    mChildren.end(), std::mem_fn(&SceneNode::isMarkedForRemoval));
    mChildren.erase(wreckfieldBegin, mChildren.end());

    std::for_each(mChildren.begin(), mChildren.end(),
    std::mem_fn(&SceneNode::removeWrecks));
}
```

This function can now be called in `World::update()`, and we automatically get rid of all nodes that request their removal.

Out of view, out of the world

Most entities that leave the current view become meaningless. Launched projectiles that have missed their enemy unwaveringly follow their path in the endless void. Enemies that fly past the screen continue to fly, although the player will never see them again, which can be costly performance-wise.

In order to reduce the amount of unnecessary entities, especially having our collision algorithm in mind, we want to remove entities that are located outside the view. Remember that `getBattlefieldBounds()` returns `sf::FloatRect`, which is slightly bigger than `getViewBounds()`. It also contains the area beyond the view, inside which the enemies spawn. We create a command that destroys all entities, of which the bounding rectangle doesn't intersect with the battlefield's bounding rectangle (that is, they are outside).

```cpp
void World::destroyEntitiesOutsideView()
{
    Command command;
    command.category = Category::Projectile
                     | Category::EnemyAircraft;
    command.action = derivedAction<Entity>(
    [this] (Entity& e, sf::Time)
    {
        if (!getBattlefieldBounds()
        .intersects(e.getBoundingRect()))
            e.destroy();
    });

    mCommandQueue.push(command);
}
```

The final update

A lot of new logic code has found its way into the `World` class; the different functions are invoked from `World::update()`, which currently looks as follows. The function names are self-explanatory.

```cpp
void World::update(sf::Time dt)
{
    mWorldView.move(0.f, mScrollSpeed * dt.asSeconds());
    mPlayerAircraft->setVelocity(0.f, 0.f);

    destroyEntitiesOutsideView();
    guideMissiles();

    while (!mCommandQueue.isEmpty())
        mSceneGraph.onCommand(mCommandQueue.pop(), dt);
    adaptPlayerVelocity();
```

```
    handleCollisions();
    mSceneGraph.removeWrecks();
    spawnEnemies();

    mSceneGraph.update(dt, mCommandQueue);
    adaptPlayerPosition();
}
```

Victory and defeat

Equipped with the Eagle aircraft, you can accept the challenge to maneuver through a mission. Depending on your skill, you may reach the end of the level and become a pilot legend. Or you fall victim to the enemy fleet and die in a horrible plane crash.

Anyway, the player should be informed by the game about his fate. In most games, there are victory and defeat conditions. In our airplane game, a mission is complete if you cross the level's border at the end. A mission is failed if your plane is destroyed. To display this information, we have written GameOverState that displays an appropriate message. Of course, this can be extended to show high scores, statistics, or save the game between multiple missions. But the basic principle remains the same. We reuse the states and GUI from the previous chapters. Since their implementation should be clear, we do not paste their code here. However, you are free to look at the original code base at any time.

Summary

This was probably the most difficult chapter up to now, as it combines all the game-related features we have developed in earlier chapters: resources, world, entities, input, and commands. Despite all the things to consider, it became apparent that the existing framework made a lot of new tasks simple to achieve.

In this chapter, you learned about essential gameplay mechanics and their interaction. We added projectiles to represent bullets and homing missiles. We let enemies spawn, follow certain movement patterns, fire in regular intervals, and drop pickups upon destruction. Collision detection and response was implemented, and we discussed performance considerations. Eventually, we managed the world's update cycle, and cleaned up destroyed entities.

Now that the game foundation has been built, we are ready to add more graphical content. In the next chapter, we are going to add a variety of visual effects to improve the appearance of our game.

Every Pixel Counts – Adding Visual Effects

8

Throughout the previous chapters, we have constantly been adding functionality. We finally reached a point where our game is playable, where all the game mechanisms are implemented. With a bit of creativity, you should already be able to write your own small game. Nevertheless, we are not going to quit now — a game is more than just gameplay. A very important part of games are the graphics. Be it cutting-edge 3D scenes in the newest real-time strategy game or the nostalgic atmosphere of a pixel-art indie title, graphics determine to a big extent how the player feels.

In this chapter, we are going to look behind the scenes of rendering. We are going to cover various techniques that are used in modern games to create graphical effects of different kinds. To mention a few:

- Texture atlases and how different objects can be stored in one texture
- Texture mapping and vertex arrays
- Particle systems to create effects such as fire or smoke
- Animations that show an object in motion
- Render textures as an alternative to render windows
- Shaders to give the whole scene a distinct look

While the previous chapter concerned gameplay and therefore didn't work a lot with SFML, this one will introduce many new features of its Graphics module.

Defining texture atlases

A **texture atlas** describes the concept of a single texture that contains multiple objects. You may also encounter other terms, such as **sprite sheet**, or **tile set** in the case of squared tiles put together. Texture atlases allow having fewer image files, which decreases the amount of switches between different textures at runtime. Since texture switching is a rather slow operation on the graphics card, using texture atlases may result in notable speedups. Till now, we used separate textures for each object: one for each aircraft, pick-up, projectile, button, and background. Every texture was stored in its own PNG file. The code design looked as follows:

- Textures were stored inside `TextureHolder`, our container storing `sf::Texture` objects.

- We had an enum `Textures::ID` to identify the different textures in a `TextureHolder`. By that, we could easily refer to different textures without knowing the actual `sf::Texture` object or the filename.

- The textures used in the scene were loaded in `World::loadTextures()`.

- They were bound to sprites in the specific entity classes such as `Aircraft`. For a given entity, data tables stored the texture ID it used.

The SFML sprite class `sf::Sprite` offers the possibility to set a **texture rectangle** (or texture rect for short), containing the pixel coordinates of a specific object inside the texture. You already came across this functionality when we implemented the tiling background for our world in *Chapter 3, Forge of the Gods – Shaping Our World*. The rectangle is of type `sf::IntRect` and stores four integral values: the x and y coordinates of the left-upper pixel (members `left` and `top`) as well as the size (members `width` and `height`).

For example, the following texture rectangle `rect` begins at (0, 15) and has a width of 30 and height of 20. The size excludes the last pixel; the pixel with coordinates (30, 35) is outside the rectangle.

```
sf::IntRect rect(0, 15, 30, 20);
```

Given a texture and a rectangle, you can initialize a sprite using the constructor, or you can set the attributes later with the corresponding methods.

```
sf::Texture texture = ...;
sf::IntRect rect = ...;
```

```
sf::Sprite sprite(texture, rect);

sf::Sprite sprite2;
sprite2.setTexture(texture);
sprite2.setTextureRect(rect);
```

If no rectangle is specified, the sprite will assume that the whole texture is used. This is what we have always done so far.

Adapting the game code

We need to extend a few parts of our code to work with texture rects instead of whole textures. First, we must remove many of our resource identifiers. All the aircraft, projectile and pickup textures will be merged to one texture, with an ID of Entities. The texture containing the three buttons is accessible via Buttons. Eventually, we only have the following identifiers:

```
namespace Textures
{
    enum ID
    {
        Entities,
        Jungle,
        TitleScreen,
        Buttons,
        Explosion,
        Particle,
        FinishLine,
    };
}
```

In case you wonder, Jungle is the new background we will paint. It is much bigger and far more interesting than the desert we had before. FinishLine is a texture used to mark the end of the level, instead of the black void. It is embedded to the scene graph using SpriteNode. Explosion and Particle are going to be introduced soon.

With the new image files in our `Media` folder, the method `World::loadTextures()` can be adapted accordingly. We also modify our data tables to store a texture rectangle in addition to the texture ID. The rectangle coordinates are hardcoded in the initialization functions.

```
struct AircraftData
{
    Textures::ID            texture;
    sf::IntRect             textureRect;
    ...
};

std::vector<AircraftData> initializeAircraftData()
{
    std::vector<AircraftData> data(Aircraft::TypeCount);

    data[Aircraft::Eagle].texture = Textures::Entities;
    data[Aircraft::Eagle].textureRect = sf::IntRect(0, 0, 48, 64);
    ...

    return data;
}
```

The last part to extend is the entities that use the textures. Now, we initialize the sprite with both texture and texture rect:

```
namespace
{
const std::vector<AircraftData> Table = initializeAircraftData();
}

Aircraft::Aircraft(Type type, const TextureHolder& textures,
                   const FontHolder& fonts)
: mSprite(
    textures.get(Table[type].texture), // sf::Texture
    Table[type].textureRect)           // sf::IntRect
, ...
{
    centerOrigin(mSprite);
    ...
}
```

Analogous steps have been applied for textures other than the one for the Eagle aircraft. That's pretty much it; the new code should now directly work with texture atlases! Visually, there will be no difference to what we had before.

Low-level rendering

Besides the high-level convenience classes sf::Sprite, sf::Text and sf::Shape, SFML provides a low-level graphics API which is more complicated to use, but allows more flexibility. In the next section, we are going to look behind the scenes of rendering and discuss corresponding techniques as they are implemented in SFML.

OpenGL and graphics cards

The graphics card architecture consists of many components. Notable are the **graphics processing unit (GPU)**, which performs computations on the graphics card, and the **video memory**, which stores data such as textures. In contrast to their counterparts CPU and RAM, graphics cards' components are highly optimized to process 2D and 3D graphics.

SFML is built on top of the **Open Graphics Library (OpenGL)**. OpenGL is, like DirectX, a specification of an interface to the graphics card. Operating systems provide an API written in C that allows applications to access graphic card functionality. Newer graphics cards support higher OpenGL versions and thus have the benefit of more modern features.

The way SFML is designed is heavily influenced by the underlying OpenGL functionality. SFML itself uses an object-oriented approach and abstracts low-level accesses away; therefore users can work with the library without even knowing OpenGL. It is, however, advantageous to be aware of basic underlying techniques, in order to see the whole picture. For specific requirements, it is also possible to mix SFML and OpenGL.

Understanding render targets

A **render target** defines the place where 2D objects such as sprites, texts, or shapes are rendered. In SFML, this boils down to the abstract base class sf::RenderTarget. Apart from clear() and draw() methods, the class provides functionality to manipulate the current view.

A **render window** is a concrete implementation of a render target. Render windows represent application windows to which you can render graphical objects. In addition, they provide facilities for input handling and configurations such as V-Sync. The class sf::RenderWindow, which we have been using all the time, inherits sf::RenderTarget and sf::Window.

A **render texture** is another realization of the render target concept. Here, you do not draw objects to a window, but to a texture. Render textures can be used to render a scene that is not immediately displayed, but can be further processed — for example, saved to a file or edited as a whole. SFML provides the class `sf::RenderTexture` which derives from `sf::RenderTarget`. Notable is the method `getTexture()` which returns `const sf::Texture&` with the render texture's current contents. As with render windows, you must call `display()` before you can actually use that texture. This step is often forgotten.

Texture mapping

We have worked a lot with textures in the game, but not explained how they are actually displayed on the screen. **Texel (texture element)** is the term used for pixels in texture space. The case where every texel in the texture corresponds to a pixel on the window is an exception. In general, transforms of the graphical object and the view affect the way how pixels are displayed on the screen.

Every graphical object on the screen consists of vertices. A **vertex** is a point that defines the geometry of the object. Multiple vertices are grouped to geometric primitives such as lines, triangles, rectangles, and so on. In most cases, we have rectangular objects (such as `sf::Sprite`) that have four vertices, namely the four corners of the rectangle. Polygons (modeled by `sf::Shape`) allow a different number of vertices.

Each vertex consists of target coordinates (the position of the point on the render target, in world units) and texture coordinates (the position in the source texture, in texels). Texture coordinates are sometimes also called UV coordinates, because the variables u and v are often used instead of x and y. The process of **texture mapping** specifies how target coordinates are mapped onto texture coordinates, in order to know which pixels have to be drawn where. This mapping is clarified in the following figure:

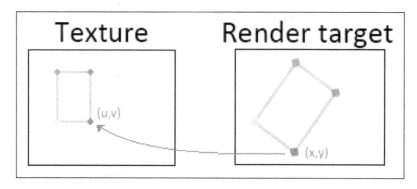

This figure only shows an aligned rectangle in the texture, the proportions of which are evenly maintained in the render target. In fact, you have a lot of freedom to place your vertices. This may result in distorted textures, but, you should just experiment yourself.

SFML provides the class `sf::Vertex` that represents a vertex of the geometric object. It has the following public member variables:

- `sf::Vector2f position`: the target coordinates (x, y)
- `sf::Vector2f texCoords`: the texture coordinates (u, v)
- `sf::Color color`: used to colorize the vertex

Vertex arrays

All geometric primitives except points consist of more than one vertex. A **vertex array** is a collection of vertices that are drawn together. A vertex array need not necessarily represent a single geometric object; it may also store the vertices of many objects.

In SFML, the class `sf::VertexArray` is used to model vertex arrays. It is a thin wrapper around `std::vector<sf::Vertex>` and derives from `sf::Drawable`. We can add new vertices to the end of the array, and access existing vertices using the index operator.

The **primitive type** determines how the vertices are interpreted to form a geometric primitive. For example, the primitive type `sf::Triangles` interprets three subsequent vertices as one triangle, the next three vertices as another triangle, and so on. `sf::Quads` interprets four subsequent vertices as a quadrilateral. When we work with rectangles, we will be using the `sf::Quads` primitive type.

A small, incomplete example should give you a rough idea how vertices, vertex arrays and render targets interact:

```
sf::Vertex v;
v.position = sf::Vector2f(x, y);
v.texCoords = sf::Vector2f(u, v);
v.color = sf::Color::Blue;

sf::VertexArray vertices;
vertices.setPrimitiveType(sf::Quads);
vertices.append(v);
...
```

```
sf::RenderTarget& target = ...;
target.draw(vertices);
```

The main reason to use `sf::VertexArray` instead of high-level classes such as `sf::Sprite` is performance. The rendering performance primarily depends on the number of draw calls, that is, the number of times the CPU invokes a draw routine on the graphics card. While sprites are easier to use and good enough for many cases, there are situations where we need to exploit the possibilities of vertex arrays.

Particle systems

Visual effects such as fire, rain, or smoke have one thing in common: they have a continuously changing nature and cannot be meaningfully described using a single sprite. Even an animated sprite is too limited for many cases, because such effects should come with certain randomness. Fire may have sparks flying in arbitrary directions; smoke may be blown away by the wind.

This is why we need another model to visualize these sorts of effects: **particles**. A particle is a tiny object that makes up a part of the whole effect; you can imagine it as a small sprite. Each particle by itself looks boring, only in combination do they lead to an emergent visual pattern such as fire.

A **particle system** is a component that manages the behavior of many particles to form the desired effect. **Emitters** continuously create new particles and add them to the system. **Affectors** affect existing particles with respect to motion, fade-out, scaling, and many other properties.

Given a particle texture, we could model each particle as a sprite; the particle system could contain `std::vector<sf::Sprite>`. The problem with this approach is that we have to draw each sprite separately. Since particle systems may easily consist of many thousands of particles, thousands of draw calls on the GPU are not unrealistic—per frame. Now consider that not only one effect must be rendered; depending on the game, the screen may contain dozens of particle systems. Clearly, we need a technique to reduce the amount of draw calls.

This is where vertex arrays come into play. We model each particle as an object with four vertices. The vertices of all particles are inserted into a single vertex array. This gives us a method to draw everything with only one draw call.

Particles and particle types

In our game, we want to create an effect for the burned propellant and the emitted smoke of homing missiles. Both can be handled in a similar way, the main difference is the color. Of course, it would also be possible to use different textures. The final result is shown in the following screenshot. You don't recognize the single particles anymore, the trace of the missiles looks like a continuous stream.

We define a class for particles that stores the position, color, and the time until the particle disappears. The `Particle::Type` data type is used to differ between smoke and propellant effects.

```cpp
struct Particle
{
    enum Type
    {
        Propellant,
        Smoke,
        ParticleCount
    };

    sf::Vector2f    position;
    sf::Color       color;
    sf::Time        lifetime;
};
```

We also create data tables for particles, in order to easily change their attributes in a central place. The required structure is shown here, the rest is as you know it, from the entity data tables:

```cpp
struct ParticleData
{
    sf::Color       color;
    sf::Time        lifetime;
};
```

Particle nodes

To render the particles on screen, they need to be part of the scene graph. We will to create a class `ParticleNode`, which can be inserted into the scene and which acts as a particle system. The class definition looks as follows:

```cpp
class ParticleNode : public SceneNode
{
    public:
                                ParticleNode(
                                 Particle::Type type,
                                 const TextureHolder& textures);
        void                    addParticle(
                                 sf::Vector2f position);
        Particle::Type          getParticleType() const;
        virtual unsigned int    getCategory() const;
        ...
```

```
private:
    std::deque<Particle>    mParticles;
    const sf::Texture&      mTexture;
    Particle::Type          mType;

    mutable sf::VertexArray mVertexArray;
    mutable bool            mNeedsVertexUpdate;
};
```

Many methods for drawing and updating are already known from other
SceneNode definitions, thus not listed here. getCategory() returns
Category::ParticleSystem, a separate category. getParticleType() returns the
particle type (smoke or propellant) which is stored in mType.

A new addition is addParticle(), which looks up the data table and inserts a
particle into the system:

```
void ParticleNode::addParticle(sf::Vector2f position)
{
    Particle particle;
    particle.position = position;
    particle.color = Table[mType].color;
    particle.lifetime = Table[mType].lifetime;

    mParticles.push_back(particle);
}
```

In the update method, we first remove all particles of which the lifetime has
expired. Since all particles have the same initial lifetime, older particles are stored
at the beginning of the container. Therefore, it is enough to remove the front element
of mParticles as long as its lifetime is smaller or equal to zero (this is also the reason
why we employed std::deque). In the middle part of the function, we decrease
the lifetime of each particle by the current frame time. Finally, every time the
particle container is modified, we enable a flag to express that the render geometry
must be recomputed:

```
void ParticleNode::updateCurrent(sf::Time dt, CommandQueue&)
{
    while (!mParticles.empty()
    && mParticles.front().lifetime <= sf::Time::Zero)
        mParticles.pop_front();

    FOREACH(Particle& particle, mParticles)
        particle.lifetime -= dt;

    mNeedsVertexUpdate = true;
}
```

The rendering part is shown next. The mVertexArray member is declared mutable, since it is not a part of the object's logical state. This allows optimizations: we only rebuild the vertex array if something has changed, and directly before drawing (instead of after each update). This way, if the particle system is updated multiple times in a row before being drawn, we do not needlessly compute the vertices each time.

After checking whether we need to recompute the vertices, we set the sf::RenderStates texture to our particle texture and draw the vertex array:

```
void ParticleNode::drawCurrent(sf::RenderTarget& target,
sf::RenderStates states) const
{
    if (mNeedsVertexUpdate)
    {
        computeVertices();
        mNeedsVertexUpdate = false;
    }

    states.texture = &mTexture;
    target.draw(mVertexArray, states);
}
```

The rebuild of the vertex array is shown in the following code snippet. First, we save the texture's full and half sizes in variables, to determine the vertex positions more easily. For size, the constructor syntax is used rather than =, because a sf::Vector2i (vector of integers) is converted to sf::Vector2f (vector of floats). We clear the vertex array, removing all vertices in it, but keeping the memory allocated:

```
void ParticleNode::computeVertices() const
{
    sf::Vector2f size(mTexture.getSize());
    sf::Vector2f half = size / 2.f;

    mVertexArray.clear();
```

For each particle, we compute the ratio between the remaining and total lifetime — this ratio in [0, 1] is used to set the particle's alpha value in [0, 255]. The alpha value determines the transparency; therefore our particles fade out continuously until they are completely invisible:

```
FOREACH(const Particle& particle, mParticles)
{
    sf::Vector2f pos = particle.position;
    sf::Color c = particle.color;
```

```
float ratio = particle.lifetime.asSeconds()
            / Table[mType].lifetime.asSeconds();
c.a = static_cast<sf::Uint8>(255 * std::max(ratio, 0.f));
```

Now the interesting part: we add four vertices for each particle, one in every corner of our rectangle. The first two arguments denote the target coordinates; the next two denote the texture coordinates. The fifth argument is the vertex color. Since we need no gradient inside a particle, the color is uniform for all four vertices.

```
    addVertex(pos.x - half.x, pos.y - half.y, 0.f,    0.f,    c);
    addVertex(pos.x + half.x, pos.y - half.y, size.x, 0.f,    c);
    addVertex(pos.x + half.x, pos.y + half.y, size.x, size.y, c);
    addVertex(pos.x - half.x, pos.y + half.y, 0.f,    size.y, c);
}
```

The function to add vertices itself is not very interesting — it builds `sf::Vertex` and adds it to `sf::VertexArray`:

```
void ParticleNode::addVertex(float worldX, float worldY,
                             float texCoordX, float texCoordY,
                             const sf::Color& color) const
{
    sf::Vertex vertex;
    vertex.position = sf::Vector2f(worldX, worldY);
    vertex.texCoords = sf::Vector2f(texCoordX, texCoordY);
    vertex.color = color;

    mVertexArray.append(vertex);
}
```

Emitter nodes

Because particles should be emitted in the places where the missiles are located, it stands to reason that emitters should be attached to missiles. Once more, our scene graph comes in very handy: we can create a new scene node `EmitterNode` for emitters and attach it to the `Projectile` node of the missile.

`EmitterNode` is rather simple, its class definition is shown in the following code snippet:

```
class EmitterNode : public SceneNode
{
    public:
        explicit        EmitterNode(Particle::Type type);
        ...
```

```
        private:
            sf::Time          mAccumulatedTime;
            Particle::Type    mType;
            ParticleNode*     mParticleSystem;
};
```

The pointer `mParticleSystem` points to the `ParticleNode` into which the `EmitterNode` emits particles. Initially, it is `nullptr`. In the update function, we emit particles if the particle system has already been initialized. Otherwise, we need to find the system corresponding to the emitter. "Corresponding" means both use the same particle type, for example, `Particle::Smoke`. We send a command through the scene graph to find the right particle system. It sets the member variable `mParticleSystem` to the found `ParticleNode`:

```
void EmitterNode::updateCurrent(sf::Time dt,
                                CommandQueue& commands)
{
    if (mParticleSystem)
    {
        emitParticles(dt);
    }
    else
    {
        auto finder = [this] (ParticleNode& container, sf::Time)
        {
            if (container.getParticleType() == mType)
                mParticleSystem = &container;
        };

        Command command;
        command.category = Category::ParticleSystem;
        command.action = derivedAction<ParticleNode>(finder);

        commands.push(command);
    }
}
```

After the emitter has been linked to a particle system, the method to emit particles becomes interesting. We set an emission rate and try to achieve it as closely as possible. Since this is not usually equal to our logic frame rate, the amount of emitted particles per frame differs. To cope with that problem, we again use accumulators, as we did for the logic game loop in *Chapter 1, Making a Game Tick*. We emit particles as long as the emission interval still fits into the current frame. The remaining time is stored in `mAccumulatedTime` and is carried over to the next frame.

```
void EmitterNode::emitParticles(sf::Time dt)
{
    const float emissionRate = 30.f;
    const sf::Time interval = sf::seconds(1.f) / emissionRate;

    mAccumulatedTime += dt;

    while (mAccumulatedTime > interval)
    {
        mAccumulatedTime -= interval;
        mParticleSystem->addParticle(getWorldPosition());
    }
}
```

Why do we separate `EmitterNode` and `ParticleNode`? Emitters can be considered purely logical scene nodes that emit particles into particle systems. They are not directly related to rendering. A particle system, however, manages the update and rendering of particles. With our current design, we can have multiple emitters that emit into a single particle system. We only need one `ParticleNode` instance per effect, even with dozens of emitters. Furthermore, both scene nodes can have different transforms. An `EmitterNode` is attached to a missile, emitting particles that take the missile's transform into account. As soon as particles have been emitted, they are managed by the `ParticleNode`, which uses the global coordinate system. It is reasonable that particles, once created, are no longer influenced by the orientation of the object that created them.

Affectors

As a counterpart to emitters, we also mentioned affectors that affect particles during their lifetime. Affectors can be modeled as functions that are applied to each particle every frame—a meaningful abstraction might therefore be:

```
std::function<void(Particle&, sf::Time)>
```

This function takes the particle to affect and the frame time as parameters. The `ParticleNode` would store a list of affectors and apply them to the particles during its update. We have not implemented affectors in our code since we don't need their functionality at the moment, but you are free to extend the system however you like!

Embedding particles in the world

That was it for the definition of emitters and particle systems. We now add these nodes to the scene graph. First the emitter in the `Projectile` constructor; we set its position to the tail of the missile (which is half the height away from the center):

```
if (isGuided()) // if this projectile is a missile
{
    std::unique_ptr<EmitterNode> smoke(
        new EmitterNode(Particle::Smoke));
    smoke->setPosition(0.f, getBoundingRect().height / 2.f);
    attachChild(std::move(smoke));
}
```

The particle system is attached to a layer node directly under the scene graph's root. Because we want particles and projectiles to appear below the airplanes, we split the existing scene layer `Air` into two layers `LowerAir` and `UpperAir`. In the following, you see an excerpt of `World::buildScene()`:

```
std::unique_ptr<ParticleNode> smokeNode(
    new ParticleNode(Particle::Smoke, mTextures));
mSceneLayers[LowerAir]->attachChild(std::move(smokeNode));
```

So far we have only considered the smoke effect, but the propellant fire works in exactly the sameway. By adding the fire particle system after the smoke, it is rendered later, so the burning propellant is still visible and not covered by smoke.

Animated sprites

Alright, now we have got particles, let's accompany them with an animated explosion. So far our aircraft have just disappeared when you shot them down. That's not satisfying. When you destroy something like an aircraft, you expect a huge explosion, don't you?

We already had a look at texture rectangles and sprite sheets. This knowledge will be used to build our animation. An animation consists of several **frames**, and we represent these frames as separate rectangles inside one larger texture, similar to what we now do with entities. Do not confuse animation frames with the game loop frames—the former represents just a state of an animation, which usually lasts for many game loop iterations.

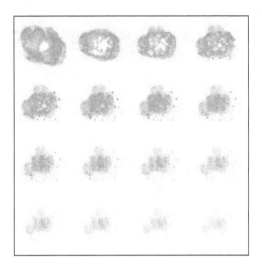

This is the sprite sheet we use for the animation. How does it work? As time elapses, we move the texture rect from one frame to the other, until the animation is finished.

We do not define the animation class as a scene node but only as a drawable and a transformable object. It can then be used by whatever scene node we want, which gives a little more flexibility when and where we can use it.

```
class Animation : public sf::Drawable, public sf::Transformable
{
    public:
        ...

    private:
        ...

        sf::Sprite        mSprite;
        sf::Vector2i      mFrameSize;
        std::size_t       mNumFrames;
        std::size_t       mCurrentFrame;
        sf::Time          mDuration;
        sf::Time          mElapsedTime;
        bool              mRepeat;
};
```

We will have a look at the functions later. As you can see we use internally a sprite. We could do without a sprite if we so desired, but it defines a lot of functions that we want to use, making our lives easier. After that comes the frame size, this vector defines the size of one frame for us. We have the values concerning frames, how many frames and what frame we are currently drawing. Lastly we have the time for the animation, the total duration, and the elapsed time since the last frame change.

So let us start looking at the actual implementation. Most of our logic is performed in the `Animation::update()` function, so it grows quite big. Because of that the function is explained in the following sections.

```cpp
void Animation::update(sf::Time dt)
{
    sf::Time timePerFrame = mDuration /
static_cast<float>(mNumFrames);
    mElapsedTime += dt;

    sf::Vector2i textureBounds(mSprite.getTexture()->getSize());
    sf::IntRect textureRect = mSprite.getTextureRect();

    if (mCurrentFrame == 0)
        textureRect = sf::IntRect(0, 0, mFrameSize.x,
mFrameSize.y);
```

In the previous code, we already have the sprite sheet divided per frame and we know how big one frame is. We have to calculate how much time needs to elapse before we progress to the next frame. If we are on the first frame, then our texture `rect` should start at the beginning of the animation sprite sheet:

```cpp
    while (mElapsedTime >= timePerFrame && (mCurrentFrame <=
mNumFrames || mRepeat))
    {
```

So while time has elapsed since we last updated, and is enough to count as a new frame, and we haven't reached the end of the animation, we perform an iteration:

```cpp
        textureRect.left += textureRect.width;

        if (textureRect.left + textureRect.width > textureBounds.x)
        {
            textureRect.left = 0;
            textureRect.top += textureRect.height;
        }

        mElapsedTime -= timePerFrame;
        if (mRepeat)
```

```
        {
            mCurrentFrame = (mCurrentFrame + 1) % mNumFrames;

            if (mCurrentFrame == 0)
                textureRect = sf::IntRect(0, 0, mFrameSize.x,
    mFrameSize.y);
        }
        else
        {
            mCurrentFrame++;
        }
    }

    mSprite.setTextureRect(textureRect);
}
```

In each iteration, we move the resulting texture rect quite easily. We move it a step to the right, all the way until we reach the end, if that occurs we move the rect down one line and start again from the start. Lastly is just some book-keeping for what frame we are on, so we know if we have reached the end of the animation.

This is the core of the animation and covers everything we need. It's very much packed together in the update function, but it is all required.

So we add it now to the aircraft such that it explodes when destroyed. Let's start with the `Aircraft` constructor.

```
mExplosion.setFrameSize(sf::Vector2i(256, 256));
mExplosion.setNumFrames(16);
mExplosion.setDuration(sf::seconds(1));

centerOrigin(mExplosion);
```

Here we set up our explosion. We define the size of one frame of the animation, the number of frames and the duration we want it to run for. We also center the animation sprite's origin, so that it is easier to position.

We will have to branch in our code to render either the normal aircraft or the explosion. It's not much but we still have to do it:

```
if (isDestroyed() && mShowExplosion)
    target.draw(mExplosion, states);
else
    target.draw(mSprite, states);
```

We cannot simply check for `isDestroyed()`, because we have no way of distinguishing between airplanes that are shot down or that leave the screen. We only want the former to explode—hence the Boolean variable `mShowExplosion`.

Also we have to remember that the animation must be updated or else it won't progress. The `return` statement prevents destroyed aircraft from further logic processing:

```
if (isDestroyed())
{
    checkPickupDrop(commands);
    mExplosion.update(dt);
    return;
}
```

This would run perfectly, except that right now the aircraft would be removed before the explosion would even be shown. We have to make sure the entity stays alive until the animation is over. We mark an aircraft for removal, as soon as it is destroyed, and either no explosion is shown (when it leaves the screen) or the explosion is finished:

```
bool Aircraft::isMarkedForRemoval() const
{
    return isDestroyed()
        && (mExplosion.isFinished() || !mShowExplosion);
}
```

And now we finally have our properly exploding planes, which give much more immersion to the game.

The Eagle has rolled!

It would be nice if the player's aircraft, the Eagle, turned around its roll axis (from nose to tail) when moving sideways. If the player moves left or right, the plane's inclination will change. Here, we don't need a full-fledged animation. It is enough to check whether the X velocity is negative (flying left) or positive (flying right), and to set the texture rect accordingly.

In the aircraft data table, we store for each plane a Boolean denoting whether it supports a roll animation. We assume that if it does, there are two texture rectangles located to right of the original rect, with the same size.

```
void Aircraft::updateRollAnimation()
{
    if (Table[mType].hasRollAnimation)
```

```
    {
        sf::IntRect textureRect = Table[mType].textureRect;

        // Roll left: Texture rect offset once
        if (getVelocity().x < 0.f)
            textureRect.left += textureRect.width;

        // Roll right: Texture rect offset twice
        else if (getVelocity().x > 0.f)
            textureRect.left += 2 * textureRect.width;

        mSprite.setTextureRect(textureRect);
    }
}
```

Post effects and shaders

You know those big budget games with dedicated graphics programmers on them?
One of the techniques they use is something called **post rendering** or **post effects**. It's
an effect that is applied after the scene has already been rendered. Using that data,
we perform whatever visual effect we want on it. One way to create effects is using
shaders, which we will delve into later.

The first thing to cover is how to perform a post effect, how it works, and then we
will actually create an effect called **bloom** using shaders.

Fullscreen post effects

Well, the effect has to be applied to the whole screen, otherwise it is pretty useless.
That is why we define a specific `PostEffect` class in order to make this a bit easier.

```
class PostEffect
{
    public:
        virtual             ~PostEffect();
        virtual void        apply(const sf::RenderTexture& input,
                                  sf::RenderTarget& output) = 0;

        static bool         isSupported();

    protected:
        static void         applyShader(const sf::Shader& shader,
                                        sf::RenderTarget& output);
};
```

This is an abstract class with some helper functions. `apply()` is the virtual function we have to define our effect code in. The `isSupported()` function checks if the graphics card supports post effects. This is only an alias for `sf::Shader::isAvailable()`; unless your GPU is ancient, it should be supported. The last function is `applyShader()`, and it is just a simple helper used internally by the derived class, so you don't have to bother with making sure you render over the entire output.

Now you might notice that the input argument to the post effect is a render texture. But up until now we have rendered everything to a render window. As you might remember, the post effect is applied on the resulting scene of the game. So we have to render the game graphics to an immediate buffer.

So in our `World` class, we create a render texture that we can use as this scene buffer:

```
mSceneTexture.create(mTarget.getSize().x, mTarget.getSize().y);
```

Not so very different than from creating a window, simpler even. We'll have to change our rendering code in the world, but thanks to the `sf::RenderTarget` interface this is an easy task. In this code, we also apply the check to see if post effects work on this computer:

```
void World::draw()
{
    if (PostEffect::isSupported())
    {
        mSceneTexture.clear();
        mSceneTexture.setView(mWorldView);
        mSceneTexture.draw(mSceneGraph);
        mSceneTexture.display();
        mBloomEffect.apply(mSceneTexture, mTarget);
    }
    else
    {
        mTarget.setView(mWorldView);
        mTarget.draw(mSceneGraph);
    }
}
```

We will get to the bloom effect later. We still have the `PostEffect::applyShader()` function left. This is where we perform the actual rendering, using a shader we will explain shortly:

```
void PostEffect::applyShader(const sf::Shader& shader,
sf::RenderTarget& output)
{
    sf::Vector2f outputSize = static_cast<sf::Vector2f>(output.
getSize());

    sf::VertexArray vertices(sf::TrianglesStrip, 4);
    vertices[0] = sf::Vertex(sf::Vector2f(0, 0),
sf::Vector2f(0, 1));
    vertices[1] = sf::Vertex(sf::Vector2f(outputSize.x, 0),
sf::Vector2f(1, 1));
    vertices[2] = sf::Vertex(sf::Vector2f(0, outputSize.y),
sf::Vector2f(0, 0));
    vertices[3] = sf::Vertex(sf::Vector2f(outputSize),
sf::Vector2f(1, 0));

    sf::RenderStates states;
    states.shader    = &shader;
    states.blendMode = sf::BlendNone;

    output.draw(vertices, states);
}
```

What we perform here is that we setup a quad using two triangles. This quad covers the entire target output. Here you see us define an instance of the sf::RenderStates class. The purpose of this class is to convey settings to the draw() call: the shader member sets the shader we want to use, while blendMode specifies the way how colors of the object and the render target are blended. With sf::BlendNone, we choose not to blend the colors, but to override all previous pixels in the render target.

You might notice that we are using `sf::TriangleStrip`, but still create a quad from it. Triangles are most often in favor as the primitive type quad has been declared obsolete in later versions of OpenGL. Luckily it is still backwards compatible, so you can use it in SFML if you want to get something up and running fast. For the difference between `sf::Triangle` and `sf::TriangleStrip` please look at the SFML documentation.

Shaders

So what is this word we have mentioned, but not really explained? Shaders themselves deserve their own book in order to be explained fully.

Previously the graphics pipeline has always been fixed. You put in vertices and you got out a fixed result based on that, you could only manipulate a very limited set of data and operations on the vertices.

Eventually came the programmable pipeline, for which there are a lot of details we unfortunately cannot cover. A **shader** in this pipeline is a program that is executed on the data you provide to the pipeline: vertices, textures, and much more. The key with shaders that makes them so desirable to use is that these operations are performed on the GPU, which is highly optimized. The CPU can then be used for other computations at the same time.

There are several different shader types, each with different purposes; however, SFML provides support for only vertex and fragment shaders. Since the API uses OpenGL as its backend, it also uses OpenGL shaders so the language used for writing the shaders is **GL Shading Language** (**GLSL**). We are afraid that this book won't be able to cover this language, but the resources on OpenGL's own webpage `www.opengl.org` are very helpful for this endeavor.

The bloom effect

Bloom is an effect which tries to mimic a defect in our eyes and cameras.

The effect has been a bit exaggerated in this demonstration picture, but this is what we are going for. When really strong light enters our eyes, it bleeds out over other parts that are not actually lit by the light. This is a visual artifact that actually does not exist in reality.

So how will we do this by using shaders? We are achieving the bloom effect in multiple shader passes. The output of a shader program can only be used as input in the next pass, which limits the possible operations per pass. Our bloom shader will consist of multiple steps; each step is implemented in its own GLSL program.

Let us start by defining a source image that we have as input to our bloom effect.

The first shader is the brightness pass; we filter out what is bright and what is not bright in the image by a simple threshold. The resulting image is mostly black:

Here we can see the different bright colors that should receive the bloom effect. Mostly, it is the bullets that we have made white just for this purpose.

If we simply added these colors to the scene colors, we wouldn't get the bloom effect. We would just get a very bright screen. That's not enough. We have to smooth out the texture. This is done by scaling down the texture and performing a Gaussian blur on it. This is done twice, so we end up with a result that is a quarter size of the original texture.

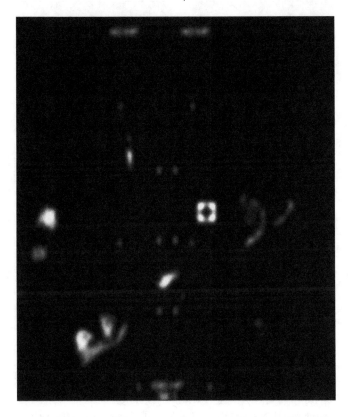

Now it's starting to look like something. What we do next is to add the blurred textures together, and add those to the original scene that we received at the start. For demonstration purposes, we cranked up the effect to make it impossible to miss. Normally you would want this effect to be more subtle.

Even the fire exhaust particles on the missile get some love from the post effect. After some further tweaking, you have a game that can really stand out.

So let's finally look at the code that is used to implement this effect. We are sorry that we will not be able to cover the shaders for you. But each one of them does one thing, so it's easy to get a grasp about what is happening in those files if you read them.

We define a class called `BloomEffect` that inherits and implements the abstract `PostEffect` class. We override the virtual function `apply()`:

```
void BloomEffect::apply(const sf::RenderTexture& input,
sf::RenderTarget& output)
{
    prepareTextures(input.getSize());
```

```
    filterBright(input, mBrightnessTexture);

    downsample(mBrightnessTexture, mFirstPassTextures[0]);
    blurMultipass(mFirstPassTextures);

    downsample(mFirstPassTextures[0], mSecondPassTextures[0]);
    blurMultipass(mSecondPassTextures);

    add(mFirstPassTextures[0], mSecondPassTextures[0],
     mFirstPassTextures[1]);
    mFirstPassTextures[1].display();
    add(input, mFirstPassTextures[1], output);
}
```

Here is the whole effect in its glory, well simplified. It goes through each step we talked about before. The only thing out of the ordinary here is the prepareTextures() function. This function sets up and creates the render textures we will need internally to create the effect. Of course, this could have been moved to the constructor, but this way the effect will always adapt to the size of the input.

```
void BloomEffect::prepareTextures(sf::Vector2u size)
{
    if (mBrightnessTexture.getSize() != size)
    {
        mBrightnessTexture.create(size.x, size.y);
        mBrightnessTexture.setSmooth(true);

        mFirstPassTextures[0].create(size.x / 2, size.y / 2);
        mFirstPassTextures[0].setSmooth(true);
        mFirstPassTextures[1].create(size.x / 2, size.y / 2);
        mFirstPassTextures[1].setSmooth(true);

        mSecondPassTextures[0].create(size.x / 4, size.y / 4);
        mSecondPassTextures[0].setSmooth(true);
        mSecondPassTextures[1].create(size.x / 4, size.y / 4);
        mSecondPassTextures[1].setSmooth(true);
    }
}
```

We have different texture sizes because the down sample process is the scaling down of the texture. So the texture itself has to be smaller as well. The rest of the functions perform the steps we explained before.

Here, you see the `sf::Shader` class in action. A reference to it is retrieved from a resource holder dedicated to shaders. The method `sf::Shader::setParameter()` passes values from C++ to the GLSL program. In the shader, you can access these values. `applyShader()` eventually performs the rendering and `display()` updates the render target.

```cpp
void BloomEffect::filterBright(const sf::RenderTexture& input,
sf::RenderTexture& output)
{
  sf::Shader& brightness = mShaders.get(Shaders::BrightnessPass);

  brightness.setParameter("source", input.getTexture());
  applyShader(brightness, output);
  output.display();
}

void BloomEffect::blurMultipass(RenderTextureArray& renderTextures)
{
  sf::Vector2u textureSize = renderTextures[0].getSize();

  for (std::size_t count = 0; count < 2; ++count)
  {
    blur(renderTextures[0], renderTextures[1], sf::Vector2f(0.f, 1.f /
textureSize.y));
    blur(renderTextures[1], renderTextures[0], sf::Vector2f(1.f /
textureSize.x, 0.f));
  }
}

void BloomEffect::blur(const sf::RenderTexture& input,
sf::RenderTexture& output, sf::Vector2f offsetFactor)
{
  sf::Shader& gaussianBlur = mShaders.get(Shaders::GaussianBlurPass);

  gaussianBlur.setParameter("source", input.getTexture());
  gaussianBlur.setParameter("offsetFactor", offsetFactor);
  applyShader(gaussianBlur, output);
  output.display();
}

void BloomEffect::downsample(const sf::RenderTexture& input,
sf::RenderTexture& output)
{
  sf::Shader& downSampler = mShaders.get(Shaders::DownSamplePass);
```

```
      downSampler.setParameter("source", input.getTexture());
      downSampler.setParameter("sourceSize", sf::Vector2f(input.
   getSize()));
      applyShader(downSampler, output);
      output.display();
   }

   void BloomEffect::add(const sf::RenderTexture& source, const
   sf::RenderTexture& bloom, sf::RenderTarget& output)
   {
      sf::Shader& adder = mShaders.get(Shaders::AddPass);

      adder.setParameter("source", source.getTexture());
      adder.setParameter("bloom", bloom.getTexture());
      applyShader(adder, output);
   }
```

If you find shaders interesting we recommend you read up on them. There is a lot of good information available on the subject, and it's a great tool to have to hand. Also definitely have a look at the shaders we have written.

Here's an example of a good and popular tutorial on GLSL:

`http://www.lighthouse3d.com/tutorials/glsl-tutorial`

Summary

Meanwhile, our aircraft shooter now deserves the name "game", as it is no longer some half-hearted sprites put together. We have seen a lot of modern graphical and rendering techniques and how they fit in our game. After an in-depth look at the rendering process (render targets, textures, vertices), we integrated a particle system for the missile, an animation for the explosion, and a shader for the bloom effect on the whole scene.

Note that there exist already implementations for many of the techniques shown in this chapter. In case you don't want to reinvent the wheel, you could have a look at the **Thor** library, which is developed by one of the authors of this book. Thor extends SFML by providing fully configurable particle systems and animations. Other features include color gradients, input and resource handlers, timer utilities, and much more. The library is available at `www.bromeon.ch/libraries/thor`.

In the next chapter we will cover how to play audio using SFML's Audio module. We will go through both streaming music and sound effects.

9
Cranking Up the Bass – Music and Sound Effects

Since the beginning of video games, sound has been a central media in games. Many games can be recognized only by listening to them. In the last few years, game industries have chosen to neglect audio in favor of better graphics; yet audio takes a very important part in a wide range of games. Independent studios in particular often put a huge effort in making games unique in their art style, which includes audio, graphics, and story. If used appropriately, music themes and sounds can have a tremendous impact on the atmosphere conveyed by a game.

In this chapter, we are going to cover the technical background of embedding audio into a game, taking the opportunity to have a closer look at SFML's Audio module. We are going to do the following:

- Play different music themes in the background
- Play sound effects that correspond to game events such as explosions
- Position sound effects in the 2D world to convey a feeling of spatial sound

Music themes

First, we want to play background music depending on the state we are currently in. We have prepared two themes: One for the menu, and one for the game itself. We'll define a corresponding `enum`:

```
namespace Music
{
    enum ID
    {
        MenuTheme,
        MissionTheme,
    };
}
```

We'll then create a class that has an interface dedicated to music playing:

```
class MusicPlayer : private sf::NonCopyable
{
    public:
                                MusicPlayer();

        void                    play(Music::ID theme);
        void                    stop();

        void                    setPaused(bool paused);
        void                    setVolume(float volume);

    private:
        sf::Music                               mMusic;
        std::map<Music::ID, std::string>        mFilenames;
        float                                   mVolume;
};
```

The method names should be self-explanatory. We have a single `sf::Music` instance that represents the currently-played music. The `mFilenames` variable maps music IDs to filenames and is initialized in the constructor. The volume takes a value between `0` and `100`; we'll initialize it to full volume. As SFML does not support the MP3 format, we'll use OGG for our files. If you are wondering how to convert between different formats, one possibility is the **Audacity** software (`http://audacity.sourceforge.net`).

```
MusicPlayer::MusicPlayer()
: mMusic()
, mFilenames()
, mVolume(100.f)
{
    mFilenames[Music::MenuTheme]    = "Media/Music/MenuTheme.ogg";
    mFilenames[Music::MissionTheme] = "Media/Music/MissionTheme.ogg";
}
```

Loading and playing

SFML uses the `sf::Music` class to deal with music themes. As already mentioned in *Chapter 2, Keeping Track of Your Textures – Resource Management*, this class behaves differently from other resource classes. Since music themes are usually long and may require a lot of memory, they are not loaded at once into RAM. Instead, `sf::Music` streams them from the source media, usually the hard disk. This means that only a short chunk is kept in memory at one time, with new ones loaded as the theme progresses. As a result, the source media must be available for as long as the music is played. For files, this means that you should not unplug an external storage device with the music on it. You can also load resources from different sources such as the RAM; in the case of music, *you* are responsible for their constant availability.

In the `MusicPlayer::play()` method, the path of the desired music is looked up in the map. The theme is loaded and possible loading errors are checked. The streaming nature is also the reason why the method of `sf::Music` to open a theme from the hard disk is named `openFromFile()` and not `loadFromFile()`.

```
void MusicPlayer::play(Music::ID theme)
{
    std::string filename = mFilenames[theme];

    if (!mMusic.openFromFile(filename))
        throw std::runtime_error("Music " + filename + " could not be
loaded.");

    mMusic.setVolume(mVolume);
    mMusic.setLoop(true);
    mMusic.play();
}
```

At the end, you can see some new statements. The `setVolume()` method sets the music's volume to a value in the range `[0, 100]`, with `0` being mute and `100` being the maximum volume. The `setLoop()` method specifies whether the theme is played again as soon as its end is reached; background themes are usually looped. The `play()` method eventually starts the music. Since music and sound effects use their own threads in SFML, you don't have to update them continuously. However, you have to keep the `sf::Music` object alive as long as the music is being played.

Music themes can be stopped or paused; for this purpose, `sf::Music` provides the `stop()` and `pause()` methods. If a theme is paused, you can resume it from the time where it was paused. A stopped music, in contrast, is replayed from the beginning. If we call `openFromFile()`, the music will automatically be stopped. The `getStatus()` method can be used to check which state the music is in. It returns one of the three enumerators in the `sf::Music` scope: `Playing`, `Paused`, or `Stopped`.

```cpp
void MusicPlayer::stop()
{
    mMusic.stop();
}

void MusicPlayer::setPaused(bool paused)
{
    if (paused)
        mMusic.pause();
    else
        mMusic.play();
}
```

Use case – In-game themes

We have seen that using music themes with SFML is very simple. We are now going to invoke the `MusicPlayer` routines in the different states of our game. First, the `Application` class gets a `MusicPlayer` instance and the `State::Context` class gets a new pointer, named `music`, to the music player.

In the menu state's constructor, we play the menu theme:

```cpp
MenuState::MenuState(StateStack& stack, Context context)
: State(stack, context)
, ...
{
    ...
    context.music->play(Music::MenuTheme);
}
```

We proceed analogously towards the game state, where we play the mission theme:

```cpp
GameState::GameState(StateStack& stack, Context context)
: State(stack, context)
, ...
{
    ...
    context.music->play(Music::MissionTheme);
}
```

If the application switches to one of these two states, the `MusicPlayer::play()` function will be called. This stops the current theme and results in a new theme being played.

When the user pauses the game, we would like the music to be paused as well. This can be handled in the `PauseState` constructor. We also define the `PauseState` destructor which resumes the music. As soon as the pause state is over, the music shall no longer pause.

```
PauseState::PauseState(StateStack& stack, Context context)
: State(stack, context)
, ...
{
    getContext().music->setPaused(true);
}

PauseState::~PauseState()
{
    getContext().music->setPaused(false);
}
```

At this point, playing different music themes in our game is completely operational. There are many ways to extend the current functionality: Playlists that play a sequence of themes in order; or smooth theme transitions implemented by continuous adaption of the music volume. Some modern games play different channels of a theme depending on the situation: In a passage where you have to pay attention, the music builds up tension; during an action scenario, the bass kicks in.

Sound effects

We have many gameplay events that can be represented by sounds: Fired machine guns, launched missiles, explosions, collection of pickups, and so on. Unlike music, sound effects are mostly very short. As a consequence, they can be loaded completely into memory, and we can also use the raw WAV format for these files without wasting too much memory. We are going to use the `sf::SoundBuffer` resource class to store the audio samples for our sound effects.

The following enumeration of sound effects is used in our game. We'll also create a `typedef` for the resource holder of `sf::SoundBuffer`.

```
namespace SoundEffect
{
    enum ID
    {
        AlliedGunfire,
        EnemyGunfire,
        Explosion1,
        Explosion2,
        LaunchMissile,
        CollectPickup,
        Button,
    };
}


typedef ResourceHolder<sf::SoundBuffer, SoundEffect::ID>
SoundBufferHolder;
```

We implement a class for the sound effects, one similar to the `MusicPlayer` class:

```
class SoundPlayer : private sf::NonCopyable
{
    public:
                        SoundPlayer();

        void            play(SoundEffect::ID effect);
        void            play(SoundEffect::ID effect,
                            sf::Vector2f position);

        void            removeStoppedSounds();
        void            setListenerPosition(sf::Vector2f position);
        sf::Vector2f    getListenerPosition() const;

    private:
        SoundBufferHolder       mSoundBuffers;
        std::list<sf::Sound>    mSounds;
};
```

The class contains a resource holder for the sound buffers and a list of currently active sound effects. Since more than one sound effect may be active at the same time, we need a container.

Loading, inserting, and playing

In the constructor, we load all of the sound effects. We do this by calling the
`SoundBufferHolder::load()` function, in a similar fashion to the textures and fonts
we loaded in earlier chapters. The first argument we pass is a `SoundEffect::ID`
enumerator, the second is the filename:

```
SoundPlayer::SoundPlayer()
: mSoundBuffers()
, mSounds()
{
    mSoundBuffers.load(SoundEffect::AlliedGunfire,
    "Media/Sound/AlliedGunfire.wav");
    mSoundBuffers.load(SoundEffect::EnemyGunfire,
    "Media/Sound/EnemyGunfire.wav");
    ...
}
```

How do we play a sound? First, we have to look up the correct sound buffer by
calling `SoundBufferHolder::get()`. We add a new `sf::Sound` instance that uses
this sound buffer to the list of sounds. Then, we obtain a reference to the sound and
call `sf::Sound::play()` to play the sound:

```
void SoundPlayer::play(SoundEffect::ID effect)
{
    mSounds.push_back(sf::Sound(mSoundBuffers.get(effect)));
    mSounds.back().play();
}
```

Instead of the `sf::Sound` constructor, you can also use the `setBuffer()` method to
initialize the sound buffer.

You might wonder why we took the `std::list` STL container. The problem with
`std::vector` is that it may relocate existing sounds as we add new ones, thus
invalidating them mid-play. Also, we cannot efficiently remove random elements from
a `std::vector` container without changing the element order. It is also important that
we first insert the sound and then play it. Otherwise, a copy would be inserted, and the
local sound object would stop playing as soon as it left scope.

Removing sounds

As soon as a sound effect has finished playing, there is no point of keeping it in the list any longer. We therefore provide a removeStoppedSounds() method which removes all sounds that have stopped. As soon as sf::Sound finishes playing, it automatically switches to the Stopped state. The method is written in a simple way, thanks to the std::list::remove_if() method and lambda expressions:

```
void SoundPlayer::removeStoppedSounds()
{
    mSounds.remove_if([] (const sf::Sound& s)
    {
        return s.getStatus() == sf::Sound::Stopped;
    });
}
```

Use case – GUI sounds

Our SoundPlayer object is instantiated as a member of the Application class, similar to MusicPlayer. It is also added to the State::Context structure:

```
class State
{
    public:
        struct Context
        {
            ...
            MusicPlayer*        music;
            SoundPlayer*        sounds;
        };
};
```

If a button is clicked, we would like to play an appropriate sound effect. We'll add a member SoundPlayer& mSounds to the Button class. We'll then adapt its constructor to take an entire Context object and initialize the reference to the sound player:

```
Button::Button(State::Context context)
: ...
, mSounds(*context.sounds)
{
    ...
}
```

In the `Button::activate()` method, which is called when a button is clicked, we'll play the corresponding sound:

```
void Button::activate()
{
    ...
    mSounds.play(SoundEffect::Button);
}
```

Several `Button` objects are instantiated in their corresponding state classes. As a short reminder, here is an excerpt of the constructor of such a state class. The context is passed to the buttons, which extracts the sound player from it. Additionally, the music theme is played in that constructor:

```
MenuState::MenuState(StateStack& stack, Context context)
: State(stack, context)
, ...
{
    auto playButton = std::make_shared<GUI::Button>(context);
    auto settingsButton = std::make_shared<GUI::Button>(context);
    auto exitButton = std::make_shared<GUI::Button>(context);
    ...

    context.music->play(Music::MenuTheme);
}
```

Now you'll hear a sound every time you activate a button.

Sounds in 3D space

The most interesting part about sound effects is yet to come. An immersive atmosphere only builds up if sounds are properly located within the game world. Like graphical objects, sounds can have a position.

The coordinate system for sounds is three-dimensional. SFML's sound API works with the `sf::Vector3f` type, a 3D vector with the members x, y, and z. SFML internally uses **Open Audio Library (OpenAL)**, an interface for low-level audio functionality, which is also the origin of the sound spatialization concepts we are going to discuss here. **Spatializing** sounds means nothing more than to locate them in the 3D space, that is, to give them a spatial representation.

The listener

The audition of spatial sound effects depends on the listener. A useful analogy is to compare the listener with your head. The listener's location and orientation can be described with the following three 3D vectors:

- **Position**: This vector describes where the listener is located in 3D space.

- **Up**: This vector tells where the top of the head points to. In SFML 2.0, the up vector is hardcoded to `(0, 1, 0)`, thus "up" lies always in the +Y direction.

- **Direction**: This vector expresses where the listener is "looking". It is a relative vector, not a position in space. SFML uses a default direction of `(0, 0, -1)`, meaning that the listener is headed towards the negative Z axis. It must be linearly independent from the up vector, so don't choose a direction with both X and Z axes set to zero. The direction vector need not have a unit length.

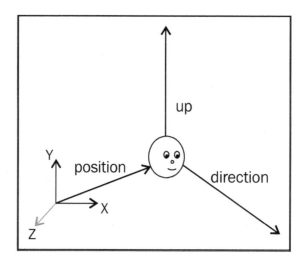

The orientation of the listener determines how sounds are perceived. If a sound is played on the right-hand side of the listener, the user will hear it in its right headphone. If you have a surround system, you will also be able to differentiate between front and rear sounds.

SFML provides the `sf::Listener` class which has the `setPosition()` and `setDirection()` methods to set the corresponding attributes. The `sf::Listener` class contains only static methods, it is not intended to be instantiated.

Attenuation factor and minimum distance

Close sounds are perceived louder than distant ones. The sound's volume is inversely proportional to its distance from the listener (we have a *1/distance* relationship, also known as the inverse distance model).

The **attenuation factor** determines how fast a sound is attenuated depending on the distance. The higher the factor, the weaker the sound becomes for a given distance or the closer the sound has to get to be played at a given volume.

The minimum distance is the distance between the listener and the sound at which 100 percent volume is achieved. If the sound comes closer, the volume will not increase anymore. If the sound goes further away, it will be attenuated.

The following figure should give you a better understanding of the perceived sound volume depending on its distance to the listener. There are two cases: Distances smaller than the minimum distance yield a constant volume of 100%, bigger distances lead to attenuated sounds depending on the attenuation factor.

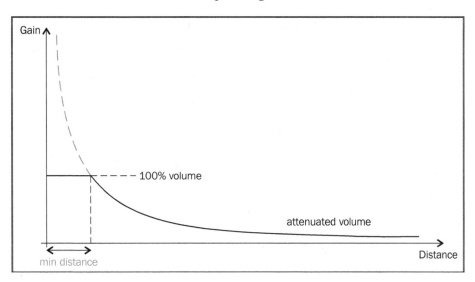

Attenuation factor and minimum distance are specific to each sound. SFML provides the setAttenuation() and setMinDistance() methods in the sf::Sound class. For sound spatialization, the setPosition() method is required to position a sound in space.

Positioning the listener

Our sounds are located in the plane of the monitor, thus their Z coordinate is always

0. But how do we place the listener? It is tempting to set the listener's Z coordinate to 0, just like the sounds. This is wrong. When you do this, a sound moving from left to right will pass directly through the listener. As a result, you first hear the sound only in the left ear, and only afterwards in the right ear. Even if the sound is very close, you will not hear it in both ears.

To get around this issue, we place the listener in a plane different than the sound — just like your head is in front of the monitor, and not inside it. The listener's Z coordinate therefore has a value greater than zero.

Let's say the 2D minimum distance is the number of world units between the listener's place in the 2D world and the sound. Since the listener itself resides outside the 2D world plane, the effective 3D minimum distance has to be computed with the Pythagorean theorem, as shown in the following figure:

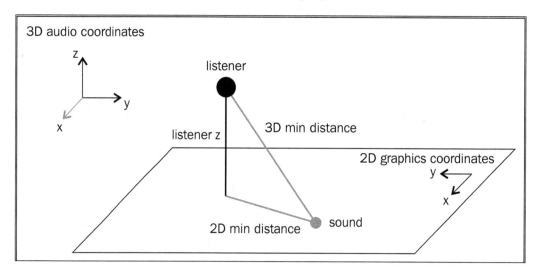

Playing spatial sounds

An important fact to keep in mind: To enable audio spatialization, the sound effects must have a single channel (mono). Stereo sounds are played at full volume, regardless of their position in space.

In `SoundPlayer.cpp`, we create an anonymous namespace for a few constants representing the measures discussed before. Don't hesitate to experiment with these values!

```cpp
namespace
{
    const float ListenerZ = 300.f;
    const float Attenuation = 8.f;
    const float MinDistance2D = 200.f;
    const float MinDistance3D =
        std::sqrt(MinDistance2D*MinDistance2D + ListenerZ*ListenerZ);
}
```

Now we need to connect the 3D audio coordinate system with our 2D graphics coordinate system. Both coordinate systems are completely unrelated; how to map one onto another depends on the use case. In the previous figure, you see how the axes of both coordinate systems are aligned.

We implement the remaining functions of the sound player, beginning with the listener's position. The X coordinate is the same in both graphics and audio system. The Y coordinate needs to be negated, as the audio up vector is in the +Y direction, but on the screen, the Y axis points downwards. For the Z coordinate, we take the constant distance between the listener and the screen plane:

```cpp
void SoundPlayer::setListenerPosition(sf::Vector2f position)
{
    sf::Listener::setPosition(position.x, -position.y, ListenerZ);
}
```

Next, we define the second overload of the `play()` function, which takes a 2D graphics position. To compute the 3D audio position, we again need to negate Y, but here we use Z=0. We also set the attenuation and minimum distance for the sound. Finally, the sound is played:

```cpp
void SoundPlayer::play(SoundEffect::ID effect, sf::Vector2f position)
{
    mSounds.push_back(sf::Sound());
    sf::Sound& sound = mSounds.back();

    sound.setBuffer(mSoundBuffers.get(effect));
    sound.setPosition(position.x, -position.y, 0.f);
    sound.setAttenuation(Attenuation);
    sound.setMinDistance(MinDistance3D);

    sound.play();
}
```

Now, we must make sure that non-spatialized sounds (such as a button click) are still played correctly. If we move the listener, all sounds will be affected, which is not always what we want. In our first `play()` overload, we make sure the sound is played directly in front of the listener, so it will have maximum volume. The `getListenerPosition()` function transforms the 3D listener position back to 2D graphics coordinates:

```
void SoundPlayer::play(SoundEffect::ID effect)
{
    play(effect, getListenerPosition());
}
```

Use case – In-game sound effects

That was a lot of theory; let's get back to the interesting stuff. We want to embed sound effects in our game and play them whenever appropriate. Before we can do that, we need access to the sound player; we let `GameState` pass a `SoundPlayer` reference to our `World` class.

Inside the world, we would like to have a dedicated scene node for sounds, so that we can use our command system to play sounds. We'll add a `SoundNode` class, which is a simple adapter to the `SoundPlayer` class:

```
class SoundNode : public SceneNode
{
    public:
        explicit        SoundNode(SoundPlayer& player);
        void            playSound(SoundEffect::ID sound,
                                  sf::Vector2f position);

        virtual unsigned int    getCategory() const;

    private:
        SoundPlayer&            mSounds;
};
```

The function definitions are not particularly interesting. The `getCategory()` method returns a new `SoundEffect` category, while `playSound()` forwards its arguments to the `mSounds` sound player. The sound node is inserted into the scene graph in `World::buildScene()`.

Anyway, this allows us to define a `playLocalSound()` method for entities, which sends a command to the sound node. As all of our current sound effects are related to airplanes, we define `playLocalSound()` in the `Aircraft` class; but it would also be possible to have it in the `Entity` or `SceneNode` base classes:

```
void Aircraft::playLocalSound(CommandQueue& commands, SoundEffect::ID effect)
{
    Command command;
    command.category = Category::SoundEffect;
    command.action = derivedAction<SoundNode>(
    std::bind(&SoundNode::playSound,
            _1, effect, getWorldPosition()));

    commands.push(command);
}
```

The `std::bind()` call might look more confusing than it actually is. It converts the `SoundNode::playSound()` function to a functor, using the following parameters:

- `_1`: This is the first parameter of `Command::action` (namely `SceneNode&`), which is interpreted as the `this` pointer of `SoundNode::playSound()`
- `effect`: This is the sound effect ID
- `getWorldPosition()`: This is the position where the sound is played

Now we've written this method once, so we don't have to fiddle with commands every time we want to play a sound. Next, we implement the sound effects for launching a missile and firing the machine gun. In the case of the machine gun, we create different sound effects for the player and enemies. In total, we only have to add two `playLocalSound()` calls:

```
void Aircraft::checkProjectileLaunch(sf::Time dt, CommandQueue& commands)
{
    ...
    if (mIsFiring && mFireCountdown <= sf::Time::Zero)
    {
        playLocalSound(commands, isAllied() ?
        SoundEffect::AlliedGunfire : SoundEffect::EnemyGunfire);
        ...
    }

    if (mIsLaunchingMissile)
    {
        playLocalSound(commands, SoundEffect::LaunchMissile);
        ...
    }
}
```

For the explosions, the approach is very similar. In order to add variety, we randomly choose one of two possible sound effects. For the pickup collection, which is performed in `World::handleCollisions()`, we proceed in a slightly different manner. Since we are in the `World` class and not a scene node, we invoke `playLocalSound()` on the player's aircraft:

```
else if (matchesCategories(pair, Category::PlayerAircraft,
Category::Pickup))
{
    auto& player = static_cast<Aircraft&>(*pair.first);
    auto& pickup = static_cast<Pickup&>(*pair.second);

    pickup.apply(player);
    pickup.destroy();
    player.playLocalSound(mCommandQueue, SoundEffect::CollectPickup);
}
```

Because we are in the `World` class, we could directly call `SoundPlayer::play()`; however, we still use `SoundNode` for symmetry reasons. If the implementation of `Aircraft::playLocalSound()` or `SoundNode::playSound()` changes, the modifications will still be applied to all spatial sound effects.

The last thing we need to do is to update the listener and remove the sounds that have finished playing. We'll set the listener to the player's aircraft position, so that the player shares the audial position of its pilot. We'll add a function which is invoked in `World::update()`:

```
void World::updateSounds()
{
    mSounds.setListenerPosition(
        mPlayerAircraft->getWorldPosition());
    mSounds.removeStoppedSounds();
}
```

Summary

In this chapter, we have covered the basic topics for dealing with audio in 2D games. We saw how the concepts are implemented using SFML classes and functions. In particular, we played different music themes depending on the application state. We also created sound effects for various in-game events, and positioned them in the world in order to enable a spatial audition.

With this knowledge, you are now able to incorporate audio into your game; a crucial component for creating an immersive gaming experience. As you have seen during this chapter, SFML makes the implementation very simple. The actual challenge is the fine-tuning and the combination of suitable sound effects and music themes in order to create a unique atmosphere.

The audio functionality completes the attempt to create a playable game that uses different sources of media. However, so far, only one player can play it. In the next chapter, we are going to improve the situation by adding multiplayer support.

10

Company Atop the Clouds – Co-op Multiplayer

After a long journey through to the book, with lots of lessons learned, we have now arrived at the last chapter. This is where we will handle a topic with growing importance in the modern times — networking. This subject shall not be overlooked as it can be very difficult to learn and implement. It is complicated enough for people to actually dedicate their careers on dealing exclusively with it. Usually network programmers are very experienced and good at it, so they can do it efficiently and provide a good multiplayer gameplay to the end users.

Obviously, even if we wanted to, we couldn't teach every single thing about network programming, good practices, and different implementations. However, we try to pass on some knowledge on how to achieve a multiplayer experience, keeping things as simple as possible. Based on the game we've built so far throughout the book, we now add two new concepts: local cooperation and actual network gameplay over the Internet.

The following is what this chapter has to teach essentially:

- Network sockets
- Client-server architecture
- Creating a protocol for communication
- Applying the concepts to our game
- Short introduction on latency problems
- Tips and tricks on cheating prevention

Let's now immerse ourselves in this complicated topic with a short introduction.

Playing multiplayer games

We've seen multiplayer games since computer games emerged – decades ago. We are used to calling friends and family to play games with us, sometimes in a co-operative mode with common goals and other times for a competitive experience. The point is that playing with someone else is usually lots of fun!

There was a time when the Internet barely existed, or simply put, people's connections were too slow to actually have a good online experience. By then, it was very usual for games to have a local multiplayer mode. This allowed a big trend for split screen and other types of local multiplayer gameplay. **Local Area Network (LAN)** multiplayer was also implemented as a way to make the experience more cooperative to players, and as a result, you could actually cooperate or fight with your friends over a cable or wireless network. Unfortunately, as time passed and the Internet became more powerful, the local multiplayer modes became less and less used, and actual online multiplayer modes started to be the dish of the day. Either mode is not extinguished or anything close to that, but the game market seems to mark a tendency for online games.

For the purpose of this book, and to cover the networking field of programming, we will be not be focusing on local modes, but rather will implement a fully-networked concept. However, fear not! We will show you a concept that game developers use a lot these days which allows you to actually have local co-op on top of a networked architecture!

Interacting with sockets

First of all, in order to go deeper in to network programming, we need to understand how computers communicate with each other. This is the technological base that everyone should know before trying to do anything with networking.

This topic is not simple by itself, but it can be approached more easily without the need to understand the deeper concepts, with the help of SFML's socket classes.

A **socket** is essentially a gateway for data. You can visualize it as a link between two applications. These applications are *virtual*, in the sense, they only matter in the network, but are not necessarily different application processes, because you can use sockets to connect an application to itself, as we do in this chapter. These sockets are the base of all networked programs; therefore, they are extremely important. As sockets are a rather complicated concept, SFML provides classes to manage them.

There are the following two main ways of communicating between multiple machines:

TCP

Transmission Control Protocol (TCP) is a network convention for transferring data between computers. This means that any operating system or platform that is connected to the Internet and therefore uses the **Internet Protocol (IP)**, which TCP is built on top of, is able to communicate in a uniform way. This is why in a networked application, we don't care who we are "talking" to, as long as the remote peer can "speak" TCP/IP, communication is possible.

For example, when you use your Internet browser, some websites will be hosted in Linux machines while others will be in Windows. Because they all use TCP/IP, it is not relevant what the operating system is, the website will be transferred to our browser and we will be able to visualize it just the same.

SFML provides two cross-platform classes for using TCP sockets: `sf::TcpSocket` and `sf::TcpListener`, which are exactly what we will use to achieve an online gameplay in this chapter. The `sf::TcpSocket` class initiates TCP connections, while the `sf::TcpListener` class listens on a certain port for an incoming connection.

Please note that TCP/IP is a high-level protocol in your operating system. When you use it, many things are being managed by the OS, which takes some weight out of your back.

The TCP protocol comes with the following features by default:

- **Packet ordering**: It will ensure packet ordering so you can assume that your data will arrive to the destination in the same order you sent it.
- **Packet restructuring**: It also provides packet restructuring facilities, completely built in. This means that if a packet is too big, it will be split into smaller ones to make the network transfer possible while still arriving at the destination in a seamless way.
- **Reliability**: It is another strong aspect of this protocol. It will ensure every that packet gets to the destination, without exceptions. If one packet fails to arrive, the protocol just stalls and is assumed to have lost its connection. However, before a packet is assumed to be impossible to transfer, it is re-sent many times in an attempt to eventually deliver it successfully.

In order to exchange data between computers, this protocol demands that a connection or a tunnel is made first. This means that before sending or receiving data, both machines must "shake hands" and create a tunnel of information between them. This is done when one of them enters a listening state on a specific port, using `sf::TcpListener`, and the other uses `sf::TcpSocket` to connect to that port. Once that connection is successfully established, data is free to roam!

A **network port** is an integer number, normally ranging from 0 to 65535, which defines a "gateway" in your network where data and connections can pass through to your application's sockets. You are free to pick what port(s) your game will use for communication as long as you do the following:

- Be careful not to pick reserved ports by your operating system.
- Avoid picking ports that are commonly used by other programs, which will cause a conflict. For example, port 80 is used very often by web servers, remote desktop apps, and others. As a general rule, avoid using ports below 1024.
- Make sure both the client and the server know the same port so communication can happen.

Besides the obligation to establish a connection in order to communicate, this protocol offers advantages such as, ordered arrival of data and reliable data sending. The first means that the order in which you send your bytes to the remote peer matters because they will get there in the same order! The latter means that the data is guaranteed to arrive at the destination. This is very good for many uses, even essential, but unfortunately, it adds an extra overhead to the network performance that some real-time games cannot cope with. Imagine you send packet A, B, and C, in order. Let's say your Internet connection isn't in its best shape and packet B keeps getting lost before arriving at the remote peer. This means that A will get to the destination, but B and C won't until B is sent successfully.

That said, we can conclude that this protocol is very adequate for file transfers and other reliable data transfers, as well as for smaller games which are less hungry for network performance. But it may be too slow for some real-time action games, which have higher speed requirements.

UDP

User Datagram Protocol (UDP) is another often used tool for network programming. Communicating data to another computer means simply pushing an array of bytes to the network, so it is very similar to TCP/IP in this matter; however, UDP has a very different set of rules.

The first important thing about this protocol is to know that it is *connectionless*. You can't establish a tunnel of reliable data. You just take your data and send it somewhere and it either gets there or not, and you are not notified of it.

This may seem strange at first. You may think "Why would I want to send data that may not even get there?" and it is normal to be suspicious about the utility of such a network protocol at first, but you'll understand how powerful it can become if made right.

The strong aspect about this protocol is that data is sent fast and there is no overhead on ensuring packet ordering or arrival. So, people usually implement a custom protocol on top of UDP that allows sending some data reliably, by sending data continuously until a confirmation of arrival is received, while other data is sent unreliably.

Another important key difference of UDP and TCP is that UDP will not split a packet into smaller parts when it exceeds the maximum limit of data size; you have to take care of that manually. While in TCP you can neglect such things, in UDP, it's important to keep packets small and efficient.

To use such sockets, SFML provides `sf::UdpSocket`. You just need to create an object of this type, bind to a port with the `sf::UdpSocket::bind()` function, and then either send data through it or check if anything was received using the `sf::UdpSocket::send()` and `sf::UdpSocket::receive()` functions respectively.

We won't be covering UDP sockets in the chapter, but the SFML documentation and tutorials on `www.sfml-dev.org` should provide what you need in order to understand them in detail.

Socket selectors

Another facility that SFML provides is the `sf::SocketSelector` class. This one is not used in the book's game, but it is very useful and will make your life easier if you choose to use it.

This class will act as an observer for your sockets. It will hold pointers to every socket you choose to register in it. Then, you may simply call `sf::SocketSelector::wait()` and it will return when one or more of the sockets receive some data. Once this happens, you handle the data somehow and call the function again. This will ensure you always are notified of packets and handle them in a simple and centralized manner.

You can call `sf::SocketSelector::add()` for any type of socket and listener: `sf::TcpListener`, `sf::TcpSocket`, or `sf::UdpSocket`.

It is this simple; you create the sockets, add them to the selector, and then call `sf::SocketSelector::wait()`. When it returns, you know one of the sockets received something or a new peer has been connected. You just check who that was by using `sf::SocketSelector::isReady(socket)` and then act upon it.

Custom protocols

We've talked about TCP and UDP so far, which are two socket types that are used widely. Programmers don't usually program anything that is "lower-level" than those two, but very often build custom protocols on top of them.

It is very useful to create such protocols as they allow us to abstract the more complex tasks of networking, and orient a network system into being more focused on a specific task. For a quick example, we can look at the FTP protocol. It allows sending files in a quick and simple way, because it has abstracted the more complex process of actually transferring that file over a lower-level protocol.

A **custom protocol** is merely a set of rules set in stone of how communication needs to happen. When a custom protocol is created, it either sits on top of TCP or UDP or even both; but it automatically absorbs all advantages and limitations of the underlying protocol.

There are many custom protocols that are used widely. For example, HTTP and FTP are two protocols that are used worldwide and are implemented on top of TCP/IP. You use them all the time without knowing; for example, when you open a web page in your Internet browser, it was received through the TCP/IP network protocol, more specifically with the rules of the HTTP protocol.

As if SFML's basic socket support weren't good enough, it also implements `sf::Http` and `sf::Ftp`, which you can use to communicate with any machine that is implementing them too! This is a fantastic tool that you can use to your advantage, for example, to directly transfer files to FTP servers, or to request web pages from remote hosts using HTTP. We won't cover such classes, as they go out of the scope of the book, but to bring up your curiosity, you could use `sf::Http` to send some data to a website that would handle it and do something useful with it. For example, that website could receive a high score information and immediately list it online for everyone to see!

We will be implementing one custom protocol as well in the upcoming section *Creating the structure for multiplayer*. It will be our own set of rules that are specific to our own game. It will lie on top of the TCP/IP protocol and you will just see how it can be used to make multiple instances of our game understand each other.

Data transport

We already know some things about how sockets behave and their inner workings, but we only talked about sending and receiving data in an abstract way. We referred to the data as arrays of bytes, which we simply send and receive, but how is it done?

Indeed, what is passed on through the network is merely a block of data, a collection of raw bytes. Therefore, it must be sent in a way that can be read again by the remote machine. Your data could be anything, text, numbers, images, sound, or pretty much anything that is digital.

For this, we pack and unpack our data into a byte array when sending/receiving it! When we use the term **packet**, we refer to a collection of bytes, which contain one or more primitives (integers, floats, and others). This is very efficient from the perspective that we don't have additional overhead for sending multiple primitives; they all go at once in the same byte array. However, we have a per-packet overhead, namely the packet headers that are required by the lower-level protocols (most notably IP and TCP/UDP).

Packing and unpacking is not a complicated thing to do, but can be troublesome to get right when done from scratch.

To add complexity to this task, you can't make assumptions on what byte ordering system the target machine is using. There are big-endian and little-endian operating systems, which mean a different ordering of bytes in memory. You can look at it as reversing the order of the bits of a variable. Therefore, for example, the number 3 in a little-endian system, when transferred to a big-endian one is not the number 3 anymore, as the bits were reversed. This needs to be taken into account.

Luckily, SFML has also solved this! You can and should use the `sf::Packet` class to address this issue. It is very simple to work with and it will make your life easier in every way, as opposed to implementing it all from scratch. If properly understanding the socket functionality is half of the work, understanding packets would be the other half into making a good networked application.

The following code shows how to pack some data and send it:

```
sf::Packet packet;
std::string myString = "Hello Sir!";
sf::Int32 myNumber = 20;
sf::Int8 myNumber2 = 3;
packet << myString << myNumber << myNumber2;
mySocket.send(packet);
```

This is as easy as it gets. You should notice the use of the operator <<. SFML implemented it to make it more simple and readable, allowing to chain many items in a single line, all being packed correctly within sf::Packet.

Then, on the other end of the network, the following code shows to unpack that same data:

```
sf::Packet packet;
std::string myString;
sf::Int32 myNumber;
sf::Int8 myNumber2;
mySocket.receive(packet);
packet >> myString >> myNumber >> myNumber2;
```

Easy enough, isn't it? Now we know to use sockets, send and receive data; but how do we know what data are we reading? An application will most likely want to act differently upon receiving different packets, right? This is where it comes handy to implement a custom protocol—a way to understand what the data really is for and what to do with it.

Network architectures

Regardless of socket types and protocols, games take different approaches in the architecture of the multiplayer mode.

We call the playable game application a *client*, network-wise, and this part of the book concerns how clients communicate with each other and who they communicate with.

There are at least two major approaches to a networked simulation.

Peer-to-peer

This architecture was and still is used in online games; however, it fits a very specific set of purposes and is used less widely than its counterpart client-server architecture.

Nevertheless, its importance should be noticed and mentioned every time networking is the topic. What defines this architecture is essentially the fact that every game client in the simulation connects to each other. You can see it in the following figure:

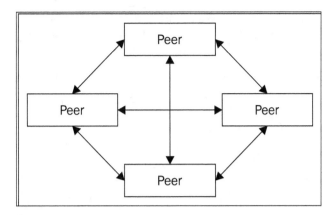

These inter-connections between all the clients, which somehow resemble a spider's web, mean that every client has a connection with every client. This way, they effectively communicate correctly, allowing chatting with each other, seeing each other's movements, and other actions. When a client means to do something, such as when the jump key is pressed and the character should jump, it notifies every other client of this, so they can see it happen too.

However, while this approach can be efficient, as the network processing is done among all clients, it introduces a nasty set of disadvantages that unfortunately can't be avoided.

The major problem with the technique is that cheating cannot be prevented. A client will just do whatever it wants to do and notify all the others of it. Players can and they will exploit your game's weaknesses whenever there are any and destroy the fun of the game to other players.

So, how will we make sure the clients can't do anything outside of the allowed actions? That's where the other network architecture kicks in!

Client-server architecture

Alright, this is a very, very important subject. This is nearly the standard as far as multiplayer gaming goes. Learn this concept well and you're gold. This will be particularly useful for nearly all networking tasks you will be doing and not exclusively games.

Why is it so important? First, because it allows a central instance to control everything, and therefore provides the possibility to implement means of security. The following figure shows how computers are laid in such architecture:

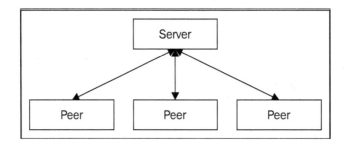

Here, you see there is a central server, or group of servers (distributed systems) that communicate with all the clients. Now, a client does not know, under any circumstances, about other client's address or information. The server acts as a proxy, or a bridge between the client's communications. However, saying the server is merely a bridge for communication is a reductive view of what it really does.

Authoritative servers

In reality, having one server manage all of the clients and be in charge of all their communications easily puts the server application under a heavy processing and networking load. It is hard to develop and maintain efficient and fast servers that can hold many clients at once. However, this cost is easily compensated by the advantages this architecture inherently gives us. The most notable feature is the authority of the server, entirely preventing the cheating and exploiting by the players.

How is this achieved, you may ask? It is easy to explain and a bit harder to get right while developing, but what happens, in essence, is that the server holds the true and absolute state of the simulation, and only the data being simulated in the server application is considered valid. This way, each client will only receive valid state information about the server and will always have correct and proper values in the simulation.

On the other hand, the server may check for every packet received from clients, and easily deduce what is possible to do under the constraints of the simulation. When the server checks a client input, it is possible to analyze it in order to know if that input is valid or is an attempt at cheating. If the server is programmed well to do these checks, its internal state remains valid and accurate. A player may modify its client to do weird things that were not programmed that way initially, that we cannot prevent, but as long as the input that comes from that client is checked, the other players won't even notice a difference, because what the cheating client sees is merely a local version and the server, which is still intact.

This is the basis for all cheat prevention in online servers. It works effectively and is an important area that must never be neglected. For the sake of simplicity, in our implementation, the server is not entirely authoritative, so cheating would be possible.

Creating the structure for multiplayer

You must be fed up with networking theory by now, and you actually want to see some code! Right, it is now time to start the concrete implementation of our game server.

In order to extend our game and add an online mode to it, we went ahead and created a new state `MultiplayerGameState`, which is very similar to `GameState` at first. In the following code snippet, you see the important parts of the class definition. As you see, the three typical state-related methods to draw, update, and handle events are again there, as well as the variables for the world, window, and texture holder. Several variables are new related to the management of different players and socket connections:

```cpp
class MultiplayerGameState : public State
{
    public:
                            MultiplayerGameState(StateStack& stack,
                                Context context, bool isHost);

        virtual void        draw();
        virtual bool        update(sf::Time dt);
        virtual bool        handleEvent(const sf::Event& event);
        ...


    private:
        void                updateBroadcastMessage(
                                sf::Time elapsedTime);
        void                handlePacket(sf::Int32 packetType,
                                sf::Packet& packet);


    private:
        typedef std::unique_ptr<Player> PlayerPtr;


    private:
        World                   mWorld;
        sf::RenderWindow&       mWindow;
        TextureHolder&          mTextureHolder;
```

```
std::map<int, PlayerPtr>       mPlayers;
std::vector<sf::Int32>         mLocalPlayerIdentifiers;
sf::TcpSocket                  mSocket;
bool                           mConnected;
std::unique_ptr<GameServer>    mGameServer;
sf::Clock                      mTickClock;

std::vector<std::string>       mBroadcasts;
sf::Text                       mBroadcastText;
sf::Time                       mBroadcastElapsedTime;

...
}
```

We changed the main menu appropriately to accommodate the newly created `Host` and `Join` options. To avoid creating one state for each of those options, we created a custom constructor for `MultiplayerGameState`, which takes a parameter clearly stating whether this state will be hosting or just joining. You can see those changes in `StateStack.cpp`. Because both modes are almost equal, it wouldn't even make sense to have another state. The only difference is that if the state is the host, it will launch a background server in its constructor and shut it down again in its destructor! By this logic, we can say that `MultiplayerGameState` is the client-side of our application and `GameServer` is the server-side.

Working with the Server

Now it is time to put our hands on the actual server! We will be dissecting the `GameServer` class to understand properly what is going on.

Server thread

To begin with, we decided to put the server in a separate thread. This is very useful in many ways. For once, server processing can be intensive and could hurt the frame rate on the client. On the other hand, if the server is running on a parallel thread, aside from improving its performance, it also allows it to perform blocking calls whenever necessary, and the game keeps running smoothly. Another plus in this approach is that our server does not communicate programmatically with the client, it communicates only via network; therefore, we don't even need to care about synchronization between the two. It is just like as if server is running on a different application!

As we have already introduced `sf::Thread` before in *Chapter 5*, *Diverting the Game Flow – State Stack*, we will skip that topic here. It is important to notice that `GameServer::executionThread()` is the thread function and that it starts running when `GameServer` gets constructed, and is stopped before it gets destructed.

Now, inside `GameServer::executionThread()` is where all the magic happens. First rule is that while `executionThread()` doesn't return a value, the parallel thread is alive. There are three main logical steps in the server thread: initialization, the server loop, and termination. Take a look at this pseudo-code:

```
void GameServer::executionThread()
{
    initialize();
    while (!timeToStop) loop();
    shutdown();
}
```

Not unlike the client-side of the game, we must do the appropriate things in the proper places. In the initialization phase, just when the server thread starts, we are going to tell the `sf::TcpListener` socket to start accepting new connections. This is what allows the players to join our server. Also, we initialize some timing variables here to be used in the server loop later. As you may notice, there isn't that much to initialize at this point as the world is still empty without any ally or enemy aircraft, and the basic variables are initialized by the constructor.

Then, we enter the server loop, which will simply keep executing until the `while` loop ends, either by a forced termination of the thread, which is not recommended, or by setting the `timeToStop` Boolean variable to `true`, effectively ending the `while` loop at the end of the next step.

Server loop

Without a doubt, this part is the most important, and while many programmers take different paths in the process of creating a server loop, we did it in a way that is not unusual to see across programs. The following is the simplified anatomy of each step in the loop:

```
handleIncomingPackets();
handleIncomingConnections();

while (stepTime >= stepInterval)
{
    updateLogic();
    stepTime -= stepInterval;
}
while (tickTime >= tickInterval)
{
    tick();
    tickTime -= tickInterval;
}

sf::sleep(sf::milliseconds(50));
```

The first two functions are going to respectively handle all incoming traffic from the connected peers and accept new connections, if there are any. Then, `updateLogic()` will be very similar to the client's `update()` functions; it will simply perform the evolution of data over time, to keep the server's state always up-to-date. The next function, `tick()`, is very similar to the previous update step, but usually executes fewer times and is used to send a snapshot of the server's state to the clients. In our case, we send updates to the clients 20 times per second. We may call this frequency the **tick rate**.

Just to be clear, the main reason `tick()` and `updateLogic()` functions are not merged is because they run at different rates. This is to save processing time and network bandwidth, as sending too many packets too often would just put a heavy load on the network with no benefits. Ideally, we want to send as little data as possible but making sure it is enough to accomplish the gameplay demands. This way, `updateLogic()` runs a lot faster to always keep the data as refreshed as possible, while `tick()` only performs as few times as necessary to make sure the client has an accurate version of the server state locally at all times.

Finally, the call to `sf::sleep()` is entirely optional; however, it is not a bad idea to tell the thread to sleep a bit and let the client's thread take the processor for itself for a little while. The bigger time you pass to `sf::sleep()`, the less time will be spent on server's tasks. It will be fine just until the server has too many tasks to perform and too little time to do them.

Before heading to the depths of these functions, let's rest a bit by looking at the data structures we will use, and how they are laid out.

Peers and aircraft

The multiplayer version of our game is a little different than its single-player counterpart. Now, each client can have one or two local aircraft objects, but many clients can be connected simultaneously. Though, one client is always one peer in the eyes of the server. A peer by itself can contain multiple aircraft. Therefore the server always knows how many clients are connected, how many aircraft are in the game and which peers they belong to:

```
struct RemotePeer
{
                                    RemotePeer();

    sf::TcpSocket               socket;
    sf::Time                    lastPacketTime;
    std::vector<sf::Int32>      aircraftIdentifiers;
    bool                        ready;
    bool                        timedOut;
};
```

The preceding code snippet shows the structure of `RemotePeer`, which is declared inside `GameServer`. The constructor merely initializes the peer's data to an invalid state, which by itself means the peer is instanced, but not yet pointing to an actual client. The socket variable is the TCP socket we mentioned earlier in the chapter that we will use to communicate exclusively with a specific peer. The `lastPacketTime` variable always contains the timestamp of the last packet received from that peer. This is used to deduct disconnections and timeouts by a simple rule: If the peer did not send any data after *n* seconds, kick it out because something is wrong, as there are packets that the client has to compromise to send regularly.

The `aircraftIdentifiers` variable is an interesting one. It holds a list of IDs of all the planes that belong to a specific peer. There is a good reason there is only an integer here: All the aircraft data is centralized in `GameServer`, and is easily referred to in there by using this integer ID, if needed.

The `ready` Boolean variable refers exactly to the valid or invalid state of the peer connection. It only becomes `true` after a successful connection and sending the world state to the newly connected socket.

The `timedOut` variable is just a flag that is set in the server logic to tell the `handleDisconnections()` function that this peer needs to be erased.

```
std::size_t                         mAircraftCount;
std::map<sf::Int32, AircraftInfo>   mAircraftInfo;
std::vector<PeerPtr>                mPeers;
```

The preceding code snippet shows where all the peers are stored, as well as the mentioned aircraft data. `mAircraftCount` will always contain the total of human-controlled aircraft in the world at a time. Their data can be queried using `mAircraftInfo`, through the `struct` declared as follows:

```
// Structure to store information about current aircraft state
struct AircraftInfo
{
    sf::Vector2f               position;
    sf::Int32                  hitpoints;
    sf::Int32                  missileAmmo;
    std::map<sf::Int32, bool>  realtimeActions;
};
```

Yes, it is very simple. It only holds the position of the aircraft and the set of real-time actions the player is currently performing, such as moving and shooting.

The size of mPeers is always the number of truly connected peers plus one. That extra peer that is never valid exists for a single purpose: To become valid once a new connection is established. And when that peer becomes valid, another invalid one is created for the same purpose! This way, new peers are always added at the end and can be removed from the middle of std::vector without problems, as the "standby" peer is always guaranteed to be at the last position of the array. The number of truly connected peers can be queried with mConnectedPlayers. There is a chance you are still struggling to understand why this extra peer is kept in the vector. Well, it had to be somewhere since sf::TcpListener::accept() requires it, so it was just a decision as any other when designing the code. Eventually, we insert the peer to the vector anyway, so it is reasonable to construct it there in advance.

```
sf::Int32  mAircraftIdentifierCounter;
```

The aircraft identifier counter is an integer that starts at 1 and grows by one every time a new aircraft is added to the world. This guarantees that no matter how many aircraft join and leave the world; new ones will always be assigned new unique identifiers. Also, we would like to emphasize the difference between mConnectedPlayers and mAircraftCount. While the former refers to unique connected peers or clients, the latter refers to unique airplanes present in the game.

Hot Seat

Our approach allows the handling of multiple aircraft in a single peer. This makes our system inherently apt to handle what the gaming community refers to as **Hot Seat** multiplayer. It really only stands for local cooperative gameplay, where the same gaming machine is used by more than one player in a single game session.

For this reason, our sample allows this mode at any time. As soon as you press the *Return* key, a second aircraft will join the game, and while you're actually playing a networked game with a real server, it will seem like one of those old-school game sessions, where you would be the friend or foe of your friends throughout the game.

Accepting new clients

About accepting incoming connections, the responsible object to do this is our mListenerSocket, which is of type sf::TcpListener. As long as the mConnectedPlayers value is below mMaxConnectedPlayers, that connection is accepted. If this condition is not met, the socket entirely stops listening for new connections, effectively rejecting them all.

The `sf::TcpListener::accept()` function is where the connection actually succeeds, generating a valid tunnel for communication between the peer and the server. It takes an already-instanced socket which is initialized in case of success. Conveniently, we have that extra peer always allocated for this purpose! That's exactly what we use to test if an incoming connection has arrived. The following is what we do:

```
if (mListenerSocket.accept(mPeers.last()->socket) ==
    sf::TcpListener::Done)
```

An important remark in this situation is that sockets have two modes: blocking and non-blocking. The main difference is that the first will hold the program from continuing execution while waiting for incoming connections/packets/responses, and the latter will never block execution, keeping the fluidity of the program. It is good to remember that we set our `mListenerSocket` as a non-blocking socket. This is due to having a fast execution of the server loop without any more threads. The calls to `sf::TcpListener::accept()` that are constantly happening, return immediately stating whether there are new connections or not. All other server sockets are set to non-blocking as well for the same reason.

So, what does it mean when `sf::TcpListener::accept()` returns a successful response? It means a new client is trying to join, whether it's the first or the nth, whether it's local or in another country, we treat it the same way. There are a few operations we must make in order to set up a new valid peer and attribute a new aircraft to it:

```
// order the new client to spawn its own plane (player 1)
mAircraftInfo[mAircraftIdentifierCounter].position =
    sf::Vector2f(mBattleFieldRect.width / 2,
    mBattleFieldRect.top + mBattleFieldRect.height / 2);

sf::Packet packet;
mAircraftInfo[mAircraftIdentifierCounter].hitpoints = 100;
mAircraftInfo[mAircraftIdentifierCounter].missileAmmo = 2;

packet << static_cast<sf::Int32>(Server::SpawnSelf);
packet << mAircraftIdentifierCounter;
packet << mAircraftInfo[mAircraftIdentifierCounter].position.x;
packet << mAircraftInfo[mAircraftIdentifierCounter].position.y;

mPeers[mConnectedPlayers]
->aircraftIdentifiers.push_back(mAircraftIdentifierCounter);

broadcastMessage("New player!");
informWorldState(mPeers[mConnectedPlayers]->socket);
notifyPlayerSpawn(mAircraftIdentifierCounter++);
```

```
mPeers[mConnectedPlayers]->socket.send(packet);
mPeers[mConnectedPlayers]->ready = true;
mPeers[mConnectedPlayers]->lastPacketTime = now(); // prevent initial
timeouts
mAircraftCount++;
mConnectedPlayers++;
```

First, we use our identifier counter to get a new ID for the new aircraft, then, we bind to it some aircraft data, namely its initial position. Then we assign that aircraft to belong to the newly created peer, using the aircraftIdentifiers struct.

Now, there are the following four things that we send to the client:

- The order to spawn itself immediately
- The current state of the world with all the current aircraft
- How big the map is
- How much distance has been travelled already inside the map

Also, we notify every other peer that this aircraft is joining, so they are aware of a new player. Finally, and not as a mandatory step, we use broadcastMessage() to send a message to all previously connected peers, informing them of the new player that just joined!

The first thing in the list is actually the last being sent for a reason: When the client spawns the aircraft, it expects the world to be configured already with the current state. This is where TCP sockets come in very useful, as they help us ensure the ordering of the packet arrival, making our game logic more consistent.

To finish, we just increment the proper peer and aircraft counters, that is, mConnectedPlayers and mAircraftCount respectively, and set the current timestamp to the peer, so it is not prematurely disconnected by lack of activity.

After setting mPeers.last()->ready to true, we are ready to instance the new invalid peer for the next connection. This happens if there are still available slots for peers in the server, otherwise, the mListenerSocket socket will go back to a sleeping state, not listening to new connections anymore. It can indeed come back to life later, if users leave in the meanwhile.

Handling disconnections

Every time the server checks the peers for incoming packets, it makes a quick analysis of whether a peer hasn't sent anything in a very long time. If that is the case, we consider that peer timed out, and it is effectively kicked out of the server along with all its aircraft.

There are two main scenarios for disconnection; the first is when a user explicitly quits the game, intentionally leaving the simulation by sending a specific packet warning the server. The other is when something is wrong with the network, and the packets are not arriving anymore—the situation that we know as **timeout**.

If in that situation, at least one peer is marked for removal by setting its `mTimedOut` flag to `true`, `handlingDisconnections()` is called, and does the following:

```
FOREACH(sf::Int32 identifier, (*itr)->aircraftIdentifiers)
{
    sendToAll(sf::Packet() << static_cast<sf::Int32>
    (Server::PlayerDisconnect) << identifier);
    mAircraftInfo.erase(identifier);
}

mConnectedPlayers--;
mAircraftCount -= (*itr)->aircraftIdentifiers.size();

itr = mPeers.erase(itr);

// Go back to a listening state if needed
if (mConnectedPlayers < mMaxConnectedPlayers)
{
    mPeers.push_back(PeerPtr(new RemotePeer()));
    setListening(true);
}

broadcastMessage("An ally has disconnected.");
```

As you can see, it iterates over every peer, and for those who are flagged to be removed, it warns every peer that those aircraft are going to disappear. Then, the proper counters are decremented again and `mAircraftInfo` is partially cleared so it doesn't contain any more data for the erased planes. The peer is then effectively released from the `mPeers` list. Finally, if it's necessary, we resurrect the listener socket to start listening again for new users and always send an "ally disconnected" broadcast message, such that the other users are aware of what happened.

Incoming packets

We saved this part for last, as it is very important and a little more complex. We will now inspect the behavior of sending actual packets and receiving them. We use the exact same concepts we previously talked about for packing and unpacking `sf::Packet`. However, every packet must conform to some rules in order for both the client and the server to understand what is supposed to happen in the presence of each packet.

All packets have a fixed identifier, sized as a `sf::Int32` for coherence. This identifier is what explicitly tells us what the packet contains and what it brings inside:

```
sf::Packet packet;
packet << static_cast<sf::Int32>(identifier);
```

The rest of the packet data depends on what the identifier actually is. All identifiers we defined are under `NetworkProtocol.hpp`. All packets that originate in the server are under the `Server`, and all the packets that come from the client are in the `Client` namespace. The following is a code snippet with those identifiers:

```
namespace Server
{
    enum PacketType
    {
        BroadcastMessage,
        SpawnSelf,
        ...
    };
}

namespace Client
{
    enum PacketType
    {
        PlayerEvent,
        PlayerRealtimeChange,
        ...
    };
}
```

By making sure that both clients and server use the same "network language" by packing and unpacking the transferred data the same way and conforming to the specification of every packet type, we achieve a sane and logical communication protocol, which we call the network protocol, custom-made to fit our needs! As stated earlier in the chapter, defining such a protocol is, in many ways, similar to how other protocols were defined, such as HTTP and FTP.

Now let's understand how packets are handled in code:

```
bool detectedTimeout = false;

FOREACH(PeerPtr& peer, mPeers)
{
    if (peer->ready)
```

```
    {
        sf::Packet packet;
        while (peer->socket.receive(packet) == sf::Socket::Done)
        {
            // Interpret packet and react to it
            handleIncomingPacket(packet, detectedTimeout, *peer);

            peer->lastPacketTime = now();
            packet.clear();
        }

        if (now() >= peer->lastPacketTime + mClientTimeoutTime)
        {
            peer->timedOut = true;
            detectedTimeout = true;
        }
    }
}

if (detectedTimeout)
    handleDisconnections();
```

What we do is essentially traverse all the properly connected peers, and for each peer, we read as many packets as there are available using the non-blocking `sf::TcpSocket::receive()` function.

For each packet received, we call `handleIncomingPacket()` and reset the timestamp in the corresponding peer, so it doesn't time out. After receiving the packet, we test this timestamp against a predefined timeout limit. If no packet was received for at least `mClientTimeoutTime`, then the Boolean `detectedTimeout` flag is set, allowing a call to `handleDisconnections()`, which will remove the peer that timed out, as it was marked for removal by setting `timedOut` to `true` on the peer.

Now, let's take a look at how we handle a packet from the client:

```
sf::Int32 packetType;
packet >> packetType;

switch (packetType)
{
    ...
}
```

As we mentioned, the packet identifier, which clearly states the packet type, depending on whether it was sent by the client or the server, is fixed to be always a `sf::Int32` value, so we begin by unpacking that header. Now, since that number matches directly with the members of the corresponding enumerator, we perform a switch on it. The preceding code snippet does not contain all cases that we handle, so we can better understand the flow of the server logic and later analyze each packet properly.

This is exactly what defines the interaction between peers and the rules of the gameplay in conformance with the network protocol we created. For example, when we get a packet from the client of type `Client::PlayerEvent`, we already know from the "specification" that we can find in the packet's data two `sf::Int32` variables: the aircraft identifier and the action identifier that matches directly the one in the `Player.hpp` file. This way, when we read such a packet, we can broadcast it back to all peers so they all make the aircraft X perform action Y at the same time.

Studying our protocol

Let's attempt a deeper understanding of the logic of our server by checking what each server packet exactly means.

Every packet in the `Server::PacketType` enum is formed by the bullet's title as its identifier. That assumed, we explain the following packed parameters:

- `BroadcastMessage`: This takes a `std::string` and is used to send a message to all clients, which they would show on the screen for some seconds.

- `SpawnSelf`: This takes a `sf::Int32` value for the aircraft identifier and two float values for its initial position. It is used to order the peer to spawn its player one's aircraft.

- `InitialState`: This takes two float values, the world height and the initial scrolling in it, then a `sf::Int32` value with the count of aircraft in the world; then for each, it takes a `sf::Int32` identifier and two float values with the position of the airplane.

- `PlayerEvent`: This takes two `sf::Int32` variables: the aircraft identifier and the action identifier, as declared in `Player`. This is used to inform all peers that plane X has triggered an action.

- `PlayerRealtimeChange`: This is same as `PlayerEvent`, but for real-time actions. This means that we are changing an ongoing state to either `true` or `false`, so we add a Boolean value to the parameters.

- `PlayerConnect`: This is same as `SpawnSelf`, but indicates that an aircraft from a different client is entering the world.

- `PlayerDisconnect`: This takes one `sf::Int32` value with the aircraft identifier to be destroyed.

- `AcceptCoopPartner`: This is used to tell the client that it is free to spawn another local plane. It takes a `sf::Int32` value and two float values with the identifier of the aircraft to be spawned and its initial position.

- `SpawnEnemy`: This takes one `sf::Int32` value with the type of the aircraft as declared in `Aircraft` class and two float values indicating where the enemy should spawn.

- `SpawnPickup`: Similar to `SpawnEnemy`, but applies for the spawn of a pickup in the world. The first `sf::Int32` value to be packed is declared inside the `Pickup` class.

- `UpdateClientState`: This takes one float value with the current scrolling of the world in the server, and then a `sf::Int32` value with the aircraft count. For each aircraft, it packs one `sf::Int32` value with the identifier and two float values for position.

- `MissionSuccess`: This has no arguments. It is simply used to inform the client that the game is over.

Understanding the ticks and updates

In the pseudo-code, we referred to the `updateLogic()`, now let's take a look at what it actually does:

```
while (stepTime >= stepInterval)
{
    mBattleFieldRect.top += mBattleFieldScrollSpeed *
    stepInterval.asSeconds();
    stepTime -= stepInterval;
}
```

Comments are probably not needed, as fixed time steps were already explained in *Chapter 1*, *Making a Game Tick*. All that is being actually updated in here is the `mBattleFieldRect` variable, which scrolls upwards into the end of the level—an exact replica of what happens in the client with the world view.

Simple enough, let's now look at a more important code, the ticks, which we use to maximize the synchrony between both server and client. Let's use some pseudo-code:

```
while (tickTime >= tickInterval)
{
    updateClientState();
    checkMissionEnd();
    spawnEnemies();
    spawnPickups;

    tickTime -= tickInterval;
}
```

The first step is to send to all clients the current snapshot of the server's state, which consists of the current scrolling of the world (`mBattleFieldRect.top +`
`mBattleFieldRect.height`) and the positions of all aircraft.

About the aircraft positioning, it is important to notice that the server is not an authority over the movement of aircraft, but rather an agent in their synchronization. When you control your aircraft with the keys, the server will obey and register your newly obtained positions and the client won't overwrite its own local plane locations with the incoming server data. Therefore, we can assume that each client is responsible for the positions of its own aircraft. The server will however dispatch each client's positions to all others!

Then, `checkMissionEnd()` corresponds to the code that will check if all aircraft are near enough to the end of the level for the `Server::MissionSuccess` packet to be delivered, effectively showing a message in the client and quitting to the menu. This check is performed by checking if all the aircraft positions are between the effective end of the level and a given offset, provided in the `endLevel` constant.

After that, both `spawnEnemies()` and `spawnPickups()` functions will be responsible for making enemies and pickups appear at random intervals and at random locations, by using the `randomInt()` utility function.

Synchronization issues

If you test this chapter's sample extensively enough, you will notice clear synchronization problems, where some things do not happen the exact same way for all clients. This is intended and accounted for. We sacrificed a bit on the final polish level of the networked simulation, so it could remain simple. We understand networking is a very complex topic which might confuse even the brightest minds at first. We could never learn everything about it in one book, let alone in one chapter. Therefore, we went with an approach as simple as possible in this chapter. We would rather have you focused in learning the concepts we directly teach so you can extend them later into a fully-polished game than to have a way bigger codebase to look and get lost in.

Taking a peek in the other end – the client

We have looked in the server extensively and have hopefully clarified all systems and learned how they come together to form a single object that services a lot of clients at once, and potentially even more aircraft! Now let's look at the other end, the client, and see how we took a jump from a single-player-only game into a fully-networked game.

Let's examine the `MultiplayerGameState` constructor first:

```
sf::IpAddress ip;
if (isHost)
{
    mGameServer.reset(new GameServer());
    ip = "127.0.0.1";
}
else
{
    ip = getAddressFromFile();
}

if (mSocket.connect(ip, ServerPort, sf::seconds(5.f)) ==
    sf::TcpSocket::Done)
    mConnected = true;
else
    mFailedConnectionClock.restart();

mSocket.setBlocking(false);
...
```

We need to deduce which IP to communicate with, in order to successfully join a game. If we are the host, we just connect to the loopback address `127.0.0.1`, otherwise, we need to connect to a pseudo-remote server. This means that in practice, the server could still be running in the same machine if the user is testing two clients in the same computer. However, if we are joining a server on another computer, we actually need a valid IP address. We get it from a file conveniently named `ip.txt`, which is created and saved in the same directory as the executable in case it doesn't exist, already containing the loopback address. Changing this file is the way to go if you want to pick an arbitrary IP to connect to.

The port used is `5000` and it is hardcoded both in the server and the client. If you try the application, make sure you don't have other games or programs conflicting with this port.

 The loopback address we referred previously is simply a widely adopted IPv4 address that points to the local host or the machine itself where it is being used.

After attempting to connect with a timeout of five seconds, we either set the client to a valid connected state, or we restart a clock that will timeout after another 5 seconds, in the meantime showing the error message stating that connection was not possible.

Most things in `MultiplayerGameState` are a direct copy of how `GameState` used to work. Though there are some changes and additions we would like to mention. In the `update()` function, besides what was already there, we now check for incoming packets from the server:

```
sf::Packet packet;
if (mSocket.receive(packet) == sf::Socket::Done)
{
    sf::Int32 packetType;
    packet >> packetType;
    handlePacket(packetType, packet);
}
```

The `handlePacket()` function is very alike to the server's `handleIncomingPacket()` function.

Then we perform some logic to update the broadcast queue that shows the messages from the server on the screen and the text that blinks prompting a second player to join in by pressing the *Return* or *Enter* key:

```
updateBroadcastMessage(dt);

mPlayerInvitationTime += dt;
if (mPlayerInvitationTime > sf::seconds(1.f))
    mPlayerInvitationTime = sf::Time::Zero;
```

Finally, we tick the client in the same way and rate we tick in the server. Instead of sending a snapshot of all the local states, the client sends only the positions of its local aircraft:

```
if (mTickClock.getElapsedTime() > sf::seconds(1.f / 20.f))
{
    sf::Packet positionUpdatePacket;
    positionUpdatePacket << static_cast<sf::Int32>(
                            Client::PositionUpdate);
    positionUpdatePacket << static_cast<sf::Int32>(
                            mLocalPlayerIdentifiers.size());

    FOREACH(sf::Int32 identifier, mLocalPlayerIdentifiers)
    {
        if (Aircraft* aircraft = mWorld.getAircraft(identifier))
            positionUpdatePacket << identifier
                                 << aircraft->getPosition().x
                                 << aircraft->getPosition().y;
    }

    mSocket.send(positionUpdatePacket);
    mTickClock.restart();
}
```

Client packets

Here's the protocol explanation for the client. The `Client::PacketType` enum contains the following enumerators:

- `PlayerEvent`: This takes two `sf::Int32` variables, an aircraft identifier, and the event to be triggered as defined in the `Player` class. It is used to request the server to trigger an event on the requested aircraft.
- `Quit`: This takes no parameters. It simply informs the server that the game state is closing, so it can remove its aircraft immediately.
- `PlayerRealtimeChange`: This is the same as `PlayerEvent`, but additionally takes a Boolean variable to state whether the ongoing action is active or not.
- `RequestCoopPartner`: This takes no parameters. It is sent when the user presses the *Return* key to request the server a local partner. Its counterpart `AcceptCoopPartner` will contain all information to actually do the spawn of the friendly unit.
- `PositionUpdate`: This is what we saw in the client's tick code. It takes a `sf::Int32` variable with the number of local aircraft, and for each aircraft, it packs another `sf::Int32` variable for the identifier and two float values for the position.
- `GameEvent`: This packet informs the server of a specific happening in the client's game logic, such as enemy explosions.

Transmitting game actions via network nodes

Now, we will take a closer look at the `GameEvent` packet, which is sent when certain actions in the game occur. We use it to notify about explosions of enemies in a way that pick-up dropping is synchronized among different clients (either, a pick-up drops at every client or not at all). However, our implementation allows you to extend it for any game action. First, we have a `GameActions` namespace which contains an enum to differ between the game actions, and a struct to store an action:

```
namespace GameActions
{
    enum Type { EnemyExplode };

    struct Action
    {
                        Action();
                        Action(Type type, sf::Vector2f position);

        Type            type;
        sf::Vector2f    position;
    };
}
```

In *Chapter 9, Cranking Up the Bass – Music and Sound Effects*, you saw that we used a dedicated scene node class named `SoundNode` to build an interface between command-based game events and another game component, in that case, the sound player. Here, we are repeating this approach: We create a `NetworkNode` class that lets objects in the scene directly send events over the network:

```
class NetworkNode : public SceneNode
{
    public:
                        NetworkNode();

        void            notifyGameAction(GameActions::Type type,
                        sf::Vector2f position);
        bool            pollGameAction(GameActions::Info& out);
        ...

    private:
        std::queue<GameActions::Action>    mPendingActions;
};
```

This class holds a queue of game actions that are going to be transmitted. The `notifyGameAction()` method inserts a new game action into the queue, while `pollGameAction()` checks if an action is pending. If so, it pops the action from the queue and stores it in the output parameter—just as you know it from SFML's `pollEvent()` function.

Now, how does this look in practice? In the `Aircraft::updateCurrent()` method, we have a check if the current airplane has just exploded and if it's an enemy. In this case, we issue a command. The `Category::Network` category is the receiver category of `NetworkNode`:

```
Command command;
command.category = Category::Network;
command.action = derivedAction<NetworkNode>(
                [position] (NetworkNode& node, sf::Time)
{
    node.notifyGameAction(GameActions::EnemyExplode, position);
});
```

The network node itself is placed in the `World` class. A `World::pollGameAction()` member function acts as a pure forwarder and can be used in other parts of the game where we only have access to the world, but not its scene and entities.

One example is the `MultiplayerGameState` class. In its `update()` function, we interpret the game action and build a packet based on it, which is then sent over the network. We fill the packet with the `Client::GameEvent` packet type, the game action type (which in our case is always `GameActions::EnemyExplode`) and the position coordinates.

```
GameActions::Action gameAction;
while (mWorld.pollGameAction(gameAction))
{
    sf::Packet packet;
    packet << static_cast<sf::Int32>(Client::GameEvent);
    packet << static_cast<sf::Int32>(gameAction.type);
    packet << gameAction.position.x;
    packet << gameAction.position.y;

    mSocket.send(packet);
}
```

On the server side, in `GameServer::handleIncomingPacket()`, this packet is interpreted. When the game action denotes an exploded enemy, a pick-up will be spawned with a certain probability. This in turn leads to a packet of type `Server::SpawnPickup`, which is distributed to all clients.

The new pause state

For this chapter, the pause state was slightly modified. The same `PauseState` class was now modified to accept an option in its constructor to either allow or deny underlying states from being updated. The "default" behavior didn't change, but if we pass this parameter as `true`, the underlying states keep updating. This was a necessity as there was no concept of pausing in a networked game, because the world is persistent. However, the user may still want to access settings or go back to the main menu!

Settings

You may now configure two sets of keys in the Settings screen! This was done by not using an application wide `Player` instance anymore, rather by using a proper `KeyBinding` structure, holding the keys that are later passed to `Player` instances at will.

The new Player class

The Player class needed to be reworked quite a bit in order to support a multiplayer mode. Players are not hardcoded anymore in a state context scope, but rather, there is one player for each human-controlled aircraft in the world.

Every player is now identified by the same identifier that classifies one aircraft, so they can be paired up fast. Also, the constructor of Player now looks like the following:

```
Player(sf::TcpSocket* socket, sf::Int32 identifier,
       const KeyBinding* binding);
```

We pass on a socket instance or a nullptr, defining whether the Player class is being used in a networked or a single-player game. This socket, if passed, is valid for sending data to the server, which we will do next!

The identifier is exactly what you'd expect, the same that maps to an aircraft too. Finally, we also have KeyBinding being passed here. We will be passing it three different things: The defined keys for the player 1, player 2, and nullptr in case this Player instance does not receive local input, but rather is controlled by the server!

As for event and input handling by the Player class, it now works a little differently too.

Now, the real-time input is only delivered to the local player aircraft—the ones with actual human players controlling them. In consequence, each client has total control over its planes along with immediate responsiveness and smoothness. At the same time, that input is sent to the server, so every client is aware of that movement.

Latency

Programming and maintaining efficient server software is already a very hard task; however, to add even more complexity to this duty, we must deal with latency too. This topic is very broad but we will still try to give you some starting tips on how to deal with these issues.

Roughly, **latency** is the delay a network packet takes to reach its destination. The bigger the latency, the more we get behind in the networked simulation, and in consequence, the gameplay gets worse.

This little nightmare is one of the hardest troubles to deal with in network programming. It will make players have a different experience based on their connection and other network conditions, that is, it will make the game very smooth for some players while completely unplayable for others; it will be a mess. Unfortunately, it is not in the hands of the programmer to deal with the network's latency at all. A programmer can at best prepare the software to behave a little better in the worst case scenarios, where the latency is high. This is usually a very hard task to get right and is one of the main reasons game development companies need specialized and experienced network programmers to achieve a good simulation for all players, independently of how bad their connection is, within reasonable limits. Latency becomes a more and more determining factor as the geographical distance between peers increases. Already the speed-of-light delay between different continents of the Earth amounts to a fraction of a second, router logic on the way through the Internet may add even more. Until a peer receives an answer, data must be sent to the other peers and back; thus, we have the delay of both ways (also called **round-trip time**). Therefore, physics significantly limits the way how multiplayer games can be played across large distances.

Latency versus bandwidth

Do not confuse latency with bandwidth: The former denotes the time delay, while the latter denotes the capacity of the link. If you imagine a link as a pipe, the latency is related to its length, and thus to the time the water requires to flow through it. Bandwidth however is determined by the cross-section of the pipe; it specifies how much water can flow through it in a certain amount of time.

You cannot make a single bit arrive faster by increasing the bandwidth. What you can do however is to send many bits in parallel, so that a bigger chunk of data still needs less time to be transmitted. The bandwidth determines how much data you can send in a certain amount of time.

View scrolling compensation

The view is now simulated both in the client and the server and updated at the same speed in both of them. However, since the updates are happening in different threads or even different machines, some discrepancies may occur occasionally. Also, when a new player joins the game, he has to be informed of how far the view currently is, so it can keep up with it. In order to keep the view synchronized between all clients and the server, the server will send the view's position in every tick and the clients will employ a little trick to smoothly resynchronize the view.

The trick is simple. When the view is scrolled, we multiply the scroll offset with a compensation factor:

```
mWorldView.move(0.f, mScrollSpeed * dt.asSeconds() *
                    mScrollSpeedCompensation);
```

Now we just need to ensure that the factor is 1 when the views are in sync, and vary it, so the view scrolls faster or slower depending on how distanced it is from the server's view position. We do this by dividing both positions whenever we get the update:

```
mWorld.setWorldScrollCompensation(currentViewPosition /
    currentWorldPosition);
```

This will keep the view synchronized while never losing smoothness, unless something is very wrong and is too far behind, which should never happen in normal circumstances.

Aircraft interpolation

After the compensation technique, we decided to implement another little trick for the aircraft synchronization. Again, this is a simple way to achieve synchronization and it doesn't give the smoothest results most often. We still wrote it so you could face different algorithms and techniques and hopefully learn from them.

Remember, that each client commands its own planes and just informs the server of what is happening locally. With this information, the server keeps track of where every aircraft that is located. In every tick, it sends that information to its peers so they can synchronize with the true simulation data.

The planes would move quite accurately anyway with the real-time input information that comes from the server, but still some desynchronization could happen eventually. Because of this, when we get the real position of the aircraft in every tick, we move our aircraft slowly into that position, so, at best, after some ticks the aircraft are completely synchronized:

```
if (aircraft && !isLocalPlane)
{
    sf::Vector2f interpolatedPosition = aircraft->getPosition() +
    (aircraftPosition - aircraft->getPosition()) * 0.1f;
    aircraft->setPosition(interpolatedPosition);
}
```

The logic is simple. If the aircraft belongs to a remote player, we will interpolate its position between the current local position and the server's position (`aircraftPosition`). We have hardcoded an interpolation "amount" of `0.1f`, which means that we will always move 10 percent of the distance between both positions. This small value avoids having the aircraft "jump" from place to place, except when the network conditions are really bad and the synchronization is suffering too much.

Cheating prevention

By now you probably are scratching your chin and asking yourself: "But is this secure? Is a hacky player able to exploit the game to its benefit somehow?"

If you answered "No" to yourself, you are correct. By all means we would like to explain you how to make every little thing cheat-proof. However, we don't want to give you the fish by bloating the code with lots of validations; but rather, explicitly writing about how you can learn how to fish.

The current game, as is, is not cheat-proof whatsoever. There are a lot of validations that are not performed, so it will only work predictably until a clever user starts doing packet-sniffing and sending things that are not really expected by our protocol.

Let's try to understand how cheating could be achieved in our particular case, and how would we prevent it by looking at a few examples:

- In the client's tick, we let the client decide where its planes are going to be at. If a user with malicious intent sent this packet after modifying, he would be able to position its aircraft in any location, effectively warping from place to place as much as he wanted. We would fix this by not accepting the new positions in the server without some validations first. We would need to check if the new position is possible. Whether it could be achieved with normal gameplay, given the aircraft velocity and previous positions. Right here we could spot on a cheater and act upon it by banning or kicking or simply logging what happened to a file.

- Another great example of how we could exploit this game is to look at the `PlayerEvent` packet on the client-side. It carries an aircraft identifier and an action to perform. However, as the server doesn't check if the identifier sent is owned by that peer, a malicious user could effectively make other people's planes shoot bullets and missiles.

We intentionally left such things uncovered so you could see how serious it can be if you don't check all the data coming from a client. Users will often try to break the server state for an in-game profit.

The golden rule to prevent cheating is, when handling a packet in the server, always ask yourself if what the client is requesting is possible! Do as many validations as possible in the server's logic. The ultimate goal for a safe online simulation is reaching that point when there is no possible combination of data coming from the client that will produce unpredicted results. Always remember, as long as the server's state is sane and controlled, there is no cheating, as hard as it may be to achieve this.

Summary

In this final chapter, you learned about basic networking concepts. We had a look at sockets, different network architectures, and protocols. We incorporated this knowledge to our game, and extended the existing design to cope with new challenges of networking. By using SFML's Network module, we implemented a mechanism to communicate with other players on the same keyboard, the local area network, or the Internet. Although we had to make compromises in some places, you should have learned a lot of techniques which you can eventually apply in another game.

Along with this chapter, also ends the book! It has been a long ride all the way and we can only thank you for reading through our pages patiently. Finally, our aircraft top-scroller has reached a state where it is not only playable, but contains many features to create an immersive experience. We began with rendering, resource and input handling, and went over to shape different states and menus with a graphical user interface. We implemented actual gameplay mechanisms, polished the appearance using a variety of visual effects, played sound and music, and eventually added multiplayer support. Nevertheless, there are hundreds of possibilities to further improve our game, there are virtually no limits!

By now, you have seen many different aspects of game development—maybe a lot of unconventional approaches—and you are certainly motivated by these ideas to create your own work. Remember, what we showed you should only be a source of inspiration, not the one and only truth. We made choices that other people would handle differently. Therefore, don't be afraid of experimenting and trying out your own ideas! Be it code design, art style, or the gameplay itself—be creative, this is the most important attribute of any game developer. We hope you have enjoyed reading this book and following the development of our game, and wish you good luck on your journey!

Index

Symbols

Thank you for buying
SFML Game Development

About Packt Publishing

Packt, pronounced 'packed', published its first book *"Mastering phpMyAdmin for Effective MySQL Management"* in April 2004 and subsequently continued to specialize in publishing highly focused books on specific technologies and solutions.

Our books and publications share the experiences of your fellow IT professionals in adapting and customizing today's systems, applications, and frameworks. Our solution based books give you the knowledge and power to customize the software and technologies you're using to get the job done. Packt books are more specific and less general than the IT books you have seen in the past. Our unique business model allows us to bring you more focused information, giving you more of what you need to know, and less of what you don't.

Packt is a modern, yet unique publishing company, which focuses on producing quality, cutting-edge books for communities of developers, administrators, and newbies alike. For more information, please visit our website: www.packtpub.com.

Writing for Packt

We welcome all inquiries from people who are interested in authoring. Book proposals should be sent to author@packtpub.com. If your book idea is still at an early stage and you would like to discuss it first before writing a formal book proposal, contact us; one of our commissioning editors will get in touch with you.

We're not just looking for published authors; if you have strong technical skills but no writing experience, our experienced editors can help you develop a writing career, or simply get some additional reward for your expertise.

HTML5 Game Development with GameMaker

ISBN: 978-1-849694-10-0   Paperback: 364 pages

Experience a captivating journey that will take you from creating a full-on shoot 'em up to your first social web browser game

1. Build browser-based games and share them with the world

2. Master the GameMaker Language with easy to follow examples

3. Every game comes with original art and audio, including additional assets to build upon each lesson.

Torque 3D Game Development Cookbook

ISBN: 978-1-849693-54-7   Paperback: 380 pages

Over 80 prctical recipies and hidden gems for getting the most out of the Tourque 3D game engine

1. Clear step-by-step instruction and practical examples to advance your understanding of Torque 3D and all of its sub-systems

2. Explore essential topics such as graphics, sound, networking and user input

3. Helpful tips and techniques to increase the potential of your Torque 3D games

Please check **www.PacktPub.com** for information on our titles

Cocos2d-X by Example Beginner's Guide

ISBN: 978-1-782167-34-1   Paperback: 246 pages

Make fun games for any platform using C++, combined with one of the most popular open source frameworks in the world

1. Learn to build multi-device games in simple, easy steps, letting the framework do all the heavy lifting

2. Spice things up in your games with easy to apply animations, particle effects, and physics simulation

3. Quickly implement and test your own gameplay ideas, with an eye for optimization and portability

Mastering UDK Game Development

ISBN: 978-1-849695-60-2   Paperback: 290 pages

Eight projects specifically designed to help you exploit the Unreal Development Kit to its full potential

1. Guides you through advanced projects that help augment your skills with UDK by practical example

2. Comes complete with all the art assets and additional resources that you need to create stunning content

3. Perfect for level designers who want to take their skills to the next level

Please check **www.PacktPub.com** for information on our titles